FROM FIRST JOB TO CAREER

From First Job to Career is an anthology that weaves together inspiring first-job stories from people across diverse industries and backgrounds, offering career seekers of all ages the chance to connect with relatable experiences and hard-earned wisdom. This collection reveals the different paths people take in shaping their careers and serves as a resource for readers to identify with and learn from others' journeys. Paired with a comprehensive review of research in vocational psychology and career counseling, the book distills key principles and provides actionable resources for navigating the job search and building a meaningful career.

STEVEN ZHOU is an assistant professor of psychology at Claremont McKenna College, where he researches and teaches on quantitative methods, leadership studies, and careers and vocation. He completed his PhD in organizational psychology at George Mason University, during which time he published twenty-one articles, obtained $40,000 in research funding, and taught six undergraduate courses. He also has several years of corporate experience in nonprofit management, human resources, and data analytics.

GRAZIELLA PAGLIARULO MCCARRON, PhD, is an associate professor of leadership studies and a higher education program faculty member at George Mason University. As a scholar-practitioner, she has more than twenty years of experience in spaces including student development, college access, adult/returning and/or first-generation learner support, workforce development, and mattering/belonging-focused curricular and co-curricular pedagogy.

FROM FIRST JOB TO CAREER

Research and Narratives

STEVEN ZHOU
Claremont McKenna College

GRAZIELLA PAGLIARULO MCCARRON
George Mason University

Shaftesbury Road, Cambridge CB2 8EA, United Kingdom

One Liberty Plaza, 20th Floor, New York, NY 10006, USA

477 Williamstown Road, Port Melbourne, VIC 3207, Australia

314–321, 3rd Floor, Plot 3, Splendor Forum, Jasola District Centre, New Delhi – 110025, India

103 Penang Road, #05-06/07, Visioncrest Commercial, Singapore 238467

Cambridge University Press is part of Cambridge University Press & Assessment, a department of the University of Cambridge.

We share the University's mission to contribute to society through the pursuit of education, learning and research at the highest international levels of excellence.

www.cambridge.org
Information on this title: www.cambridge.org/9781009376990

DOI: 10.1017/9781009376983

© Steven Zhou and Graziella Pagliarulo McCarron 2025

This publication is in copyright. Subject to statutory exception and to the provisions of relevant collective licensing agreements, no reproduction of any part may take place without the written permission of Cambridge University Press & Assessment.

When citing this work, please include a reference to the DOI 10.1017/9781009376983

First published 2025

A catalogue record for this publication is available from the British Library

Library of Congress Cataloging-in-Publication Data
NAMES: Zhou, Steven, author. | McCarron, Graziella Pagliarulo, author.
TITLE: From first job to career : research and narratives / Steven Zhou, George Mason University, Graziella Pagliarulo McCarron, George Mason University.
DESCRIPTION: Cambridge, United Kingdom ; New York, NY, USA : Cambridge University Press, 2025. | Includes bibliographical references and index.
IDENTIFIERS: LCCN 2024061431 (print) | LCCN 2024061432 (ebook) | ISBN 9781009376990 (hardback) | ISBN 9781009376976 (paperback) | ISBN 9781009376983 (epub)
SUBJECTS: LCSH: Vocational guidance. | Career development.
CLASSIFICATION: LCC HF5381 .Z45 2025 (print) | LCC HF5381 (ebook) | DDC 331.702–dc23/eng/20250217
LC record available at https://lccn.loc.gov/2024061431
LC ebook record available at https://lccn.loc.gov/2024061432

ISBN 978-1-009-37699-0 Hardback
ISBN 978-1-009-37697-6 Paperback

Cambridge University Press & Assessment has no responsibility for the persistence or accuracy of URLs for external or third-party internet websites referred to in this publication and does not guarantee that any content on such websites is, or will remain, accurate or appropriate.

For EU product safety concerns, contact us at Calle de José Abascal, 56, 1°, 28003 Madrid, Spain, or email eugpsr@cambridge.org.

This book is dedicated to all of the individuals who shared their stories with us and to all those on the career and lifelong learning journey.

Contents

List of Tables	*page* x
Acknowledgments	xi

Introduction		1
	Why Stories?	2
	Overview of the Book and How Readers Might Approach the Volume	3
Chapter I	An Overview of the Changing Nature of Work, Career Research, and Career Education	5
	1.1 Career Research and Development in the US and Around the World	6
	1.2 Salient Theories of Career Development	9
	1.3 Career Development Theory Limitations in a Holistic Context	14
	1.4 Career Guidance and Development Work in Education	20
	1.5 Career Development in Higher Education	21
	1.6 Career Development Theory and Student Development Theory	23
	1.7 Conclusion	26
Chapter II	First Job and Career Narratives	27
	2.1 On Leaning into Risk-Taking: Sophie's Story	27
	2.2 On the Long and Windy Path: Caleb's Story	31
	2.3 On Persistence in Pursuing Accounting: Katie's Story	35
	2.4 On Reaching Out for Help: Cam's Story	38
	2.5 On Alternative Definitions of Success: Wyatt's Story	41
	2.6 On Unconventional and Unexpected Paths: Meera's Story	44
	2.7 On Getting the Most Out of That First Job: Aiden's Story	46
	2.8 On Trying Something Out, Just to See What It's Like: Sara's Story	48
	2.9 On Doing Something Completely Different: Bailey's Story	50
	2.10 On Starting a Career in the Army: Ronald's Story	52
	2.11 On Persistence from an International Student Perspective: David's Story	56

2.12	On Finding a Job in the Interim: Arlene's Story	58
2.13	On Confidence in Your Value: Axel's Story	60
2.14	On Being Hungry: Gregor's Story	64
2.15	On Lifelong Government Careers: Sid's Story	66
2.16	On Overpreparing in Your Job Search: Daniel's Story	68
2.17	On Changing Plans and Taking Risks: Taylor's Story	74
2.18	On Recovering from Being Blind Sided: Tabia's Story	76
2.19	On Saying Yes to Everything: Korey's Story	80
2.20	On Coincidences: Adnan's Story	82
2.21	On Finding a Path Internationally: Maara's Story	86
2.22	On the Challenges of Being a Person of Color in Finance: Afi's Story	89
2.23	On Adapting to Nonlinearity: Tristan's Story	92
2.24	On Setting Your Own Pace: Kyla's Story	95
2.25	On Reflecting on Times of Desperation: Ray's Story	97
2.26	On Throwing the Plan Out the Window: Dana's Story	100
2.27	On Proving Your Worth: Colton's Story	101
2.28	On Staying Open to New Directions: Thomas' Story	103
2.29	On Pivoting from Your Original Career Path: Mika's Story	105
2.30	On Faking It Until You Make It: Darius' Story	107
2.31	On Starting a Career Later in Life: Tori's Story	109
2.32	On Leaving a Hostile Work Environment: Allen's Story	110
2.33	On Starting at the Bottom of the Ladder: Dex's Story	112
2.34	On Being Employee Number Seven: Sheri's Story	114
2.35	On Being a Lifelong Learner: Warren's Story	116
2.36	On Faith through Disabilities: Gerald's Story	118
2.37	On Managing Your Expectations: Ronan's Story	120
2.38	On Making the Most Out of Your Degree: Nolan's Story	123
2.39	On Working Hard in Any Position: Zara's Story	125
2.40	On Selling Out: Irena's Story	127
2.41	On the Challenges of Sexism at Work: Macie's Story	130
2.42	On Loyalty to a Company: Esther's Story	131
2.43	On Bouncing Back: Aba's Story	133
2.44	On Inventing a Role: Sia's Story	134
2.45	On Start-Up After Start-Up: Dario's Story	136
2.46	On Breaking Traditional Expectations: Angela's Story	137
2.47	On Figuring It Out through Trial and Error: Glenn's Story	140
2.48	On Finding Value in Less-Than-Ideal Circumstances: Kara's Story	143
2.49	On Resilience: Nathan's Story	145
2.50	On Focusing on the Here and Now: Mason's Story	147
2.51	On Patiently Waiting for Your Moment: Jed's Story	149
2.52	On Negotiating Your Salary: Ray's Story	153
2.53	On Standing Up for Yourself: Clara's Story	154
2.54	On Being Pushed Harder Than Expected: Klein's Story	156

	2.55	On Widening Your Job Search: Devon's Story	158
	2.56	On Relying on Your Network: Rafaela's Story	160
	2.57	On the Immigrant Experience in the US: Domenico's Story	162
	2.58	On Being a Serial Entrepreneur: Claudia's Story	163
	2.59	On a Lifelong Career in Hospitality: Reagan's Story	166
	2.60	On a Lifelong Career in Nursing: Barbara's Story	168
	2.61	On Just Starting a Career and Looking for Next Steps: Molly's Story	171
	2.62	On Taking the First Step: Melinda's Story	173
Chapter III	Making Meaning of Career Narratives		175
	3.1	Introduction and Context	175
	3.2	Core Themes and Resources for Practice	178
	3.3	Summary and Conclusion	189

Appendix A: Methodology   191
Appendix B: Participant Demographics   194
References   195
Index   204

Tables

1.1	Stages of career counseling development in the US	page 7
1.2	Foundational student development theory families and select reference resources	24
3.1	Core career themes emerging from participant narratives	176
3.2	Self-audit prompts: the first job	179
3.3	Resources for navigating first job expectations and adjustments	179
3.4	Self-audit prompts: networking	180
3.5	Resources for building meaningful professional networks and connections	181
3.6	Self-audit prompts: identity	182
3.7	Resources for engaging in identity-conscious career conversation	182
3.8	Self-audit prompts: risk-taking	184
3.9	Resources for navigating career risk-taking, career agility, and pivots	184
3.10	Self-audit prompts: exploration	185
3.11	Resources for navigating career exploration and finding your "why"	186
3.12	Self-audit prompts: self-efficacy	187
3.13	Resources for fostering self-efficacy	188
3.14	Self-audit prompts: resilience, perseverance, and persistence	189
3.15	Resources for fostering resilience, perseverance, and persistence	189
B1	Participants' self-reported identity and demographic details	194

Acknowledgments

First and foremost, we thank the individuals who so generously shared their stories for this book and offered empathetic, encouraging, and strategic words of counsel to those on career and lifelong learning journeys. We thank the many colleagues who scaffolded this work along the way, especially those who aided us in recording the important stories featured here – Lauren Campbell, John Aitken, Renee McCauley, and Stephanie Atkins. Friends, thank you for your hard work in engaging so meaningfully with each of the storytellers, ensuring that their narratives are shared authentically and their voices are represented clearly. We also thank Jessie Cannon for her inspiring perspectives as a critical reader.

Steven recognizes that this book would not be possible without the support and mentorship of his faculty advisors – many in his academic doctoral program (Dr. Stephen Zaccaro, Dr. Philseok Lee, Dr. Lauren Kuykendall, and Dr. Richard Klimoski) – as well as and, especially, Dr. Graziella Pagliarulo McCarron. He thanks Graziella for believing in this vision and offering her incredible insight and effort to help bring this book to fruition. Steven also extends his thanks to his mentors from prior undergraduate and graduate experiences, especially Dr. Ben Postlethwaite who introduced Steven to the book inspiring this project – *Working* (Terkel, 1974) in his undergraduate class. Steven also thanks the many other mentors who helped him navigate his own first job search not too long ago. Finally, Steven expresses his gratitude to his family and friends, especially, and most important, his wife Ruth Zhou, who have put up with so many hours of listening to him talk about his work or offering to read drafts of papers on careers and organizational sciences.

Graziella, first and foremost, thanks her collaborator, colleague, and friend Dr. Steven Zhou; sharing in this journey together has been a true delight. She also extends her thanks to the communities of scholars and practitioners who have inspired and created the foundation for this text. She thanks the myriad career counselors who have made it their lives' work to serve as a bridge between hopes and realized dreams. Finally, Graziella expresses her gratitude to her friends, family (especially Keith and sweet Oliver), and the larger community of caring, thoughtful people around her who inspire and energize her every day.

Introduction

Whether after college graduation, graduate school, or even high school, we have all been in that place of searching for our very first "official" job. For many of us, this phase of life was characterized by an endless stream of applications apprehensively forwarded into the job search abyss – with nothing but "Thanks for applying!" and a months-late "We're sorry, we've moved on with other applicants" in return. Yet, after struggles with fluttery stomachs, self-doubt, bruised egos, and well-practiced interview handshakes, some of us finally landed that first job. Or, perhaps more appropriately, we landed a job experiment.

But, perhaps, that first job was far from what we thought we would be doing, even more distant from what we had been studying, and, at times, a few steps backward – for example, an accounting major selling pharmaceutical products, an engineer with a master's degree making company coffee runs, an art history major researching cancer prevention, a food-runner turned loan officer.

Too often, job seekers are told – frequently implicitly – that they need to have it all figured out: Finish school, choose your career path, get a job right away in the right field, and work your way up the professional ladder. There is a set path you should take. The path is linear, straightforward, and predictable. But if we examine the larger career development pathway, we will notice that this narrative is inconsistent with the realities. The "traditional" narrative of stability, predictability, and certainty is flawed or, at the very least, informed by antiquated notions of what career trajectories "should" look like. Such narratives can leave today's career seekers disillusioned and discouraged.

A new narrative is needed, one informed by the actual experiences of people from different walks of life – people returning to the world of work after caring for family, folks who are entering the workforce fresh from decades of schooling with multiple graduate degrees, or folks finding that first job after working through challenges to complete high school. In this book, we share these experiences through story, and we aim to demystify the early career journey by presenting a tapestry of experiences from individuals across various fields and backgrounds. Thus, this book focuses on the stories of 62 people with a range of experiences and career paths, each recounting the road to first jobs and careers. This text highlights each of these participant's answers to questions such as *How did you get that first job? What was the job, relative to your initial career interests? Where are you now? How did you navigate family and reconcile aspirations with the actual?* and *How did you experience identity and/or culture as part of career path?*

The stories captured in the process of participants' authentic reflections on these questions paint a more accurate picture of what it is like to start a career, with all of the stress and disappointment, joys and fulfilling moments, and twists and turns that come with engaging in the world of work. Each story offers a glimpse into the multiple and complex ways people have overcome obstacles, seized opportunities, and carved out professional paths. These narratives serve as a reminder that there is no singular route to or definition of success; rather, success is composed of a series of personal milestones and learning moments that shape our professional lives.

Why Stories?

Why stories? In a world overflowing with advice on career-building, it is the personal story that truly resonates and inspires. In fact, it was Studs Terkel's (1974) *Working*, an anthology of people talking about what they do for work, that inspired this book. The stories in this text seek to capture the essence of diverse early career paths, highlighting the unique journeys individuals take to find their first jobs. Stories have a way of connecting us on a human level, transcending generic advice, and offering real, relatable experiences. They provide a window into the struggles, triumphs, and unexpected turns that characterize the job-seeking journey, especially for those just starting out in their careers.

Readers of this book will engage with a variety of voices – recent graduates, career changers, stay-at-home parents, and those who left higher education early in pursuit of other goals – across a range of industries (e.g., banking, farming, law, hospitality, medicine). As you take in these stories, we hope you find not just guidance but also encouragement and a sense of solidarity with those embarking on their own career paths. Through the power of storytelling, we hope to amplify our capacity for empathy, learn from others, and find the motivation to persevere and succeed in our own endeavors. The stories give us an opportunity to ask, "How did they do it?" and honor a long-standing tradition of oral histories and narrative anthologies.

Overview of the Book and How Readers Might Approach the Volume

While honoring the power of story, we do so in a scholarly context. We ground participants' stories in a review of historical and contemporary literature on career decision-making and development. This review, presented in Part I, provides a summary of the academic research geared toward broad audiences, offering best practices for individuals (and their supporters, e.g., career development professionals) in the search for their first job. Just as our experience informs our need for a new narrative about the first job search, this review synthesizes contemporary research on career development models, approaches, and practices to offer tangible takeaways for those engaging the twenty-first-century world of work.

Part II of this text presents the 62 stories so generously shared with us – each titled and organized by the main themes that emerged from each narrative. The index may help if you, as a reader, hope to look for stories specific to your industry or field of study and/or educational background. However, we encourage you to sit with and hold space for all of the stories. You never know, despite being a biology major, your motivation for and about work might be reinforced by the story of a budding musician!

Based on Part II's narratives, Part III offers a reflection on how these stories converge, diverge, and connect with the theories reviewed in Part I. Here we include helpful resources such as self-audit and reflection questions for career seekers as well as career development professionals. And offer helpful text- and web-based resources. We hope to offer readers ideas on how to address weighty and critical questions such as *What do I do if I'm unable to finish college? Should I go to grad school or get a job first? How do I bring my whole self and my multiple identities to my career planning process? Who can I look to for support and mentorship?* and *How can I define success for myself?*

As authors, we believe that this book is for anyone searching for a job – especially their first job ever or new work in the context of career change – as well as folks who might be supporting those searchers. Whether you are newly out of high school, college, or graduate school, or returning to the workforce after decades working inside the home to care for family, we hope you find inspiration in these stories and tangible guidance to support your journey.

CHAPTER I

An Overview of the Changing Nature of Work, Career Research, and Career Education

> *Career guidance operates within a tradition of concern for the welfare of the individual and a respect for the dignity of each person. It eschews a haphazard or serendipitous approach to career choice for one that is more coherent and structured. The aim is to maximise the vocational potential of each person for themselves and the world-at-large.*
>
> (Perera & Athanasou, 2019, p. 2)

In the opening passage, Perera and Athanasou (2019) offer an encouraging perspective on the purpose of career guidance as a pathway for shepherding individuals toward a calling that speaks to realizing their personal promise and contributing to collective benefit. In the nearly 175 years since the introduction of career guidance as a societal necessity for supporting the "transformation from agricultural collectivism to industrial individualism" (Perera & Athanasou, 2019, p. 28), much has changed with respect to the vastness of career choices and the methods for supporting individuals in their career discernment (Guichard, 2022; Maree, 2020). Central to making meaning of the personal narratives in Part II of this text is familiarity with the arc of career guidance and the changing nature of work. Therefore, the purpose of this chapter is to explore this changing nature of work as well as the history of career guidance and development both in the US and globally, including the salient theories on career development from structured paradigms to the more fluid and systems-inclusive models we understand today. Our discussion on theory will also examine the limitations of career research as it pertains to underserved, historically marginalized, and non-Western peoples whose unique lived experiences shape their world of work. Additionally, we speak to the place of career guidance and development in pre- and postsecondary education. The history, theory, and discussion in this chapter are explored in a way that offers a lens through which readers can interpret the many personal narratives ahead.

1.1 Career Research and Development in the US and Around the World

In his review of the history and development of career counseling in the US, Pope (1997, 2000) posited that the evolution of career counseling and the nature of work were informed by major societal changes, the impact of those changes on the lives of the populace, and, in turn, the necessary training and retraining of workers to keep society functional. Pope distilled these societal shifts into six critical stages (see Pope, 2000). Table 1.1 summarizes the shifts and changes that advanced vocational and career guidance into the late twentieth century as a necessity for the success of both the larger economy and individual lives. Though Pope's (1997, 2000) stages pause in the late 1990s, several other scholars have spoken to the current, twenty-first-century US career development landscape. In the following section, we explore this landscape and examine what is meant by the "changing nature of work."

1.1.1 The Changing Nature of Work

Savickas and Savickas (2019), in their recounting of the history of career counseling, pointed to the career themes of the twenty-first century as "transactional" (rather than relational) in nature, with a focus on "short-term efficiency in which both employers and employees act as businesses" (p. 38). They further differentiated the new, twenty-first-century nature of work by positing that "the new employment contract calls for repeated adaptation and personal responsibility in constructing boundaryless, protean, and intelligent careers" (p. 38). While twentieth-century careers were built around a mutual loyalty between employer and employee, Savickas and Savickas offered that the twenty-first-century markets would thrive on flexibility (e.g., the "gig economy") that spoke to workers' individualism and adaptation to, in Bauman's (2017) coinage, a "liquid life." In fact, the rapid growth of the gig economy signals a potential shift in the nature of work from a static, lifelong career to a flexible, ever-changing career. While such a shift offers workers a sense of individualism, freedom, and flexibility, it also poses potential threats to financial stability and exploitation – especially in the gig economy space.

In addition to changes ushered in by market forces, biosocial changes also play a role. One such change came in the form of the COVID-19 global pandemic. In considering the pandemic in tandem with the changing nature of work, Hooley (2023) contended "that the pandemic

Table 1.1 *Stages of career counseling development in the US*

Stage	Time period	Key elements of the stage
1	1890–1919	• Job placement and vocational guidance began as demand for workers shifted from agricultural spaces to the industrial economy. Vocational guidance was also influenced by opposition to the exploitation of workers. • Frank Parsons (1909), the progenitor of career counseling, established the Vocation Bureau in the Civic Service House in Boston in 1908, the first formalized career counseling space. • Self-assessment tools for vocational guidance emerged. • In 1911, the Boston Vocation Bureau launched the first career development publication (the *Vocational Guidance News-Letter*, now *Career Development Quarterly*). • In 1913, the National Vocational Guidance Association (now the National Career Development Association [NCDA]) was founded. NCDA sets standards and provides professional support and enrichment for the career development profession.
2	1920–1939	• Catalyzed by the Great Depression, vocational guidance entered educational counseling in schools and industry. • The growth of unions and unemployment fostered employment training programs such as the Civilian Conservation Corps – partly overseen by the US Office of Education.
3	1940–1959	• Conditions after World War II led to the growth of professional practice in counseling, in particular career counseling as services were instituted to support veteran job placement and to tend to the new demographics of the higher education student body catalyzed by the GI Bill of Rights. • Interest in fostering science and technology professionals emerged as the US entered the outer space race.
4	1960–1979	• Sentiment around the Vietnam War and the Civil Rights Movement created a desire for meaningful work among young people eager for societal change. In response, President John F. Kennedy tasked a vocational education task force that led to the establishment of the 1963 Vocational Education Act. The act provided for expanded career education programs that supported the transition from the "old" economy to the new. • Career development programs began to emerge in organizational and corporate environments – for example, companies such as IBM and Pacific Bell established career services centers.
5	1980–1989	• The US realized a transition from the industrial economy to one centering information and technology. Once again, workers were called to "retool" for a job transition. • Private practice career counselors gained notice as essential to supporting a US workforce in job transition. Additionally, outplacement counselors emerged to help workers find new employment as companies downsized and/or changed.

Table 1.1 (cont.)

Stage	Time period	Key elements of the stage
6	1990–2000	• The Perkins Vocational Education Act of 1984 and the Omnibus Trade and Competitiveness Act of 1988 codified, respectively, provisions for vocational education targeting underserved groups and technological job training. • NCDA conducted three national, inaugural large-scale surveys gauging the beliefs and attitudes of the US workforce. • Survey findings led career counseling professionals to conversations around the changing demographics of the US workforce, focusing on culturally inclusive career counseling. Discussions that centered on the range of gender, racial, and ethnic identities in the workplace were prevalent. • Career development was affirmed as a lifelong process, as opposed to one focused on immediate postgraduation changes. • Access to career guidance was supported by better technology. • Enactment of the Americans with Disabilities Act (1990) established legislation for the protection of individuals with disabilities in hiring spaces and employment processes.

both exerted a massive impact on the labour market conditions within which individuals were developing their careers and profoundly shaped individuals' psycho-social worlds, shifting what they believed was possible and what they wanted from their careers" (p. 41). Nearly overnight, the shape, location, and rhythm of work changed. According to some, this change was simply an acceleration of key trends in the employment arena that were already on the horizon – for example, remote work, use of automation and artificial intelligence, and e-commerce (Lund et al., 2021). With this acceleration comes the undeniable realization that career guidance is even more critical now in the wake of new possibilities for the future of employment, as well as new challenges for individuals and the labor market as a whole (CEDEFOP & Organisation for Economic Co-operation and Development, 2021). For example, traditional career guidance methods of preparing and matching individuals to stable, long-term roles within specific industries must now shift to helping individuals develop resilience and adaptability in the face of changes to remote work patterns, technology in the workplace, and new competitors in the market. As such, we look to theories on career development to inform this complexity in guidance and a work landscape with many possible futures.

1.2 Salient Theories of Career Development

To state that the published material dedicated to exploring and explaining career development theory is robust would be an understatement. From the progenitors of early theories (e.g., Holland, 1959, 1973, 1985, 1997; Super, 1990, 1994) to the scholars who have evolved and expanded on those theories (e.g., Duffy et al., 2016), researchers have interrogated conceptualizations of career development – and their integration and convergence with other disciplinary tenets (e.g., psychology, sociology; Patton, 2019) – in great depth. A cursory search of the local library's career development literature catalog will yield such recent seminal works as the *International Handbook of Career Guidance* (Athanasou & Perera, 2019), *Career Development and Counseling* (Brown & Lent, 2020), the *Oxford Handbook of Career Development* (Robertson et al., 2020), and *Career Development and Systems Theory: Connecting Theory and Practice* (Patton & McMahon, 2021). Given the vast body of already existing and extensive literature on career development theory, the purpose of this section of Part I is not to regurgitate the full scope of what is known but rather to focus intentionally on some of the milestone theories that are relevant to and may inform how we can think about work and career in the twenty-first century. Our goal is to illustrate how career development theory has been and can continue to be reframed to serve individuals and the diversity of their lived experiences, especially as readers consider the range of individual narratives in Part II of this text.

With respect to an organizing framework for our discussion of career development theories, we borrow Yates's (2020) schema that placed theories into two distinct categories, with the caveat that there is much overlap between them: (a) content theories (focused on identity and environment) and (b) process theories (centering career learning and psychological resources). We do so with the full understanding that theories cannot operate in a vacuum and must be understood in relationship with each other and in the context of individual lives. In the following section, we briefly describe these theories and explore some of their limitations.

1.2.1 Content-Focused Theories of Career Development

A central aim of content-focused theories is identity, which can be defined as "an individual's sense of self defined by (a) a set of physical, psychological, and interpersonal characteristics that is not wholly shared with any other person and (b) a range of affiliations (e.g., ethnicity) and social roles" (American Psychological Association [APA], n.d., para. 1). Cognition of self – including needs, abilities, interests, values, and skills – forms the basis of person–environment theories of career development. Theories of person–environment fit find commonality in the understanding that individuals possess certain characteristics or "vocational personalities" (Holland, 1997) that suit them to specific types of work or job climates (Juntunen et al., 2019). Career development researchers often point to Frank Parsons, founder of the Vocation Bureau in the Civic Service House (see Table 1.1), as the first scholar-practitioner to conceptualize the importance of person–environment fit in vocation (see Guan et al., 2021). Parsons (1909) outlined three critical principles central to vocational choice, explaining that every individual needs the following:

> (1) a clear understanding of yourself, your aptitudes, abilities, interests, ambitions, resources, limitations, and their causes; (2) a knowledge of the requirements and conditions of success, advantages and disadvantages, compensation, opportunities, and prospects in different lines of work; (3) true reasoning on the relations of these two groups of facts. (p. 5)

Subsequently, and aligned with Parsons (1909), theories of person–environment fit assume that congruence between the individual characteristics and the nature of the job climate will lead to positive outcomes (e.g., increased job satisfaction). Though there are many person–environment fit theories we can discuss here, next we focus on a few specific frameworks given their constancy in the larger career guidance and career development conversation.

Theory of Vocational Choice. The Theory of Vocational Choice emerges from the work of John Holland (1959, 1973, 1985, 1997) and relies on typology to establish an understanding of individuals and the environments in which they work. Holland introduced six personality types – realistic, investigative, artistic, social, enterprising, and conventional (RIASEC) – with which to classify individuals and, in turn, determine vocational fit and success based on interaction with the job environment. Four conceptualizations within the Theory of Vocational Choice represented how a person might relate to the environment: (a) congruence (i.e., fit between person's RIASEC types and those of the environment), (b) differentiation (i.e., the degree to which an individual's interests are clearly defined), (c) consistency (i.e., the extent of commonality between an individual's dominant or preferred types), and (d) identity (e.g., stability of an individual's talents and goals) (Holland, 1959, 1973,

1985, 1997; Juntunen et al., 2019). Today, Holland's theory can be found in databases such as the O*NET (www.onetonline.org), the primary source of occupational information in the US, with RIASEC ratings (among many other metrics) for over 1,000 occupations. Job seekers can take a RIASEC interest profiler and browse for occupations based on their RIASEC scores.

Theory of Work Adjustment. The Theory of Work Adjustment (Dawis & Lofquist, 1984) contends that job satisfaction is an outcome of how closely people's abilities are linked to work requirements *and* how closely the rewards of the job role align with an individual's values (e.g., achievement, comfort, status, altruism (i.e., fostering harmony), safety, and autonomy). In the model, Dawis and Lofquist (1984) accounted for the notion of "adjustment behavior" – how an individual changes the work environment to align with abilities and values or, alternatively, changes themselves to align with the work role. The Theory of Work Adjustment prioritizes salience of identity (and even shifts in identity) in the context of work and offered a space for more nuanced, culturally relevant ways of thinking about vocation (Juntunen et al., 2019).

Values-Based Career Theory. Brown (1995, 2002, 2016) developed Values-Based Career Theory to capture the role that an individual's values (e.g., cultural, work) play in their vocational choices and experiences in tandem with personal demographics and systemic norms. Brown contended that sociocultural values – such as collectivistic or individualistic family, community, and societal leanings – informed an individual's work values but was careful to draw a line at monolithic perspectives within culture, noting that, "there is considerable diversity within the values systems of people from the same cultural groups and extensive overlap in the cultural values held by people from different cultural groups" (Brown, 2002, p. 49). As with the RIASEC interests, job seekers can search the O*NET system based on this set of work values: achievement, independence, recognition, relationships, support, and working conditions.

Theory of a Protean Career. In their development of the Theory of a Protean Career, Hall and Mirvis (1995) likened the twenty-first century's nature of work to a "new career contract" that would shift "organizational" careers to "protean" careers "driven by the person, not the organization, and that will be reinvented by the person from time to time, as the person and the environment change" (Hall, 1996, p. 8). Given that the role of "the self" and self-directedness were central to the Theory of a Protean Career, the theory speaks to content- and identity-oriented theories of career development – the goal of a career was no longer ladder climbing but psychological success, from job security to employability, from work-self to whole-self, and from managed to self-managing (Hall, 1996; Hall et al., 2018).

Psychology of Working Theory. Duffy et al., (2016, 2017) conceptualization of the Psychology of Working Theory emerged from considerations of sociology, vocational psychology, intersectionality, and multicultural psychology and was keenly focused on the pursuit of decent work. For the purposes of the model, decent work included "(a) physically and interpersonally safe working conditions, (b) access to health care, (c) adequate compensation, (d) hours that allow for free time and rest, and (e) organizational values that complement family and social values" (Duffy et al., 2017, p. 206). The authors were clear to center concepts of power and equity with careful attention paid to the role of multiple and intersecting identities in the types of work to which individuals had access. A central tenet of the theory was to eschew a "single axis" view of identity and, instead, capture the fullness of human experience (Duffy et al., 2016). Thus, we position the theory with content theories centering the self but acknowledge that the Psychology of Working Theory can straddle the worlds of both content and process.

1.2.2 Process-Focused Theories of Career Development

Process-focused theories of career development center the cognitive organizing, schemas, contexts, and sorting that individuals undertake as they make decisions about career options (Yates, 2020). As we offer the non-exhaustive summary of salient process-focused theories next, we reiterate that there can be substantial overlap between these models and content-oriented frameworks. As such, we ask that readers engage this discussion with a holistic lens.

Life-Span Life-Space Theory. Super's (1990) Life-Span Life-Space Theory emerged from a focus on self-concept and the presupposition that career development was a process that evolved over the course of an individual's entire life through a series of moments rather than singular decisions. From Super's perspective, a career was conceptualized as "the life course of a person encountering a series of developmental tasks and attempting to handle them in such a way as to become the kind of person he or she wants to become" (pp. 225–226). The Life-Span Life-Space Theory was grounded in four major constructs: (a) career development is a lifelong process (i.e., life span) that includes developmental tasks in growth stages ranging from childhood to late adulthood and retirement;

(b) depending on individuals' engagement with other parts of the life space (e.g., home, school, community), their valuing of work may change; (c) a series of life roles from son or daughter to student and, finally, pensioner are enacted in the four theaters of life – home, school, workplace, and community; and (d) individuals' self-concept (part of identity) will shift and change depending on how they view their roles over time.

Chaos Theory of Careers. Pryor and Bright's (2003, 2014) Chaos Theory of Careers was informed by the authors' desire to formulate a career development theory that accounted for individuals' uniqueness, complexity, and holistic context as well as situational complexity, connections in the world, change, and the limitations of human control (i.e., chance). In revisiting their theory 10 years after its introduction, Pryor and Bright (2014) underscored the model's relevance to modern career development challenges that were inclusive of new and dynamic technologies, constant change, globalization of employment, enmeshed economies, and "the contractual and episodic nature of much contemporary employment" (p. 5). Central to the Chaos Theory of Careers is an acknowledgment of the complex micro and macro systems as well as the predictable and unpredictable events that influence career decision-making.

Social Cognitive Career Theory. Speaking to elements of Bandura's (1977) conceptualization of self-efficacy (i.e., the extent to which an individual believes they can successfully perform a particular behavioral task), Lent and colleagues (1994) developed Social Cognitive Career Theory. The model centered "the interplay between three 'cognitive person variables' that are seen as playing key roles in career development: self-efficacy beliefs, outcome expectations, and personal goals" (Lent et al., 2014, p. 114). In other words, the Social Cognitive Career Theory posited that when individuals believe they possess (or can possess) a specific skill set (i.e., self-efficacy) and that fulfillment will come from using those skills (i.e., outcome expectations), they will cultivate a preference for certain activities and shift toward a career in an aligned field (i.e., personal goals) (Yates, 2020).

Career Construction Theory. Intended for use in a global context that invites in a range of diverse perspectives and lenses on career, Career Construction Theory (Savickas, 2005, 2013) "explains the interpretive and interpersonal processes through which individuals construct themselves, impose direction on their vocational behavior, and make meaning of their careers" (Savickas, 2013, p. 147). The model is grounded in the belief that career development and decision-making evolve from a series of adaptations that lead to integration between person and work environment.

Individuals actively cultivate adaptability through the development of four capacities: (a) concern for one's vocational future, (b) control over one's vocational future, (c) curiosity about types of work, and (d) and confidence and self-efficacy to pursue goals and aspirations (Savickas, 2013). Given its focus on construction and personal agency in the career learning and decision-making process, Career Construction Theory allows for individual narratives and stories to emerge that speak to how vocation is constructed.

As noted earlier, both the content-focused career development theories and the process-oriented theories highlighted here are not exhaustive, but they have weathered time, and some have been reframed to meet the modern moment. While arguably there may be no doubt about the salience of the models shared, many career development models were not only created in the context of Western and White norms (Juntunen et al., 2019; Yates, 2020), but are also subject to the times in which they were created (McMahon & Arthur, 2018) – which naturally leads to limitations in their applicability. In the following section, we discuss such limitations regarding theory applications for People of Color and minoritized communities, communities which identify as non-Western, and/or communities of the Global South.

1.3 Career Development Theory Limitations in a Holistic Context

As we think about the nature of work and career guidance and development in the US and around the world – and how this learning can help us understand and support job and career seekers broadly – we must consider all elements in a holistic context. Specifically, we must center understanding of the societal and cultural context (i.e., the localisms) that inform how people make meaning of their lives, the work they do, the work they aspire to do, and the overall impact on themselves, their families, and the larger collective. Especially as we digest the narratives in Part II of this volume, we must give considerable space to the tension between localist ideas and pursuits about work/career and the "universalist" (Sultana, 2023), Westernized, or monolithic ideologies with which individuals may struggle (e.g., linear career paths and educational attainments). Sultana's (2023) work posited that those who guide must ask the following questions of themselves: *Which forms of being are valued by my approach to career guidance? How do the theories I work with affirm or deny the worldview of those I serve?*

Asking such questions about *why people work* is critical to interrogating theories in this postmodern, twenty-first-century space and developing career guidance practices that honor the whole individual. Some scholars offer that career guidance work requires that counselors and clients be informed by a life-design model of career counseling (see Hartung, 2019; Savickas & Savickas, 2019) that "addresses the twenty-first century question of 'How do you want to be?' instead of the twentieth century question of 'What you want to be?'" (Savickas & Savickas, 2019, p. 39). However, life design is scaffolded by a constructionist paradigm that assumes people's agency in creating the narrative of their lives. Therefore, we must be careful with this assumption in the face of systemic oppressions and social inequities that may suppress individuals' career options. For example, an individual of immigrant origin from a low-income household aspiring to become a computer scientist may face significant challenges in accessing the necessary resources such as advanced courses, computing power, expensive software, and social networks for mentorship and internships. Despite their interest and potential, these systemic inequities may limit their ability to fully engage with the life-design model of career development. Next, we will examine more closely the relationship between underserved communities, career guidance, and the nature of work, but we must pause here and acknowledge that though the radical changes from twentieth- to twenty-first-century approaches may inform accelerated progress, the capacity (or desire) for working individuals to write their own career story is not universal.

1.3.1 Limitations of Theory for Service to People of Color and Broader Marginalized Communities

In the US, racial and ethnic diversity in the workforce has increased significantly, yet, commenting on this increase, Kantamneni and Fouad (2023) noted that the growth does not speak to the disproportionate unemployment rates for People of Color or disproportionate representation in specific occupations – including careers in engineering or medicine – when compared to White counterparts. While career development theory and vocational research in general has evolved to include (or been revised to include) identity elements such as race, ethnicity, and gender, understandings of what factors play a role in the career choices for minoritized groups – particularly with respect to race and ethnicity – are still understudied and opaque (Flores et al., 2019; Kantamneni and Fouad, 2023). To this point, McWhirter and McWha-Hermann (2021), in their work focused on social justice and career development, found "that the historical focus on higher-income settings and workers with relatively privileged status reflects the neoliberal underpinning implicit in most of VIO [vocational and industrial/organizational] psychology" (p. 1). Further, Flores and colleagues (2019) contended that, when it *is* generated, vocational research that *does* focus on racial and ethnic groups does so in a monolithic way without unpacking the nuances of within-race or within-ethnicity nuances that affect the career development process. The authors applauded the Psychology of Working Theory (Duffy et al., 2016) for its inclusion of identity in context with respect to career development and decision-making, but they urged the reframing of theory to ensure that it is (a) scaffolded by culturally sensitive research, (b) grounded in empirical assessment with People of Color, (c) connected to interdisciplinarity, (d) aligned with psychological and educational science, (e) rooted in intersectionality, (f) steeped in an understanding of systemic oppressions and structural bias, and (g) considerate of the impact of environmental disasters (e.g., Hurricane Katrina) on the long-term employment of vulnerable populations. As career development theory looks to its next evolution, the limitations associated with inclusion of minoritized groups must be foregrounded.

1.3.2 Limitations of Theory for Service to Non-Western and Global South Communities

While the societal changes that informed the US career development and vocational guidance evolution are reproduced in some form around the globe, the "largely overlapping waves or cycles in the economy, industry ..., psychology in general, and career counseling in particular" (Maree, 2020, p. 68) may present differently in any given country. Maree (2020) offered that a nation's positionality in terms of factors such as affluence and modernity (e.g., Global North versus Global South) can inform if and how career counseling is a consideration. To this point, Keshf and Khanum (2021) – in their study of career guidance and counseling needs in Pakistan – offered that, while the benefits of career guidance and counseling were many, the practice was still evolving in their landscape. The authors not only spoke to nation-state factors that influenced the availability of career guidance resources such as the economy, infrastructure, and politics but also familial and social culture around work roles. Keshf and Khanum's work informs an important discussion about the actual and assigned value of career development opportunities based on a country's national fabric (e.g., norms, needs, affluence). This latter point is evidenced by Malach-Pines and Kaspi-Baruch (2008), whose research – scaffolded by Hofstede's (1991) cultural difference model – examined the nexus between culture and career choice, noting that culture played a role in the meaning made of work, perspectives of traditional versus contemporary views on career, and factors that influenced career (e.g., family).

While it is beyond the scope of this book to examine the overlapping and historical societal structures that fostered the nature of career guidance and work across the range of countries on earth – a range than can span 194–237 nations depending on perspectives on sovereignty (see Saunders, 2024; US Central Intelligence Agency, n.d.) – we must center an important dialogue about how societal forces manifest uniquely in every nation. We must also consider what this means for how we assume career development from a non-US lens. Yates (2020) offers: "Most of the career literature is Western, written in English, and assumes an individualistic culture. It presupposes that people have a choice and want to use their careers as a means of achieving self-actualization..." (p. 133). Thus, "traditional" theories require disruption toward returning career development practice to its roots of advocating for decent work and serving the underserved (Gutowski et al., 2020). Such disruptive dialogue is essential to understanding the breadth of individuals' journeys in a holistic light that is reflective of Sultana's (2023) discussions of work and career "localisms and particularisms." Sultana argued that we cannot have a conversation about the texture of work and career guidance on the international stage until we understand that the dominant understanding of "correct" or "good" career development, guidance, and nature of work is privileged and shaped by *who* and *what* entities define the terms. The author contended that,

> with vocational psychology being complemented and even challenged by philosophy and the social sciences – we are still missing in-depth anthropological/ethnographic accounts that would help us understand the extent to which our theories, with their universalising tendencies, are both plain wrong, and equally plainly dangerous (Sultana, 2011). (Sultana, 2023, p. 265)

This tension between localisms and universalisms certainly applies to career development theory and gaps in how some of the most seminal works engage individuals across difference. For example, while Holland's (1959, 1973, 1985, 1997) work is foundational to career development practice, several studies have presented critiques with respect to applications in non-Western and/or non-US contexts (see Juntunen et al., 2019). In their research examining the fit of the Theory of Vocational Choice to the career development needs of South Korean college students, Lee and colleagues (2022) found that the explanatory power of the model was a better fit for students who identified as men than students who identified as women, contending that the personality types in the model could be interpreted and understood differently across gender and at the intersections of gender and culture. Additionally, Fu and colleagues (2019), in their examination of university students in China, underscored the potential limitations of the concept of "congruence" in Holland's model noting that an individual's fit with environment alone may not explain satisfaction and that, in fact, external forces (e.g., support from local relations) could also be a significant factor. To this point of external relationships, Fu and colleagues observed the following about Holland's model: "In collectivist cultures, the supports from and barriers to the collectivist context of an individual may be considerably stronger determinants of the individual's career development in comparison with congruence" (p. 213).

In addition to critiques on applicability of existing theory, we would be remiss to not mention limitations in the sheer availability of empirical work on measurement equivalence between countries. For example, taking a critical look at Lent and colleagues' (1994) Social Cognitive Career Theory, Sheu and Bordon (2017) conducted a meta-analysis of several international studies and discovered that studies including Asian and European participants were abundant, but this was not the case for African and South and Central American contexts. Summarizing some of the model critiques shared here, in their work focused on career guidance from an international lens, Perera and Athanasou (2019) spoke to the complexities of career development across country and culture as follows:

> On top of the existential problems facing each individual, there are systemic factors (sex, age, religion, ethnicity, race, nationality, geography, disability) that influence choice. These factors are moderated by a host of other factors such as economic, social and even geopolitical factors in the case of refugees. Added to this cocktail of influences are myriad personal attributes in the form of values, interests, aptitudes, and adaptability. Vocational guidance is a broad church. (p. 3)

McMahon and Arthur's (2018) perspective about limitations was even more wide sweeping and focused on the very meaning of the word "career" as understood across communities around the world. They contended: "The middle-class connotations of 'career' also warrant consideration. Career development's emphasis on paid employment disenfranchises those whose careers concern voluntary work and work in the home" (p. 12). McMahon and Arthur went on to note that "a common criticism of the foundational career theories is that they do not adequately accommodate the careers of women and groups other than white, middle-class males, as mentioned previously" (p. 13), and that "with the internationalisation of career development, concerns have been raised about the appropriateness of the Eurocentric nature of career theory that has been exported to and imported into countries with vastly different cultures and traditions from where the theories originated" (p. 13). Echoing this last point, Ribeiro (2020) also expressed concern that the bulk of foundational theories had been devised and applied in the Global North and did not necessarily transfer to contexts in the developing countries of the Global South, which may claim different socioeconomic and political features and as well as variance in cultural milieu. Similarly, in elaborating on Global North contexts, Maree (2020) contended that career development may speak to "storied" approaches that imagine an individual's holistic self in the conceptualization of a career future – that is, the "How you want to be?" question posed by Savickas and Savickas (2019). But such storied approaches may be less congruent within the context of developing nations (Maree, 2020).

Examining this Global North/Global South relationship, variance in theoretical applicability, and the need for Global South agency, Ribeiro (2020) highlighted the urgent need for the co-creation of career research that represented both the Global North and the Global South so that the communities in the Global South could "help renew and democratize the field of career development (Ribeiro, 2020, p. 235) and reclaim their own narratives and epistemic truths. Supporting this latter point, Bengtsson (2022) underscored the idea of epistemic justice for communities who had otherwise been silenced or erased in the career development arc. Understanding whose voices are silenced and whose are amplified is critical to creating career development frameworks that speak to the holistic nature of human existence. Thus, as we consider the way forward for career development theory, its limitations with respect to global efforts are rather clear. We join the call for a reframing of career research that is centered on more critical perspectives of career choice and development, which attend to power and unmask dominant ideologies situated in privileged contexts (see Thomsen et al., 2022). This reframing is in few places more essential than in educational spaces, which nurture the workforce pipeline. Therefore, in the following section, we speak to the connection between career guidance, educational contexts, and necessities for advancing holistic career development.

1.4 Career Guidance and Development Work in Education

In the Coalition for Career Development's recent report on the condition of career readiness in the US, Solberg and colleagues (2023) underscored that "launching future-ready youth" (p. 11) for both advanced schooling and the world of work is a critical part of the K-12 responsibility set. While counselor–student ratios are problematic across the US, the authors highlight that longitudinal studies affirm the linkage between middle and high schoolers' participation in such readiness counseling programs and wages in adulthood, with the impact more significant for underrepresented and marginalized youth (Solberg et al., 2023; see also Covacevich et al., 2021). Of note here – and central to the work of this volume – is that "future ready" does not necessarily have to equate to "higher education ready," and the work of preparing youth for the world of work is multipronged and inclusive of both college degree and nondegree pathways. As readers will find in the range of narratives in Part II of this text, many of our interviewees found success in the unlikeliest of places, despite never attending or completing college. To this latter point, Eddy (2023), in her analysis of changes on the work horizon posited that, rather than forcing a singular focus on a particular type of education or a particular type of career, educators and families should embrace that

> We'll need to transform our spaces of learning and prioritize skills development. The change involves helping kids see that the job isn't the end-goal. Instead, they should strive to find a happiness that exists at the intersection of what they're good at, what they can be paid for, what the world needs, and what they love. (p. 8)

Again, for youth from historically marginalized and systemically oppressed communities, holistic readiness programs offer what Mann and colleagues (2020) referred to as the "capacity to aspire" (p. 10). And, here, recalling our discourse in the career development theory section of this chapter, we note the caveat that this US-based perspective may assume Western ideologies around agency and future-making. Yet, in this context, Solberg and colleagues (2023) highlighted several key practices that would support capacity-building – if desired – toward postsecondary engagement.

Two such practices encouraged that educators and stakeholders should (a) leverage technology to provide quality career advising to youth (e.g., chatbots for career coaching, gamification of career readiness scenarios); and (b) engage employers and community partners to champion career readiness and provide youth opportunities for experimenting and learning (Solberg et al., 2023). Underscoring Carnevale and colleagues' (2023) employment prospects and wage data, Solberg and collaborators contended that, while not a path for all, postsecondary education – two- or four-year – could substantially boost individuals' work and earning possibilities. The question then becomes, if/when students enroll in higher education, what becomes of "future readiness" preparation? In the next section, we spend a few moments describing the career development texture of institutions of higher education and offer a brief discussion on the intersection of career development and one of the most critical elements of college and university work – student development and, by extension, student development theory.

1.5 Career Development in Higher Education

In his contribution to Buford and colleagues' (2023) volume on *Mapping the Future of Undergraduate Career Education: Equitable Career Learning, Development, and Preparation in the New World of Work*, Hooley (2023) offered a clarifying definition of what we mean by the "changing world of work" in the context of postsecondary students' preparation. He wrote:

> The "changing world of work" groups together a set of commonly anticipated changes to working life and presents them as a largely inevitable future. These changes are strongly focused on technological innovations with particular attention given to automation and artificial intelligence, growing digital connectivity, big data.... The changing world of work discourse also addresses several wider contextual challenges for our working lives, including demographic change, globalisation, the "great" (post-2008) recession, environmental change and urbanisation, but these big contextual issues are often viewed as secondary to the technological transformation (the fourth industrial revolution) that is presumed to be driving the future. (Hooley, 2023, pp. 39–40)

Hooley's assertions about the new world of work – offered from a global lens – are particularly salient because they not only underscore the potential challenges and rewards for working individuals writ large, but they also offer a snapshot of what may greet college and university students as they prepare for the first job or their long-term career. Given that so many of the narratives in Part II of this volume intersect with individuals' higher education pathways in terms of anticipation, preparation, and expectation, we feel it appropriate to speak to career guidance and development work in postsecondary – particularly US-based – environments. We do not aim to privilege postsecondary education as a preparatory avenue but to provide context.

Career guidance in higher education is far from novel, having been articulated as one of the primary responsibilities for student affairs staff in the early 1930s by the American Council on Education's (ACE) (1937) seminal publication, *The Student Personnel Point of View (1937)*. This guiding document describing student personnel work asserted that the main aims of such work included "assisting the student throughout his [sic] college residence to determine upon his courses of instruction in light of his past achievements, vocational and personal interests, and diagnostic findings" (ACE, 1937, p. 4) and to support the student in "articulating college and vocational experience" (ACE, 1937, p. 5). Given the great transitions in society and in the nature of work since the document's creation (see Table 1.1), career counseling in college environments has had to move on from a singular focus on vocational and placement guidance. In their historical recounting of college career services, Grimmett and Severy (2024) offered that placement models "worked well with small numbers of graduates joining a stable, lifelong career path, usually with the same company" (p. 130) when career paths were linear in nature. However, "those career paths no longer run a straight course, and most graduates will leave their first jobs within one to three years" (Grimmett & Severy, 2024, p. 130). Given the career paths of the contemporary college graduate as well as a deeper need for a more engaged career guidance paradigm, scholars suggest that higher education career services have steadily progressed from reactive (i.e., placement-focused), to proactive (i.e., counseling and typology-focused), to interactive (i.e., coaching, networking), and, in the last decade, to hyperactive (i.e., multi-faceted, connectedness, life-design thinking, chaos theory based) (Dey & Cruzvergara, 2014). In fact, Trinity College's career services unit – the Career and Life Design Center (https://careerlifedesign.trincoll.edu) – serves as an example of what this contemporary counseling model might look like in higher education.

With respect to the context shared here, arguably, career services work is not just about career development and planning alone – along with the larger dialogue on the complexities of student care, it has "grown and evolved along with colleges and universities to represent the breadth and depth of personal, academic and professional development" (Grimmett & Severy, 2024, p. 129). Critical to this expansion of aims and responsibilities for career services practice in higher education is the understanding that "the impact of coming to and staying in college does not translate into equitable opportunities for all" (Jehangir et al., 2022, p. 104), and, thus, career development work must take place with a nuanced understanding of each student's narrative – to include social location, environmental factors, historical treatment, and knowledge and networks relevant to decoding the college experience (i.e., social and cultural capital; Garriott, 2020). In short, career guidance in higher education cannot be informed by career-oriented practice and theory alone; it must include a holistic approach to guiding the student as a person. As similarly expressed in our discussion on theoretical limitations earlier in this chapter with respect to career guidance on a global scale, educators who are helping students develop a career identity must consider the whole student – thus, we must examine the nexus between career development theory and student development theory.

1.6 Career Development Theory and Student Development Theory

In the first portion of this chapter, we discussed some of the most salient career development theories in the larger career guidance and counseling arena. While these theoretical underpinnings offer context for higher education career services, their application would be incomplete in postsecondary environments without the simultaneous consideration of student development theory. Scholarship on college student development began to emerge in the mid twentieth century as student affairs (e.g., student activities, counseling/advising, orientation; see Nuss, 1996) formalized on college campuses. Student development theory, scaffolded by interdisciplinary thinking across such fields as psychology, sociology, education, and anthropology, can serve scholars and practitioners in describing college students' concerns, explaining elements of students' experiences, predicting how best to serve students, generating new theory, fostering student growth through customized experiences, and assessing intervention effectiveness (McEwen, 1996; Oxendine & Taub, 2023). Foundational student affairs scholar-practitioner Lee Knefelkamp (1982) contended that "[student development] theory can serve as a 'common language' that allows student affairs professionals to communicate with one another about students and about student affairs practice" (p. 380), and, akin to career development theory, student development theories are "understood as social constructions rather than objective value-free realities.... The foundations of many theories are rooted in Western/Eurocentric paradigms that inherently cannot be applied in many contexts of varying perspectives" (Oxendine & Taub, 2023, p. 117). While it is beyond the scope of this volume to examine all student development frameworks and their evolution over the course of the sociocultural timeline, in Table 1.2, we offer a snapshot of foundational student development theory families as well as cornerstone and contemporary scholarship centering those theories.

Table 1.2 *Foundational student development theory families and select reference resources*

Theory family and focus*	Reference resources
Psychosocial theories Concerned with developmental tasks throughout the lifespan, which can be presented in recursive phases or stages. Considers environment and an individual's intrinsic factors. **Cognitive-structural theories** Concerned with the development of individuals' reasoning and thinking. Individuals move from stage to (a more complex) stage as they encounter challenges that require new thinking. **Social identity theories** Concerned with how students develop identity (e.g., race, ethnicity, sexual orientation, gender, and class) and considers an understanding of multiple identities and intersectionality.	Abes, E. S., Jones, S. R., & Stewart, D.-L. (Eds.). (2019). *Rethinking college student development theory using critical frameworks*. Taylor & Francis. Duran, A., Abes, E. S., Stewart, D.-L., & Jones, S. R. (2024). Looking back, moving forward, and everything in between: Revisiting student development's relevance and enduring concepts. *Journal of College Student Development, 65*(2), 121–136. Garvey, J. C., Harris, J. C., Means, D. R., Oerez, R. J., & Porter, C. J. (Eds.). (2020). *Case studies for student development theory: Advancing social justice and inclusion in higher education*. Routledge. McClellan, G. S., & Kiyama, J. M. (Eds.). (2023). *The handbook of student affairs administration* (5th ed). Wiley. Patton, L. D., Renn, K. A., Guido, F. M., & Quaye, S. J. (Eds.). (2016). *Student development in college* (3rd ed.). Jossey-Bass. Schuh, J. H., Jones, S. R., & Torres, V. T. (2016). *Student services: A handbook for the profession*. Jossey-Bass.

* Note: Adapted from Oxendine and Taub's (2023) overview of salient theories.

Although not explicit in Table 1.2, here we also draw attention to the concept of intersectionality with respect to identity development and expression. Intersectionality was first brought into larger parlance by Black feminist leaders and activists such as Anna Julia Cooper (1892) and then formally conceptualized by Crenshaw (1989). The concept served as a framework to name the explicit marginalization experienced by Black women at the intersection of systemic sexist and racist oppression. In more contemporary and broader conversations, intersectionality shines a light on the insufficiency of considering individuals in context if single social identities (e.g., race alone, class alone, ability alone) given that this narrow approach does not take into the account the complexities of multiple and intersecting identities and how those intersections engage with societal systems and structures. Collins (2009) and Collins and Bilge (2020) described the matrices of domination inherent in intersectionality because of the "overlapping and conflicting dynamics of race, gender, class, sexuality, nation, and other inequalities" (Cho et al., 2013, p. 788) that result in individuals experiencing multiple forms of discrimination (e.g., a Black woman may experience both racial and gender discrimination simultaneously). With respect to students and student development theory, Duran and Jones (2019) highlighted the role of intersectionality in students' overall identity development and, thus, student development. As we consider the links between student development and career development, keeping the salience of identity (as well as psychosocial and cognitive development) in the forefront is critical for shaping career guidance in higher education that is inclusive and responsive. Severy (2018) shared in her work exploring career development and career identity in the context of emerging adulthood theory (see also Arnett, 2000, 2015):

> (T)here are personal, contextual, and experiential differences that influence an individual's progress through developmental tasks. Even focusing on one subset of the population, those emerging adults pursuing degrees in higher education covers a wide range of individuals. Understanding how social structures are helping or impeding emerging adults is important for educators and career development professionals who want to be helpful. (p. 85)

Understanding these social structures and how they influence students' psychosocial, cognitive, and identity development *in tandem with and in relation to* career development is nonnegotiable in the changing world of work and global context. Garriott (2020), in his exploration of career development frameworks for first-generation and economically marginalized students, spoke to students' academic and career development in the context of structural/institutional conditions, social–emotional crossroads, career self-authorship, and cultural wealth, which supports the notion that career development cannot be separated from student development. How students evolve in their developmental tasks, how they think and reason, and how they engage who they in the context of larger systems are critical to career meaning-making.

1.7 Conclusion

The purpose of Part I was to examine the changing nature of work, engage key historical milestones in the career counseling and guidance landscape, and speak to a spectrum of career development theories, their limitations, and their intersection with educational spaces. As we move into exploring the 62 participant narratives in the next section of this volume, we hope that the frameworks offered in this chapter provide context and, ultimately, serve as an avenue through which promising practices for holistic career development are informed.

CHAPTER II

First Job and Career Narratives

2.1 On Leaning into Risk-Taking: Sophie's Story

The biggest thing is that the first job that you get doesn't have to be the end. Just because it's the job that you have, doesn't mean that you need to stay there for the rest of your life.... I strongly encourage taking that risk and taking that chance. I feel like it'll give you so much more to live for, otherwise you get stuck, and you get stagnant in whatever it is that you might be doing.

I started looking for a job in January 2013, knowing I was graduating from college at the end of April 2013. Now, my degree is in psychology with a minor in social work. So, I knew that this first job might not necessarily be in the field. I wanted to get my Marriage and Family Therapy (MFT) license, so I was also applying to graduate school. I was at college in Los Angeles (LA) at the time, and I applied to both LA graduate schools as well as Northern California graduate schools. And then, when I got accepted into the University of San Francisco (USF) in the middle of February, I decided to focus my job search in the San Francisco Bay Area.

I was open to almost anything in terms of a job to pay the bills. That being said, I wasn't trying to work in retail, and I wasn't trying to work in food service. But I had a lot of experience with anything computer related, with any sort of customer service type of position. So, initially, customer service was probably the biggest keyword I was looking for. It was that, or office administration, or office assistant. During my last two years of college, I was working at the [college] operating center, that's the generic phone number that everybody calls, and I would then transfer the call to public safety or to another professor. So, my phone etiquette and my verbal customer service were very on point. I also had a little bit of an office background; I had helped my mom at her job at various times throughout my summers growing up. I was also very computer savvy, as far as particular computer programs. So, in terms of customer service or customer relations, I was very comfortable, probably a little overqualified for the jobs I was applying to. But I didn't have too high of an expectation for my first job. I knew that the first job that you get out of college, 97 percent of the time, is not going to be the exact amazing thing that you're always looking for. I knew I didn't necessarily need or want to keep my hopes too high. But still, I didn't get any jobs for several months.

Eventually, by March, a month before graduation, I was in a fit of concern, and I emailed my mom. I was thinking, "Well, what am I going to do? I need to find a job, I'm graduating soon, I need to make money because grad school is expensive." So, my mom told me that their receptionist was leaving at the beginning of May, and she suggested that I apply for that job. I thought a lot about it. On one hand, it was back home, and it was a company that I was intimately familiar with. My mom has been there for over 20 years, and I've grown up with a lot of her coworkers, and they've seen me grow up. The downside? Well, I would be working with my mom every day.

So, my mom told me to send my resume to Andy, who is the boss and the owner of the company. Now even though I've known him for most of my life, I kept it very professional. I sent an email saying something like, "Hey Andy, my mother mentioned that the position is opening. I wanted to let you know that I was interested. Here is my resume, let me know if you have any questions or concerns." I'm sure that my mom probably vouched for me. And realistically, everyone in that company, especially all of the partners, knew who I was. About a week or so later, I was given the approval to start. There was no official interview. Andy and I just emailed back and forth about the logistics. We probably had our first in-person conversation the Monday that I started working, and it was at that time that we hammered down some of the logistics, what my pay was going to be, and things like that. But considering it was a receptionist position, which is relatively straightforward, there wasn't a whole lot of interviewing.

My first day was April 30. I graduated on Friday, drove home on Saturday, and started work on Monday. That was the other downside, I got absolutely no summer vacation after graduation. I remember my first day walking in, I was pretty excited to have a job. I knew I was incredibly lucky. I knew that there were few opportunities like this, immediately after college. That's the thing when you get to senior year of college, everyone is so concerned about what you're going to do after college. Because there's no longer a road map of what you're supposed to do. When you graduate from high school, 98 percent of the students are probably going to go to college. After college, what were you supposed to do? You're supposed to get a job. Well, where are you going to find a job? I knew I was incredibly lucky to be able to get a job, so I was excited to start. I was interested to learn more about the background of the stuff I had heard about over the years because my mom talked about her job. I also wanted to be able to get to know the other coworkers on a professional level. They've always known me as my mom's daughter, so I wanted to be able to talk to them on my own, with me as their coworker.

The job itself was pretty basic. As a receptionist, I would answer calls, sometimes do some letter writing for the legal side of the business, and do a lot of scanning for the accounting people. I helped Andy finalize a lot of his letters. He would write things out, and then I would type up everything and prepare it for his signature. I loved the family vibe of the company. The company was so small, and the next person who had been recently hired before me had been there for at least eight years. So, this is a long-standing company, and my mom has been there since I was six, so she's been there for almost 20 years. Everyone knew about each other's spouses and their children. Some of the employees were around when children were born and watched them grow up. It was very much a family, and I really appreciated that.

But I quickly realized that this was not the field that I wanted to be in. I know what my mom was thinking. She never explicitly stated it, but I know she was thinking that if I worked there long enough, I would want to be an accountant. And I was like, no, this is not happening. It just got really tedious after a while, especially knowing that this was not the field that I wanted to be in. I also ultimately realized that I was getting underpaid. Funnily enough, my mom actually was the one who told me a couple years ago. Now, I was never necessarily bored. Our clients were always so interesting. And we'd have office gossip about what's happening with this client and what's happening with the money after this person died, stuff like that. But it just got tedious. I knew that I could be doing more.

It actually took me a couple of years before I found the drive again to go back to graduate school. Even though I had gotten accepted into USF, some financial struggles were happening at the time, so I deferred my admission for a semester, and then, ultimately, I rejected the offer. And so, it took me a couple of years until I actually went back to grad school.

Eventually, I left Andy's company at the end of 2017, after about four years. So now I'm working at a jewelry store. If you're from the Bay Area, you've probably heard our commercials. I am a customer service associate here. I've been here for over a year, with my second anniversary coming up in November. Last year was actually really crazy, I switched jobs three times. I left Andy's company at the end of 2017, and then I was doing DoorDash full-time for a few months until I realized that it just wasn't sustainable. Then I got referred to a part-time position at a food catering start-up that my boyfriend had been working at. I worked there for another few months before I landed this job at the jewelry store company.

My advice to someone currently looking for their first job is … Don't limit what you're willing to do. I think one of the things that I regret is that I refused to work in food service or in retail. I've heard so many horror stories about retail positions and food jobs that it scared me away from doing anything like that. But at the same time, a job is a job. So, it comes down to what you're willing and able to sacrifice. Had I needed to actually maybe pay more bills, I would've just taken anything. I wouldn't have cared how demeaning it might have been because it was necessary for me to live and for me to survive. But looking back, I definitely limited myself in what I was willing to do. If I could do it again, I would definitely broaden my horizons, and maybe look in a different location.

One thing that I'm realizing now is that I want to live somewhere else and experience what life is like in a different location. I've lived in California my entire life, and other than the four years that I went to college, I've been in Northern California my entire life. I'm kind of getting that itch to see what it's like to live somewhere else. I've heard a lot of great stories about people who broaden their search to literally everywhere and find an opportunity in a different city. They couch surf for a little bit, but now they've settled, and they're having a good time. It's those experiences that I think could be really helpful in gaining a wider knowledge of what you're comfortable with, what you're not comfortable with, and where you want to go.

The biggest thing is that the first job that you get doesn't have to be the end. Just because it's the job that you have, doesn't mean that you need to stay there for the rest of your life. I'm almost done with my MFT program now, and I've told my employer that I expect to leave at the end of this year. That's why dealing with retail during the holiday season wasn't as big of a deal, because I knew that my time here was limited. I know people often get comfortable with their jobs, and if they get comfortable, they feel like they can't branch out, that they can't risk it all to find something else. I strongly encourage taking that risk and taking that chance. I feel like it'll give you so much more to live for, otherwise, you get stuck, and you get stagnant in whatever it is that you might be doing.

2.2 On the Long and Windy Path: Caleb's Story

You have to expect the unexpected, but you also have to put yourself out there. Nothing fell really in my lap, everything came from me going above and beyond what I was initially asked. Then people saw that there's value here, that my talents are not being fully utilized in this role.

I went to a tiny liberal arts college for undergrad, and I majored in political science and history. Which, in hindsight, maybe didn't prepare me so much for "real world" jobs. But I graduated, and then after that, didn't really know what to do. I did some contract work, stayed at home, made a little money, saved up, and then went to get my master's in public policy. I figured I could actually get some practical skills this way.

So after graduating with my master's, I started applying to jobs in Washington, DC. I applied to anything I could find that was remotely related to policy work, though I was particularly interested in nuclear nonproliferation because that's what I did my internship in. I applied to be a program assistant, policy assistant, program administrator, research assistant, really kind of any of those "working with somebody who was obviously much more senior" types of positions. Most of it was grunt work, editing documents and such. But that was where I figured I would have to get my foot in the door. And I applied, applied, and applied some more. All I hoped for was just for one person to see my application, that I would get longer than the 12 seconds on average somebody looks at your resume. I mean, we all had the resume template, right? And it all felt so generic, so I would try to customize it for each job. If I read an article by someone who worked at that place, I would reference that article and try to really personalize it to show that I'm connected to the work that the organization is doing.

But I just didn't get anything for months on end. I got tired of waiting, so I just decided to throw it all into the wind and see what happened. So I just straight-up moved to Washington, DC in July or August of that year. No job, and no apartment, I just slept on some couches and took temp work to make ends meet. I did that for several months, working conferences and the registration booth, and even some catering work. Now this was in 2011, so it was right in the economic downturn, people were still struggling to find work, and I knew other friends who were still working as baristas. I tried not to get discouraged, but it was tough. I remember sitting there thinking, "Okay, I've invested a lot of money in my education to come to this job." But then even the jobs I was applying for paid only $30,000 or $40,000 a year. So, what was it all for? And I remember I had made a decision, I think it was December, I said if I didn't find anything by February, I said I would have to go home, and I'd have to reassess. I had prospects back at home that I could have taken, but it was like I could go back and work as curriculum support at my high school. It felt like that was going to put me into a life that I was not looking forward to. I felt like I had a dream, I really did have a dream that I was going to be able to come out here and make a difference. Blame that maybe on too much watching of *The West Wing*. But I just believed that that was what I was coming to do.

And then finally I got lucky. I was working a temp job as an admin for a think tank in DC. And they treated me really well, even though I was just an admin, they recognized I had a master's degree in public policy, so they worked really hard to try to help me find something. That led to a connection with a science policy think tank, and they didn't have anything available, but one of their people had just started as a director over at an organization supporting engineering education. So they passed my info over to him, and he happened to have an opportunity for an entry-level job doing help desk work. So that's where I started, as a program assistant, essentially a help desk worker. I was answering questions about the foundation's Graduate Research Fellowship Program. I remember walking in, so nervous, on my first day. I was nervous because I couldn't fail. It took me so long to get that job, I had to be great at it. I can't afford to fail, but also this is what I said I wanted, this is my foot in the door.

There's also all the complexities and concerns around race as well. I was just worried that anything that I didn't do well would be a negative, not just for me, but for everybody who looks like me. And so it was just this pressure to really succeed.

I remember showing up on the first day, not knowing what the dress code was, so I came in wearing a full suit and tie. Everyone else was wearing T-shirts and jeans. I think, even though I saw what the culture was, I still wore button-downs and slacks probably for the first six months. I remember coming in not knowing what people supply you with on your first job. So I had a pack of pens, and a pack of Post-it notes, so I came in with this backpack essentially full of school supplies because I wasn't sure what I would have at my cubicle.

But there was also this weird sense of, "I've made it." When I walked up, they walked me to my cubicle, there with my name on that cubicle. And it was kind of like, this is my spot. This is where I belong. That felt really awesome. It really felt like, okay, after all of this, there I am.

I remember I took a picture, and I posted it on my Facebook because for me it was truly a symbol. As I was as proud of that, as I was of my degree because I had finally got my name on the board somewhere.

Now that being said, it wasn't exactly a dream job. I made like $40,000 a year, which wasn't a lot for DC. I was living with four other people in a shared house. I was walking to work most time because I didn't even have enough money to constantly load my Metro card. I remember I usually had enough money to get through half the month. And so I would load the card for half the month, and I would just use it on days when it was cold or rainy, or I'd take the bus on days when it was cold or rainy, and I would take the bus because the bus was cheaper than the Metro.

Despite all that, I learned so much on that first job. My manager, even though she was hands off, she was very good at connecting with people on a personal level, checking in, and asking how people were, ensuring that people were taking care of themselves. One thing that she always did was she would bring back little trinkets from wherever she traveled. It meant so much to me. I don't know if anybody else felt it, but as a sensitive and very empathic person, I did. The fact that you took some time while you were on your vacation, and thought about us, said a lot to me. So I've carried that with me. I check in on my team, and when I go on travels, I bring back trinkets, because I find that we spend so much time at work, that they do become very much part of our family. Sometimes we spend more time with work colleagues than we do with our own families, right? And in some things, I also try to do the antithesis, by creating an environment in which people never feel like they're just heads down working clock in clock out. I believe that what I do and what we do here at my current institution, and really everywhere that has these goals, is around passion. It's passion work. I like to try to see that. I love to see people laughing while they're working, I love to see people willing to stay after and going above and beyond because they know that it's going to make a difference. And also, the very last thing, is that I always tell people if they're starting a role with me, on the first day I'm very clear about what the dress code is and what will be on their desk!

Anyway, I worked my way up from that first job. Now initially, I thought, answering phones and answering questions about a fellowship program didn't really seem like I was changing the world. But after some time, I realized that I could actually help people, even in that position. I grew pretty quickly, so I went from an assistant to an assistant program manager. And then from an assistant program manager to a program manager there, and I did that within the four years. During that time,

I realized that our organization really struggled with getting diverse applicants, so I started working on that. By the time I became program manager, I was in charge of our outreach program helping them find and encourage diverse applicants. And that actually set the tone for me working in diversity in STEM [science, technology, engineering, mathematics].

So while I would have never expected that I, a person who was interested in nuclear nonproliferation, would end up doing diversity, I've worked my way all the way up to now being a chief diversity officer at a school of engineering. So it was a very windy path that I would have never, as I started off, drawn the map that way. But the destination at which I ended up is exactly where I think I was supposed to be.

My advice to someone currently looking for their first job … is that you have to expect the unexpected, but you also have to put yourself out there. Nothing fell really in my lap, everything came from me going above and beyond what I was initially asked. Then people saw that there's value here, that my talents are not being fully utilized in this role.

I remember I was in my first job in the help desk role, there was an evaluation tool that we used, and I think I had mentioned how not many people stepped up to offer assistance in helping our boss. I went to her and said, "Hey, is there anything that I can help you with?" And she was doing some evaluation stuff, and she was like, "Well, maybe, do you know how to do pivot tables?" I said absolutely! I got back to my desk, and I had no clue how to do pivot tables. So I went on Google, and I watched the e-how videos on how to do pivot tables, and I watched it three or four times and tried and tried again until I got it right. I did that, and my boss liked it, and pretty soon I took over a lot of the reporting duties.

So again, it may not have been in your skill set initially, but that's why we're lifelong learners, right? You have to find out where the need is, and learn it, and then do it. Whether it's picking up an e-how, or picking up an additional book to try to figure out how to become a better editor, whatever it may be, that's what you have to do to put yourself out there.

And I think for people of color, know that coming in, you already have some bias possibly against you. Use that as encouragement and empowerment. Say, "I know what I bring to the table, I know that intrinsically as an individual I am capable, that I am not the stereotype." The more you challenge assumptions and the more you challenge opinions, the people that come behind you, because they had that real-world interaction with you, no longer are they basing it on a stereotype, now they're basing it on a literal interaction with someone. And now that implicit bias comes up in their first thoughts, they can wave that away because their real-life experience will have said, "No, I met someone that was African American that didn't have the highest GPA [grade point average], that didn't have the right upbringing, that didn't speak English as their first language, and they ended up being one of the greatest employees I ever had."

That I think is what changes perceptions, it changes views and ultimately allows us to be much more interconnected and supportive of one another in a global society.

2.3 On Persistence in Pursuing Accounting: Katie's Story

If you're specifically looking to be an accountant, just apply, apply, apply. Remember that not getting an internship does not mean that there isn't a spot for you as a full-time hire. Getting an internship offer could just be maybe more on your interview skills, and they might've needed a little bit more work. It has nothing to do with your ability to actually perform, so my advice is I wouldn't judge yourself too harshly on having an internship or not.

During the fall or spring of your third year in college, all the top accounting firms are interviewing for their internship program. So in our accounting classes, that's when our professors were encouraging us to look for summer internships. They told us we should never get an unpaid internship if it's going to be in accounting. They gave us guidance for getting an internship and how that process works. Actually, the top accounting firms were a new concept to me, because I did not grow up close to a big city. So that was the first time that I had heard about the top accounting firms.

At that time, I thought I wanted to do tax accounting. I actually didn't get any offers from the other accounting firms that I applied to. I was scared after that; it was a big hit to my ego and self-confidence. I felt like I had just totally bombed my interviews, felt like maybe I wasn't quite good enough, even though I was a top performer in my classes. However, just talking through that process with professors as well as family members, I kept being told that even if you don't get an interview for an internship, that does not mean that you can't apply for a full-time position even at one of the top accounting firms. So even if you don't get an internship, which generally results in an offer, they still do hire full-time hires who have not done an internship.

This all changed for me when we had a class one day where our professor brought in a couple of alums who were working at accounting firms to come do a presentation. The two alumni essentially turned it into a recruiting event. Even though they didn't recruit directly at our school, they came in and gave a small presentation, but then we went out to dinner afterward with their recruiter. I sat next to the recruiter, and we got to talking about school and my personal life, I told her that I had applied for tax internships. She told me that I didn't strike her as somebody who belongs in the tax, she told me that my personality seemed better suited for audit. So she invited me to interview for an audit internship at their company, and then I ended up getting the offer for the summer. This whole experience was sort of by luck, especially because my college wasn't very big, so I had to compete against my fellow classmates for a lot of the same internships from companies that were regularly recruited at our school.

This summer internship was probably the best experience I had in college. While I had the opportunity to see a couple of different companies and help the team with whatever they needed me to do, I wasn't working a busy season, so I had time to explore and learn different things. And they organized the internship well with our cohort, so we would do class activities together and have fun. It was amazing to get to see the inside workings of a business, to actually sit in their offices and see behind the scenes. It's like going behind the scenes of a movie. I learned to ask questions, be eager to volunteer for small tasks, show up on time, and all the other basics of making a good impression in an internship.

Generally, in accounting, if you don't screw up your internship, you'll get a full-time offer. Toward the end of the internship, you would get your performance feedback from the various teams that you have worked with, every person was assigned to a partner, and the partner would call you in and share with you the feedback on your internship. And then basically you would get your offer in that meeting.

So the next year when I started full time right out of college, I was considered a first-year associate (a "newbie," they called me). When I started with the firm, I had two main engagements: one public company in the oil and gas industry with quarterly filings, and a nonpublic company with a September 30 year-end. The different year-end dates worked well with my schedule, so I could help out on other engagements as needed. As a first year, most of my work was in auditing cash, auditing accounts payable, and doing some limited controls testing related to the areas of the financial statements that I was responsible for. But really when you show up, you're never really working alone, because you don't know what you're doing. There are always senior employees coaching you through it, letting you try it, and then taking over after you show that you can get it right. What I learned was to take notes, ask questions, group your questions together, then ask my coach for help. Auditing is essentially testing, you're doing tests to make sure that what the company says in its financials is materially accurate. I loved testing, I loved working in Excel, and making things look nice and neat and organized.

I haven't left my company, I'm still here 14 years later! For me, I was always focused on the next goal. When I got started, I wanted to be promoted to senior. When I was a senior, the next step for me was to be a manager, and so on. It's been the right path for me so far. I've moved industries, I've moved countries, and I even did a three-year rotation in Switzerland when I was an experienced senior. At my company, it's always an upward trajectory. It's a pentagram where your performance is measured against five different expectations. You're not expected to meet the next level for each of the five areas, but after a few years, if you're exceeding expectations in those areas, then you'll get the promotion to the next level. So now I'm a director, and the next step would be a partner.

My advice to someone currently looking for their first job is ... Everyone should have an open mind and flexibility when it comes to taking a job right out of college. No decision on a job is permanent; you can always change. However, before saying you don't like this, you should speak to somebody. Sometimes the soft skills that you're learning on a job aren't as apparent as the technical skills. But soft skills are such an important thing to learn, and they take a little bit longer to learn in a career development pathway. A lot of times, people miss the learning opportunities or even the experience that they're getting if they're in a tough situation. Maybe you're actually learning incredibly important soft skills in stress management or working with a difficult situation. So if you're in that place, it's about assessing if you're having a tough time now but learning from it, or it's a bigger problem and you're not on the right career path. We've had people leave because they wanted to be a yoga instructor, but right out of college, they thought they needed to get a job in finance where it's stable and pays well. That's why I'm saying that nothing that you do is permanent, you can always change careers. There's nothing wrong with that, getting some experience under your belt and then deciding, is this what I want to keep doing, or do I want to do something else.

If you're specifically looking to be an accountant, just apply, apply, apply. Remember that not getting an internship does not mean that there isn't a spot for you as a full-time hire. Getting an internship offer could just be maybe more on your interview skills, and they might've needed a little bit more work. It has nothing to do with your ability to actually perform, so my advice is I wouldn't judge yourself too harshly on having an internship or not. If you join a bigger accounting firm, it provides a lot of value to stay long enough to get experience in coaching and overseeing work performed by at least one or two junior staff.

2.4   On Reaching Out for Help: Cam's Story

Don't be afraid to reach out to anyone and everyone and just let them know that you are looking. I think some people are scared to do that because they fear that it may look like you're asking for a job. But it's not that, it's really saying, hey if you hear of anything, please know that I am on the market. You just never know what's going to turn up in someone's circle.

I remember my first part-time job, starting at age 12 in a bakery. My years working in a bakery helped me build up proof that I could show up on time, was disciplined, knew how to deal with the public, and knew how to be managed. Plus while I was in college, I had work-study all four years, and I mostly worked in the dean's office and in residential life. So I was fortunately able to have some good things to put on my resume just to show that I had in fact been subject to employers' rules and expectations before. And then my senior year, I was fortunate enough to get an internship with a woman who was on the board of visitors for my college at the time. She ran an executive search firm, and I was able to actually work for her my senior year. So I commuted about two hours driving, two days a week, for my entire senior year.

At this point, I knew I wanted to work in HR [human resources]. I knew I had to start as a HR assistant, or something similar like running payroll, just to get my foot in the door. I actually got married after my junior year of college. My husband got a job in Oklahoma, so then my search switched specifically to finding something in Oklahoma. Now this was 20 years ago, so there were no online postings. I would search through newspapers that my parents mailed me from Oklahoma for job postings, and I applied to many different HR assistant roles across a variety of industries. I ended up having to move to Oklahoma after graduation without a job!

It was a lot of work applying for these jobs, and I often felt anxious, and out of control, like things were out of my hands. I wanted people to respond. I was frustrated because college degrees weren't all that prolific back then, so I felt like I was more than qualified given all of my work experience and my good grades. People were telling me that I had to apply for everything, even if that meant going to our local hamburger restaurant. Now in my mind, I was sitting on $80,000 in loans, and I wasn't going to go work a minimum-wage job. But I knew I had to have something, I knew I couldn't rely on my parents or anyone to provide for me. It was truly, when I graduate, how am I going to eat? So I applied everywhere, at the hamburger shop, McDonald's, Lowe's, and Safeway. I think that's one of the biggest challenges I've seen particularly in the generation just following me. I have a cousin who's just five years younger than I am, and she recently got laid off, she absolutely will not apply to those places. She says, I have a bachelor's degree and 18 years of experience, and my thought even then is that it's better to be underemployed than unemployed.

"There was one professional employer organization" at the time in Oklahoma, and they were really kind of taking off, so I thought it would be a perfect place to get started in HR management consulting. Once I moved there, I called and mailed handwritten letters to this company at least once a day for a week straight. I had family and friends in the area, so I asked around constantly to see if anyone knew someone at this company.

And eventually, they called me in to interview, maybe just to get me to stop calling them! I interviewed with the vice president of HR and another HR manager. They asked why I wanted to work in HR, and why I was so eager to work there since I had called so many times. I had my answers ready based on the research I had done on the organization. I knew they had made it on the Best Places to Work surveys, they had a great reputation for employee satisfaction and professionalism, and so forth. They asked about my HR experience, so I told them about my time on the executive search committee and gave them my references, which at the time were printed letters that I carried around. I remember one specific question was, "Are things black or white or gray?" I thought for a while about that question, between my own upbringing and what I knew about the strictness of certain labor laws, but I answered, "They're mostly gray, up until the point that some things may be black and white." And she said, "Perfect." She explained how in HR a lot of decisions have to be weighed based on the individual and the circumstances, so discernment is important in the job. So that's what I remember about the interview, and they called later that afternoon, and I started three days later.

I remember my offer actually. It was $17,500 salaried, with good benefits like a 401k match, two weeks of vacation, and all the medical benefits. I was so excited my first day, I showed up in a fancy suit with high heels and a little paper sack with my lunch. I got my own desk in an office with a window. I couldn't wait to set up my email signature, record my voicemail, get my business cards, and organize some textbooks onto the bookshelf. Probably that whole first year, I sat right next door to our CEO [chief executive officer] and the VP of HR was next to him, so I could always tell when he was leaving. That first year, I never left before he did. No one told me to do that, I just kind of had a sense that that would be better for me. I volunteered for everything. I was meticulous in how everything was ordered and organized, and I had a clean desk, I just found almost any possible way I could to always say yes, no matter the question. I bugged everyone with questions so I could learn more, like when I went down to the benefits department and asked all sorts of questions about coinsurance and reinsurance just so I could understand things better.

In the years since, I've worked so many different jobs. My husband went to graduate school, so I ended up working as the HR manager for an airline company back in California. Then I went to work as an EEO [equal employment opportunity] and dispute resolution consultant for a large bank with 80,000 employees nationwide. During that time, I had kids, got divorced, and I even went to law school. So finally, more recently, I moved back to Oklahoma, worked in the state government HR, and then started a search firm company as one of the founder's first employees. Now, I'm in Dallas as the VP of HR for a large portfolio management company.

My advice to someone currently looking for their first job is ... first, during your job search, don't be afraid to reach out to anyone and everyone, and just let them know that you are looking. I think some people are scared to do that because they fear that it may look like you're asking for a job. But it's not that, it's really saying, hey if you hear of anything, please know that I am on the market. You just never know what's going to turn up in someone's circle. To the extent that somebody has a church community, I think that's a fantastic place to reach out to people. If you were in a fraternity, sorority, or social club, they often try and do a good job building a network. Ask your professors, the ones who know you well, ask them how they got their first job, or what approach did they take. Yes, it's going to be awkward, but I think showing that interest is enough to get people to consider referring you.

When you get that job, be hungry, be insatiably curious, be the nicest person in the office, and be the one most willing to say yes to additional work. I think a lot of my success has been because of the things I've been willing to do. I would take the initiative to restock crackers and sodas, go around and clean up after a company party, and other quiet little tasks to show that I was more focused on the company than myself. I also don't think it's successful if you bring attention to it. It has to be something that you don't talk about, but others may just eventually pick up on. And be nice to the support staff, receptionists, assistants, and secretaries. I think in almost every job, they've been some of my closest connections. Always ingratiate yourself with the people who are really doing that hard work and support them. It's really to the extent that you can build up others, eventually, it'll start to reflect really well on you. There's no job that's beneath any of us, every job is meaningful.

The other thing is, if you are bored at work, that is your fault. That is not your employer's fault, that is always your fault. If you have a functioning mind and ability to communicate, go find something to do, ask for something to do, make up something to do, or look around and see what needs doing. Quietly ask somebody else if they need help, and eventually, if you ask enough people, you will get additional work to do. I mean, that's not going to work on a production line or something, but in most corporate environments, you can always find something more to do. People who wait for work, don't move up. It's the people who hungrily go out and find work and take ownership of it who get promoted.

One last thing, admit you're wrong early and often. Accountability is such a rare trait, and so if you do something wrong, unintentionally or intentionally, own it and say, that was my fault, but here's how I suggest we fix it, and here's how I'm going to make sure I don't do it again. That is something that just makes everyone on the team want to work with you.

2.5 On Alternative Definitions of Success: Wyatt's Story

My life is a life of spectacular failure, followed by very incremental and steady improvement. I was very egotistical when I left for college, followed by a pretty far fall down from where I was, or where I thought it was at least, during college. So I would say to anybody who's experienced that same feeling, be patient. Be patient and consistent. There's no reason to hate yourself, just because you didn't live up to a standard that society had set for you or you set for yourself. Allow yourself to grow.

I didn't graduate from college. I left and came home, and I was looking for something that paid money. I wasn't really specific about what I needed. I had some previous job experience in high school and on summer breaks where I would do some service work. So I started by searching for something in the service industry, ideally a higher-ranked restaurant because that meant I would get paid more.

So I just went walking around downtown Austin with a resume. I literally had no idea where the higher-end restaurants were, so I just walked into stores randomly to introduce myself. I was pretty terrified, but this was what my dad had advised me to do. I had left college because I was pretty badly in a state of depression. Walking into those restaurants was something I had never done before. So eventually I walked into this restaurant called John's, and the general manager immediately sat me down for an interview. It definitely freaked me out a little. I was only prepared to say hi, and the manager just said, let's sit down and have an interview. I felt like I was spitballing and messing it up. But at the end, he said okay, sounds good, let's get you started as a food runner. I started the next week.

This was a big turning moment for me, walking into a restaurant and getting a job. I felt pretty unstoppable. When you leave college, the world tries to tell you that you're a disgrace, they try to tell you that you're not worthy of achieving something, and I was in a pretty bad state. And I'm not in a bad state anymore, so that became a turning point in my therapy to be able to go in and learn that I could support myself. Now, there were still plenty of struggles. But it was so important to me to be able to go and be a successful adult and live by myself and support myself.

This first job was very physically taxing. We had a Pork Chop Friday, where they had this big iron skillet and they put a pound and a half of pork chops on it, and that was their promo. So when four people ordered it, that meant up to 25 pounds on your shoulder and arm, carrying that across the restaurant, serving it, then going back and getting another one. I looked at it as kind of a therapy for myself. I needed something where I could feel like I was working hard and be proud of that. I knew in the back of my mind that if I work hard enough, they're going to promote me to be a server, so I don't have to carry these as often. It was very impressive to them, I suppose, that I was working as hard as I was.

In about a month, they promoted me to server. I went into the office, and I was getting about 38 hours, and I just asked if can I do something extra to get my 40 hours, because I can't pay my rent. And so at that moment, he promoted me to server. As for benefits, it's a restaurant. So there are no benefits, they don't pay for health insurance, they don't do any of that. For me, I was young, I didn't really need health insurance, and so I lived by the skin of my teeth. I didn't really know how to manage money at the time, nobody had taught me, so we got paid out in cash at the end of every night, and I really didn't know how to put money in a savings account. I didn't know how to make sure I had enough for rent by budgeting a certain amount every month. I had no budget, all the typical young adult stuff that you hope you learn as a teenager before you become an adult, I have no knowledge of it. So it was all learning by hard knocks.

For whatever reason, the management at that company was pretty awful. Once I left, and I worked with other servers at other restaurants, everybody knew that John's is just kind of like this pit that servers fall into, and it's tough to get out, because they learn bad habits and they don't do well. Looking back on it, it was easy to understand that John's was probably not the best place for me to work at the time, but it was a job and it was something that I needed to be able to recognize what a good workplace looks like. The management wasn't good. One of the managers would come in and get angry at people for no reason. Another would put us into sections with too many tables with low sales, making it impossible for us to earn enough in tips.

Eventually, I started looking for a new job. I found a place where I stayed for about five years, and I ended up training servers for them and traveling all around the United States opening restaurants and training servers for them. Looking back, I would say that I would always give places a year. You never know how something might improve over the year, especially in the service industry. And what really got me through that season was hope. You need to develop a sense of hope in yourself every day you walk through the doors of any job. That hope has to come from within you, and you need to do whatever you need to inspire that hope, inspire that dream, and inspire that feeling. There's this axiom of 1 percent change every day. If you're improving yourself by 1 percent every day, over the year you have 365 percent change. So for me, the hope always came from the idea that I can improve myself today.

Since then, I've moved on to several different jobs. I wanted to move into a world of daytime hours, so I ended up at a company selling health insurance over the phone. It was a very challenging job, but it had the best support system that I've ever seen in a job. I had a great mentor who taught me how to work in sales, and I had some minor successes. I got married, so I started looking for a job with less hours. She was an attorney, so we weren't hurting for money at that point. But my experience allowed me to learn a bit about the banking industry. I started as a teller, I moved into a personal banker, and then I very quickly found that the people who make the most money in the credit union were the mortgage people. So a couple of months ago, I finished all the certifications I needed to get my mortgage license, and now I'm deep in the mortgage industry in Colorado. I work for a CEO who is about 10 times smarter than I am, so it's hard to keep up. He's teaching me how to negotiate and have clients and find leads and all kinds of crazy mortgage stuff. To me, I feel like I've just taken off on a rocket, and I'm just trying to hang on.

My advice to someone currently looking for their first job is ... my life is a life of spectacular failure, followed by very incremental and steady improvement. I was very egotistical when I left for college, followed by a pretty far fall down from where I was, or where I thought it was at least, during college. So I would say to anybody who's experienced that same feeling, be patient. Be patient and consistent. There's no reason to hate yourself, just because you didn't live up to a standard that society had set for you or you set for yourself. Allow yourself to grow. You've got to find someplace to take root, and then continue to water yourself, continue to seek out improvement, even when you're tired because you're going to see the fruits and the results of those improvements. Not now obviously, if you plant an apple tree, you don't get the fruit today, you get the fruit far down the road. I would say to anybody who's in that situation, find some good character people, find some good associations, and be patient.

2.6 On Unconventional and Unexpected Paths: Meera's Story

> *Unconventional methods are fine. I started out as a freelancer and as a temp, and then I worked my way up. This isn't what I wanted to do at the beginning. I didn't grow up a sports fan, so all my college friends are stunned that this is my career path. It's ok to change your mind and it's okay to do something different, because we're not locked in.*

I graduated with my bachelor's and wanted to work in the entertainment industry. I didn't know exactly what that was, so I was constantly searching. I was living at home, so I wasn't worried about paying for stuff, so I took a lot of jobs as a freelancer. I worked on a lot of movies, TV commercials, and student film festivals. I also had a part-time office job where I was somebody's assistant.

I had this vague idea of wanting to work in the entertainment industry, but I didn't really know exactly. I wasn't a writer or an actor, so I didn't really know exactly what I wanted. I just knew that I wanted to work for a large studio. I interviewed at a talent agency, some assistant jobs in entertainment, and others. Our main job search engine back then was Monster, but in the entertainment industry, most of it was word of mouth.

For those two years, I talked to as many people as possible. I learned to tell everyone possible that I was looking for a job. I learned to always have an elevator pitch ready so if someone asked me what I was interested in, I had something to say. I guess hustling is a way to describe it, but it was really to just be prepared for whatever scenario you come in touch with.

Eventually, I was talking to this complete stranger at a bookstore because we were looking at the same book. I told her I had just finished some part-time contract work on a show and was looking for new jobs, and she mentioned that she worked at a temp agency and gave me their contact information. So I called them, and a week later, I started working as a temp at this company that eventually hired me for a full-time job.

For the first three months as a temp, I worked for this popular TV channel clearing commercial copies. For example, when you watch a TV show and you're watching the commercials, my job was to make sure that the right commercial that the advertiser wanted was airing at the right time. I remember when I was hired, my job wasn't really well explained because they were just scrambling to get someone into the role. Then I ended up getting hired permanently by a different network in the same department, and I stayed in that job for many years.

In television, there's always a very immediate deadline. Each day was pretty routine in terms of when reports were due, so the job itself was very structured. But the challenges were always changing; you never knew which advertiser or show would create a problem on a given day. I stayed in my division for years, moving from network to network, going from administrator to senior administrator to supervisor. Then I moved to the sports division in the same company as a manager, then I became the director. So now, 13 years later, I'm at the same company as the director of programming. I also got my MBA [master of business administration] along the way.

My advice to someone currently looking for their first job ... is to learn as much as possible and meet as many people as possible. People tend to be more forgiving of your mistakes when you're starting out or you're younger. A part of me wishes when I was younger that I had been more aggressive and more of an advocate for myself in getting promoted and asking for what I wanted. I would always encourage people to just go for what they want, which is such a cliche, but it's a cliche for a reason.

Also, unconventional methods are fine. I started out as a freelancer and as a temp, and then I worked my way up. This isn't what I wanted to do at the beginning. I didn't grow up a sports fan, so all my college friends are stunned that this is my career path. It's ok to change your mind and it's okay to do something different because we're not locked in. We don't have to be locked into the decision we made when we were 22.

2.7 On Getting the Most Out of That First Job: Aiden's Story

Looking back, my first job was the foundation that helped me get to where I am currently. It's where I met amazing people, learned from their experience, learned best practices, learned how to make work more efficient, and learned how to help the organization's bottom line. I still stay in contact with about seven people on a daily basis that I worked with or worked for.

I completed my college degree in finance and information systems, so I was looking for some type of financial analyst job, sales operations, or reporting and analytics. At one point I was interested in investment banking, but after speaking to people about that job and that field, I lost interest in that area. So I really focused my search on data and analytics jobs.

It ended up that the internship I had after my junior year of college ended up leading to my first full-time job. I had applied on their website for the internship, but my mom happened to know the hiring manager and was able to get me in contact with them, so that sped up the process to get me hired. I actually had offers from two other internships also, which I had just applied to without any connections.

There were a few folks I met at my internship that were particularly helpful. They would make time throughout their days and weeks to sit with me and go through their roles. They would explain what the job was like as a full-time job, and they taught me the processes, systems, and Excel files necessary to do the job. I think it was those people within that team that made the internship extremely beneficial because they were always willing to help if I got stuck on a project that I was working on or if I had a lot of questions. For the internship itself, at the end of the time, there was a project and a presentation. The project was being presented to leadership, and the project would really help the company improve and optimize its processes in the sales operations team that I was a part of. What was great about that was, five months later, when I did accept the full-time job, that same project that I was working on was still being used by the company. That was really cool to see that my internship work wasn't just some random project for those three months, but it was something that the company was actually going to use.

Anyways, after the internship, I still had to go through a formal interview process, which included the same team I had worked with over the summer. That process was still stressful, because I knew I was graduating college, and the fun and games will soon be over. I was going into the real world, so I needed a career, a job, and money. So in the meantime, I still looked elsewhere. I was on LinkedIn, talking to friends, looking for other jobs. I didn't really use the career center at my university, just online resources. It really came down to doing my own research. Doing research about a company or about the job, whether through websites or by asking friends, was incredibly important to figuring out what career I wanted for myself.

But at the same time, you can only stress so much about it, you can't let it take over your life. I knew that at some point in time, the right job would come my way, and that would be the start of my career. I also always knew that my first job wasn't going to be my dream job. I was assuming that on my first job was going to learn a lot, and I'm going to make some mistakes along the way, but it's going to be the foundation and where I start on the learning process. And then going from there would be where I would work towards finding that dream job, or at least a job that fits me better after having a couple of years of experience under my belt.

So when I finally did get the full-time offer from this payroll company, it worked out great, I started a month after graduation. It was a normal 8 to 5 job, about a 30-minute commute, with the full slew of benefits. I remember my salary was $60,000 but no bonus or equity. In terms of the day-to-day, it was mostly optimizing their Excel-based reporting and bringing that into Tableau to make it more efficient and enhance their visualizations. I worked for a director of sales operations, and we supported national accounts with clients of over 1,000 employees. I wasn't working too closely with leadership, it was mostly just day-to-day reporting, cranking out numbers, and so forth. As time went on, I got more experience and became more comfortable running meetings, having conversations with senior leaders, and doing more technical forecasting analysis.

About a year and a half later, I was promoted to senior analyst. It was mostly just the same work with a new title. Then after about two years, I got to work on this big "scorecard" project to visualize all the different metrics associated with sales performance for any given sales representative. That scorecard was rolled out to the entire organization's sales team, even after I left the company. I eventually made it to manager level, which is when I started looking around for new opportunities. The job was like a 75 percent match to my dream job; I loved all the data reporting and analytics, but I didn't love doing it for a payroll company. So then I moved on to a meal kit delivery company where I spent about two years, then a few months at a third-party insurance company. Now, I'm at a large national grocery retail chain, and I'm still in sales operations and analytics.

Looking back, my first job was the foundation that helped me get to where I am currently. It's where I met amazing people, learned from their experiences, learned best practices, learned how to make work more efficient, and learned how to help the organization's bottom line. I still stay in contact with about seven people on a daily basis that I worked with or worked for. And even today, I still reach out to them for advice on certain things, just because most of them have 10 or more years of experience. So having them as a resource in my pocket was extremely helpful and has proven to be pretty beneficial for future jobs as well.

My advice to someone currently looking for their first job ... is that you should go in knowing that your first job may not be your dream job. However, if you could get an amazing experience, if you could take in as much knowledge as you can if you could learn from extremely knowledgeable folks within that industry, that's going to be the most valuable thing even if it's not your dream job. Because then from there you can take that to the next job. I would also say that, if you can be in an industry that you know you have an interest in, find a job there. You'll probably enjoy any job in the right industry, just because you're interested in the industry. And again, that first job is going to be such an important foundation for you. It may not be your dream job, but it will give you the experience and knowledge you need to further your career.

2.8 On Trying Something Out, Just to See What It's Like: Sara's Story

Don't just get any job, but rather get a job that you're interested in and then be flexible. Back then, it often felt like whatever job you got, it'll be your job for the rest of your life. Now, I've learned that you should always be willing to learn and decide what you like or don't like.

As I finished my college degree in business, I was looking for pretty much any job to get experience in. I worked in my family business a bit while growing up, and I had some internship and tutoring experience. I knew a bit about HR and mediation, so I thought I might want to go into that field. This ultimately led me to a staffing job.

I remember using online search websites like Craigslist, but it felt like I was sending job application after job application into this dark hole with no results. I would have to invest so much time to apply and write the cover letter, and I wouldn't know if it was even going to be worth it. So I learned to focus on leveraging my network of friends or family. I would ask around, does anyone do this job or work for this company?

I would interview them, to see if it's something I would like to do, before even applying.

Eventually, I got into this staffing agency as an office assistant. I basically just helped other people fill out applications, test them for skills, and then put their files away. It felt like a waste of time, like I was wasting other people's time, and I wasn't really helping people. There was a season where we helped this other big candy chain company with their staffing needs, so that was a bit more fun because I could actually help others get jobs and get paid, but it was still just temporary. I know that temporary work is better than no work, but I still felt like there was a better use of my time and talents than just basically temporarily using people for work.

Also, I wasn't for office politics or even the expectations of office culture. I remember there was a lot of free time or downtime. I think I also felt a little insecure because they weren't training me fast enough, and I was just kind of sitting around a lot. I was only at the company for a few months, because once I realized what it was, I didn't really like it. It's even harder to have those conversations of, "This isn't working for me."

Eventually, I found another job in the social services arena as an employment specialist, where I would help other people get jobs. And then from there, in the same organization, I went to the youth center to help youth find jobs. At this point, I had a two-year-old, and I was still only making $15 an hour, so I needed to find a way to make more money. So I decided to go back to school to become a teacher, and I've been a high school teacher ever since. Even though that first job was difficult and so different than what I wanted to do or ended up doing, it at least taught me that I had to believe in my work and that I had to believe in the value I was adding to helping people.

My advice to someone currently looking for their first job is ... don't just get any job, but rather get a job that you're interested in and then be flexible. Back then, it often felt like whatever job you got, it'll be your job for the rest of your life. Now, I've learned that you should always be willing to learn and decide what you like or don't like. You're scoping out the company as much as the company is scoping you out. Sometimes you try it for a bit, and it doesn't work out, but you still find out what you liked or disliked about that organization, and you can take that with you to the next job. That's definitely got me where I'm at now, and I'm super happy.

Oh, and people say that you don't use your degree, like me with a business degree but now I'm teaching. Actually, I still think it's valuable. I do some work in life insurance and securities and some entrepreneurial stuff as side jobs when I take a sabbatical from teaching. So the degree is still helpful for that.

2.9   On Doing Something Completely Different: Bailey's Story

Before I started my job, I actually was thinking of going to graduate school, and I had an acceptance from another university. But I wanted to get some experience in interviewing, really just for fun and to practice . . . it never occurred to me that I was actually going to take one of those jobs. The actual program that I was hired for was a management development training program within a large bank. . . Who would have ever hired me, a political science major?

I actually started my job before graduating college. While I was a senior, because I was a political science major, there's usually not a lot of help with job placement in that particular major, but there's quite a bit of help with the business school students. So I attended job fairs in the business school, and that's where I got all of my interview opportunities. I needed it because prior to that, I really had no practical job experience other than teaching some fitness classes.

Before I started my job, I actually was thinking of going to graduate school, and I had an acceptance from another university. But I wanted to get some experience in interviewing, really just for fun and to practice. Back then, recruiters would come to the business school and go to job fairs, and you would talk to them and get their phone number to apply for a job; this was before there was such a thing as online job applications. I remember I got pretty far in the process with this jewelry company, and I interviewed for some jobs in sales and management. I felt pretty invincible actually, mostly because I already had a graduate school option lined up, so I just went in super relaxed. I probably shouldn't have been if I were really serious about getting a job. But for me it was more of an enjoyable process; it never occurred to me that I was actually going to take one of those jobs.

The actual program that I was hired for was a management development training program within a large bank. And at that point, the recruiters were looking for students with a well-rounded background, not necessarily business majors, which was very interesting. Now this position is in Manhattan, New York. I'm a kid from a small east Texas town, and I stayed in the bubble with my small college in Texas. Who would have ever hired me, a political science major? So when I interviewed, I really didn't think I would get the job. But the interviewer and I really hit it off, and I thought it was fun. I even encouraged my boyfriend at the time, now my husband of 30 years, to apply, even though he was a speech major. Believe it or not, both of us got a callback and a paid trip to New York City to do a second interview in their office in the financial district. And again, we went thinking it was just for fun, not thinking it was serious. But lo and behold, the interview went great, we were two of the 50 students that they recruited for this program from throughout the United States.

That was the best feeling ever. Both of us got this job, despite being political science and speech majors. We both went into this thinking it was just an experiment for fun, but then we realized this was such a great opportunity just to see where it went. Plus it paid super well (something like $35,000 back then), even though we had to move to Manhattan where dollars don't go anywhere. But even though it was super exciting, it was also so scary. We had to move to a completely new culture, a new state, half a country away, and do things we had no experience doing.

Now the program was structured very competitively and with intensive training for three months. They brought consultants in to train us on different areas of banking, and then we would practice, get evaluated and tested, and then rank within this group of 50. It was mostly regular hours, but also lots of overtime working on presentations and projects. Then based on the rankings, we got assigned to an area of the bank anywhere in the US and rotated every few months, which meant lots of travel. I had one assignment in Long Island, where I was the manager of a call center, and that meant getting up at 6a to travel an hour and a half to get out there. I also had a few months in luxury and second mortgages, helping people get mortgages on items like boats, planes, and vacation homes. I was on the 46th floor of the World Trade Center for some time.

Now remember, I never, ever, saw myself in banking. I loved the management part of it. I couldn't believe the amount of money they spent on us with the various trainers and consultants they brought in. I was a naïve kid, 22 to 23 years old, and I loved it. But it was stressful with the constant ranking and competition. The higher you rank, the better your placement. But my husband and I ended up finishing after a year in third and fourth place.

So from there, I stayed at the bank for a few years, but eventually, we both decided to move on. I went back to graduate school for organizational communications, and my husband went to law school. I worked in a consulting firm for a few years, then a medical system doing marketing work, and then I taught at a local college. After we had kids, I took care of the kids and mostly did volunteer work. Now I focus on philanthropy, local development and fundraising, and serving on several boards.

Looking back, I'm so thankful for the opportunity at this bank. It was such an education, learning the industry, learning how to work with different types of people and the diversity I was exposed to, and learning skills like making presentations and public speaking. A lot of those presentation skills are what prepared me most for things I've done later in life.

My advice to someone currently looking for their first job is ... what do you do if you don't know what you want to do? Honestly, I know that there's a lot of pressure on students when they graduate to find the perfect first job. Allow yourself some grace. Students today have to commit upfront, and I think that deprives them of the opportunity to develop as a well-rounded educated person, as opposed to going headstrong in one area. In that first job, you learn so much about yourself, what you like, what you don't like, and the environment you want to work in. Do you want to work independently, do you want to work with a group? Do you like to be heads down over a spreadsheet? Or is that your worst nightmare, looking over a spreadsheet?

Allow yourself the grace to change. Now I do believe you ought to stay in a job for at least a year or two, I think there's a lot to learn in any job, I don't think you need to jump ship immediately. Maybe managers will see potential in you in a different area and are willing to move you into that role.

And then for those who had just gotten the dream job or a great job, take every opportunity. Enjoy the training sessions! There are some people who think that that is the biggest snooze. But I say get all the training you can because it makes you such a better employee, and you can take that with you. You never know when you're going to use those skills. Even as a nonemployed person at this stage in my life, I use all those skills that I learned on the first job, and I give those back to non-profit companies all the time through helping with fundraising, communication, grant writing, speech making, presentations, and looking over balance sheets.

2.10   On Starting a Career in the Army: Ronald's Story

Looking back, one of the most important things I learned in the army was how important it was to take care of your people.... I realized if you take care of others, they'll take care of you. It's a relationship. That was really burned into my head during my 19 months as a platoon leader, and it's stuck with me. As a professor now, I look out for my students, first and foremost.

On Starting a Career in the Army: Ronald's Story

I wasn't that creative of a child. My father had gone to West Point. He had been a career military officer, and I guess in hindsight, that career looked appealing to me. So I applied to West Point and a nearby university, where I had a four-year ROTC [Reserve Officers' Training Corps] scholarship. I ended up deciding to go to West Point, which I knew was going to be more challenging than ROTC. I also thought that, if I was going to be in the military, I might as well jump in with both feet. That's what West Point felt like. You spend the whole time training, you're in the pool from day one. Now I imagine if I'd gone ROTC, I could have had a similar career, and I have friends in the military who went through ROTC. So in hindsight, it probably didn't matter as much as I thought it would, but looking back I'm happy with my choice.

So during your last year at West Point, you pick which branch of the army you want to go into, and they line you up according to your class rank. Each branch has a limited number of spots, so they go down the list and the top-ranked person picks what they want, and then the next, and so forth. I ended up selecting infantry, which was my top choice. It's interesting that there were about 200 infantry slots and 1,000 in the class, and many people at the top of the class wanted to go into branches like engineering. I wanted to do infantry because, in my view, that's what I thought the army was about. I wanted to jump out of a plane, run around, shoot things, whatever else in my early twenties. Plus my dad was also an infantry officer, so I knew what that life was going to be like.

I went down to a fort in Georgia for six months going through the infantry officer basic course. A lot of it was training I'd received at West Point, but now they were focusing on training me to be a leader of a 40-person platoon. They trained me on the technical level, the different weapon systems, how to assemble and disassemble them, maintenance, and everything you need to know about equipment. They also trained me on tactics, like how to maneuver in the woods, how to set up an ambush, and so forth. After that, I went to an airborne school, then finally ranger school where you take everything you've learned and put it to the test.

At ranger school for 72 days, they limit you to about two hours of sleep per night, drop you down to about 1,000 calories per day, and push you and stretch you as much as they can. We started in the woods of Georgia, then the mountains, then the swamps, and finally the deserts. You typically were marching 20 miles a day with a 60-pound pack. It was very physically and mentally demanding. I think the washout rate is about 50 percent. But they wanted to get you to that point, to the point when you couldn't even pick up your own pack, you needed someone to help you get it onto your back for you. They wanted to see how you would respond when you're completely wiped out and miserable.

So what do you do? For me, one thing was just the realization that this was a challenge and I had to overcome it. They weren't asking me to do things I couldn't do. I could always take one more step. And I knew my father, and many others, had gone through this. Plus I needed to in order to pursue my career in infantry, so I had that career preservation thought going into my head. They also pair each person with a buddy, and I had a really good one. One of the biggest dangers of ranger school is when you start droning. Droning is the word they use when you're not thinking clearly. People walk off cliffs and break their legs and then they get thrown out. People start getting cuts on their hands that they don't clean, and then they get an infection, so a percentage of people get thrown out for medical reasons. So my buddy and I would check each other every day, make sure we got any medication we needed, and take care of one another. If you look out for each other, your chances of making it through go way up.

But at the end of it, what you realize is that everything you learned works, and you can push yourself much further than you thought you could. That's really helpful to know, especially if you end up going to war. In combat, you find yourself in just horrible conditions, and what you need to do is push through them. Not just combat. Even now, if I find myself feeling sorry for myself in hard times, I know it's okay, I can just push through it.

Anyway, my first unit was a rifle platoon with 44 people. I remember probably months ahead of time, I would rehearse in my head what I was going to say to my platoon the first time I met them. And that was an incredible moment. My 19 months in this first role were phenomenal. We had two kinds of days. Some days were garrison, which is when we're in the barracks or the wood for training and working out, maintaining our equipment, and other practices like going to a rifle range. As a platoon leader, my job was to make sure the sergeants who led each squad within the platoon were providing the proper training. When we did larger exercises out in the woods, that's when we really got to lead. I would take a command from the company commander, then write out a platoon order to give to the squad leaders, and we'd rehearse a raid.

I was very fortunate in that the sergeants who worked for me were some of the best that I ran into over 22 years in the Army. I also had great people to learn from. I was having fun, I was learning, our platoon was getting better, and we were training at a very high level, but it was challenging. One of the things that the army does very well is to bring everyone back together to train for their next jobs. After I got promoted from platoon leader, I went back to Georgia for more training to be a company commander. After seven years in the army, they sent me to graduate school and then gave me an assignment to use what I learned. I got a master's in industrial engineering, and then I went to a think tank in DC. I did well there, so they ended up sending me on to get my PhD, and then I went back to the think tank. I was then deployed to Iraq, but coming out, I ended up in the Naval Postgraduate School. I taught there for four years, and that took me to the end of my career in the army. At that time, my son was visiting various colleges, and I ended up meeting with the head of the business department at one of the colleges. We struck up a conversation, and a couple of years later, that led to me taking a job as a business faculty at this college. Now, I'm almost at the end of year eight here. I teach decision science, which is very related to the industrial engineering degree I started.

Looking back, one of the most important things I learned in the army was how important it was to take care of your people. I remember we had this young kid who was doing very well, and he had the chance to go to sniper school, which would have been a great step for his career. But we had these platoon evaluations coming up, and my platoon was going to be evaluated, and without this young kid in my platoon, it could have led to poorer evaluations. So selfishly, I wanted him to stay with our platoon. But my platoon sergeant pulled me aside and said, no you don't understand, you need to look out for your people first and foremost. The others will pick up whatever slack there is if this young kid isn't there. He turned out to be right. I realized if you take care of others, they'll take care of you. It's a relationship. That was really burned into my head during my 19 months as a platoon leader, and it's stuck with me. As a professor now, I look out for my students, first and foremost.

My advice to someone currently looking for their first job is … you need to find something where you know you're going to like the job, and there's a decent chance you're going to love it. All jobs will get hard at some point, and you're going to end up questioning whether or not it was the right decision. If you're just doing the job for money or for some other reason, you might very quickly find yourself unhappy and wanting to move on to do something else. But I know for me, I was confident in what I wanted to do, and those first 19 months really helped me stay with the army for 22 years.

If you're specifically interested in the military, I would say you need to first figure out what branch you want to be in. Do you want to run up and down hills like I did, do you want to fly helicopters, or do you want to fire artillery or drive around in tanks? To most people, that's just all being in the army. But those are very different careers and very different experiences. They require different skill sets. I think it's very important for a ROTC cadet to figure out what's going to be the best fit for them. Talk to as many former soldiers as you can and learn from their experiences. Take advantage of the training you get in the summer, where the army tries to expose you to all these different branches. I think the same is true for a ROTC cadet as it would be for just anybody. You need to find something you like doing, something that you think you're going to enjoy. Because life's not always great. There were times I was out with my platoon, it was pouring down rain, and I was not having a good time. But most of the time, the majority of the time, I was having a blast.

2.11 On Persistence from an International Student Perspective: David's Story

If a company doesn't get back to you or doesn't treat you well as an applicant, it means they're not really a company that cares about their reputation or people in general.... So, don't be mad if the company doesn't get back to you, since they clearly don't care that much about people anyways.

I had just graduated from college, and I wanted to work in the same city I was already in, to stay there because I was already established and living with friends in the area. It was very convenient for me to not have to move out of state or out of the area. I was mostly looking for jobs in hospitality, education, or marketing. I applied to a lot of marketing coordinator and administrative coordinator-type jobs. My minor was in nonprofit management, so I applied to a lot of nonprofit companies, event management, and other types of jobs. I applied to something like 150 jobs and got about 25 interviews. Most of the others, I never heard back from. Some even reached back out to me after I already got a job. I realized that to get an interview, I really needed to know somebody at the organization. I learned to reach out to people I knew at an organization and just let them know that I had applied for a job there, and when I did that, I usually got a call a few days later to interview.

That whole process was very frustrating. You're trying to work for a company, and you don't know when they're going to get back to you. Some companies have application processes that are so long, that you have to send a resume and then manually fill in stuff you already had on your resume, then they don't even get back to you! So it was painful, and it felt like most companies don't care very much about the people who apply. It was very unprofessional and inconsiderate. When I ended up working in human resources, I made it a point to always get back to applicants to let them know of an update, even if it was that we had closed the job.

I ended up applying to and working in HR at the same college that I graduated from. They were looking for somebody familiar with the college, and I had worked in about six different departments across the college during my time as a student. Plus I had completed an internship in DC at a magazine, so I knew a bit about managing websites and fundraising. But also, I loved the college I graduated from, and they knew that. In the interviews, they asked about my leadership background, my passions, my faith, and my knowledge about the college. I was ready for most of their questions since I knew the college so well.

I was nervous on my first day. I didn't know what to expect, and I thought everything I was going to do would be a mistake. I went through all of this orientation on insurance and risk and college services, and I read the policy manual of about 300 pages. Because I was working in HR, I needed to know all of this. They gave me 16 hours to read the whole manual and then meet with every single person who worked in the department. The job gave me so much exposure to the college and the other side that I didn't see as a student. I had access to hiring systems, payment policies, job applications, and data on current employees. But I also learned of weaknesses. For example, we had all these policies, but we didn't always follow all of them depending on the circumstances. We had to be careful not to get into major conflicts with other departments or superiors.

I ended up staying for nine months, then I went back to school for a master's degree. But I took with me things that I learned in that first job. I had a lot of exposure to Excel, and I did a lot of LinkedIn Learning classes. I also saw from the many job applications how important connections and references were. I also learned to see trends in other people's career trajectories, and it encouraged me to find my own trend for when I apply to my next organization.

My advice to someone currently looking for their first job is … if you're in that phase of searching and being disappointed at not having any responses like I was, remember that how a company treats you as an applicant reflects how they'll treat you when you're hired. If a company doesn't get back to you or doesn't treat you well as an applicant, it means they're not really a company that cares about their reputation or people in general. When I worked in HR, I wanted to make sure that all applicants, even those who weren't hired, had a positive view of the college and felt like we cared about them. So, don't be mad if the company doesn't get back to you, since they clearly don't care that much about people anyway.

Also, connect with as many people as possible. Ask them where they work, so you can have a connection with them. In the future, if you know somebody who knows somebody, it's easier to get into that company and to get a reference. As a hiring manager, getting an email that has someone's resume as an attachment, when you already have so many others in the system, makes a huge difference.

2.12 On Finding a Job in the Interim: Arlene's Story

I definitely didn't go into my first job thinking that it was what my first choice would have been. I was very happy about the job, but I was bummed that I wasn't starting grad school. But now looking back on it, that experience that I had was really valuable to me.

I started applying for jobs in the fall of my senior year, also while applying for graduate schools. I actually really wanted to go to graduate school, I didn't really want to work. I didn't do any internships while in college, besides some bartending and working in the family business. I actually remember in junior year I had extreme anxiety because I applied to something like 50 internships and got maybe five interviews, but I didn't get any offers. So I focused on graduate programs, and I interviewed at several graduate schools. But I didn't get into any of the programs, so I went back to looking for a job.

I applied to jobs like a data analyst role at a big tech company. That was the only other job that I got pretty far along in the interview process for. Luckily, my college did a pretty good job of giving us resources if we wanted them. Maybe some students weren't as aware of them, but I met with the career center advisors, I got help on my resume, and I got letters of recommendation from professors. I mostly searched for jobs on websites like Indeed and LinkedIn, then I would apply on the actual company website. I had read that Indeed or LinkedIn job listings could be old and outdated, so I would find the job on those sites and then apply on the company website if the job was still open. It was a lot of anxiety. I applied to a lot of jobs, and I didn't hear back from the majority of them. There were definitely weekends when I was crying because of how stressed out I was, thinking I was going to have to move back home with my parents. I couldn't believe how competitive it was.

Looking back, I'm honestly one of the lucky ones. It felt like everybody was out there getting these really great jobs with six-figure salaries, and since I wasn't one of them, I was a failure. That just isn't true. I later found out that so many people graduated without a job, and I at least had one a few months after graduating.

So I ended up getting a job through a friend of my boyfriend. My boyfriend and I were talking about moving to Utah, where he wanted to be. His friend found out about this job, and I thought it was pretty cool so I applied and got a recommendation from his friend. This company does a lot of hiring on referral; they incentivize it pretty heavily for employees to refer their friends. The interview process was the longest I have ever been through. It was two months and something like five to seven interviews, which was a lot for an entry-level job. But the more I learned about it, the more I realized that it could fit into my long-term career goals. The job was at a research company, and because my end goal was to be in a PhD program, I thought that working there would look pretty good. I wouldn't be in the specific field of study that I wanted, but I would get some research experience.

The job was interesting. On a positive note, it did help me get a head start on my statistical and data analysis knowledge. It gave me some behind-the-scenes industry knowledge that was helpful. I had amazing autonomy, I got to do some of my own research while I was there, and there was a lot of room for growth. By the time I left, I had gotten a 50 percent pay raise in a year, which is kind of unheard of, and that was two promotions in one year. It was definitely one of those millennial tech company cultures, with beanbag chairs in the office, people longboarding around, and that kind of thing.

But one big issue with my first job was that there was no diversity in the workplace. A lot of that is probably because of the office location, so I can't speak to any other office locations. The biggest problem that I saw was some misogyny and definitely gender pay gaps. Also, you work a lot. You come in at eight, you work till five, you go home, and you work another three or four hours. And they expect that. If you want to do well there, there is not really such a thing as work–life balance, they kind of churn and burn, especially with their entry-level employees. They don't expect you to stick around for very long, but they expect you to work really hard while you're there.

I ended up applying to graduate school later that year. I only applied to one, which was located in the area I wanted to live in. I got in and left my job to start the program. And for a PhD program, it's beneficial to have a diversity of people who come straight from undergrad and people who have work experience. So for me, having that industry knowledge helped me be one of those people with work experience. Plus in my field of study, which is business, it's hard to research things in business if you've never had a full-time job. But I don't necessarily think that people who are coming straight out of undergrad should be excluded, I think that there's value in that too.

My advice to someone currently looking for their first job is ... I definitely didn't go into my first job thinking that it was what my first choice would have been. I was very happy about the job, but I was bummed that I wasn't starting grad school. But now looking back on it, that experience that I had was really valuable to me. In terms of advice, I would tell people that nothing is permanent. I think when I didn't get into grad school the first time around, I was really tempted to be like, well that's just not my path, I'm just not smart enough to do it. So when I took my job, I was thinking, I don't know when I'm ever going to make time to go back to graduate school. But now, here I am in a PhD program. So, there's nothing permanent.

2.13 On Confidence in Your Value: Axel's Story

Don't second guess why you're in that room. If you got through the interview process and you got the job, you've already proven yourself to be worthy of doing the job. Now just prove that you can do the job and do it well.

I was a political science and sociology double major at college. I did the honors program for political science, and I wanted to do something in politics or public policy. I also was an intern in Washington, DC, the summer before my senior year. I really liked DC. I wanted to live in a city where it was dense, I could use public transit and not have to have a car. So I was applying for jobs in San Francisco, Seattle, New York, and DC. Plus, DC jobs are usually related to public policy and politics, which is what I was interested in. I applied for jobs in political consulting, jobs to work as a legislative assistant or a staff assistant in a congressional office, and jobs based in the knowledge economy but the subsector was public service or public policy.

I didn't always know exactly what I wanted to do. I actually spent my first year undeclared. I thought I was going to do tech journalism because I read a lot of tech journalism outlets and I loved technology. I wanted to move to the Bay Area and work in marketing or sales or comms or reporting in tech. But I didn't commit to it just yet, and when I actually learned about journalism, I didn't feel like writing so much and then having editors change everything. Then I found sociology and political science and decided it was fun. There was a moment around junior year when I thought about going to grad school because I didn't know what else to do to get into politics. I knew people went to law school but I didn't want to do that. Then I did an honors program, which was kind of a mini-grad school experience with a thesis and everything. I also was in student government, and I liked that a lot more. I ended up spending all more time doing that. I considered doing Teach for America for a while, but I didn't find anything that I really wanted to do or any location that I wanted to move to. So, I went home and started applying for jobs.

I applied for jobs all across the board. Some jobs were simple, just go wear this shirt for a nonprofit and get people to donate or sign a petition. Others I was definitely not qualified for, like they wanted years of experience and a master's degree, but I applied just to shoot my shot. I had nothing to lose. Actually, writing my honors thesis was really helpful. It helped me develop skills in writing and research and laboring over a piece of contact. And then the student government work was really important for building emotional intelligence skills, having people report to you and having to report to people, and working with colleagues. I also worked part time in the alumni office, where I had to clock in and out and do tasks, even if I didn't like it. This was all really important. I remember being at a happy hour early in my career, and this guy at work told me that one of the things they were impressed about me was that I actually showed up to work on time and not hungover. It was a bit sarcastic, but seriously, here I am this guy in my 20s, I show up on time, I listen to meetings, I get stuff done quickly, and am responsive, and that's a win for them. You have to prove yourself as worthy.

Anyways, I focused on nonprofit and public sector jobs. I used some websites that are dedicated to those types of positions and jobs on the Hill. I kept my LinkedIn updated and nice. I didn't have too many personal contacts in DC, so nothing really came out of my personal connections. It was mostly job searching on the internet, which is crazy telling somebody that I found my job by just applying for it on the internet.

For me, I did not want to go back home. I liked being independent, even in college, although that was in kind of an inflated sense since you're just using debt to pay for stuff. For me, the job search was to just get out of my home, I didn't want to live at home with my parents. I had some friends with jobs lined up after college, and I was always a little bit jealous.

I wanted to find something to start right after college also. I had other friends who were happy living at home and just floating by, but I had different expectations for myself. So I got lucky and eventually was able to get out of home.

Eventually, I got a job as an assistant at this nonprofit. I was one of the youngest people there. I got very lucky when my boss wanted someone with two to five years of experience, but the budget didn't allow him to do that, so he downgraded the job to an entry-level position. So I got that job. It was great, but it was also a little bit lonely because all my coworkers were in their late 20s or 30s, my boss was in his 40s, and senior directors and VPs were in their 50s and 60s and 70s. I felt like a little kid who cheated the system. Another thing that I got lucky on was that my team didn't care what age I was, they cared about whether or not I could get the job done. Obviously, age helps because you would know more, and if you know more, you can get stuff done quicker. But our organization as an institution didn't really go above and beyond to take care of the younger staff. We didn't have a young professionals group, we had to do that informally ourselves. I was always a little bit jealous of friends who worked at bigger firms or on the Hill, and they had a cohort of young professionals to do training together and hang out with. Whereas for me, I would always have my work life and personal life separated. Also, my pay was a little bit above average for a 501c3. I mean DC is an expensive city, so it wasn't like I had a ton of money, but I could pay my bills on time.

The job was a good fit for my career, mostly because my immediate manager was a great guy. He really made sure to take care of me and build my career up. I could see people in the institution trusted him and liked him and gave him responsibilities. Plus I liked the people I worked with, and I liked learning about new stuff. My organization had a lot of different issues and topics that we wanted to explore, so that kept me active. Also, I felt like I was important, I was helping the institution do good work in the universe. I felt like I was working at a place where I wanted to keep going to work. You know, you could go work for big companies and get a lot of money, but I'd ask, am I actually making the world a better place, or I'm just trying to get a paycheck? I felt like I was making the world a better place, or at least not harming the world.

Since then, I've been promoted twice, and I moved to a different team. I got out of state fiscal policy and into both state and local public policy. I'm also working with some institutional nonprofit management operations. I've seen coworkers leave, I've seen new coworkers come in. I've been able to travel for work, go to conferences, and help contribute to research projects. It also has some cons. For example, I come across a lot of folks who are really smart in one issue, so you always feel like you aren't as important with them because you're not the issue expert, but there are also times when you see that being good at a lot of different areas allows you to be successful and help those specialists be even more successful. So now, five years later, I'm a senior associate at this same nonprofit I started at.

My advice to someone currently looking for their first job is ... don't necessarily settle. Unless the location is so great that at least you get to go to the location and use that as leverage to get a new job. Or the money is so great that you can financially support yourself and do things, and then get the right job later. But don't necessarily settle. There were times when there were jobs that I was applying for that, in retrospect, I would have been taking a step back in my career development. Remember the long game. You will eventually find something as long as you keep at it.

Also, don't compare yourself to others to make yourself feel bad or feel better. If anything, look at others, and see what you read about their jobs and what you don't like about their jobs, and figure out how you can take that information to improve your own life. The other thing is to be willing to take risks, and don't always make the safest choice that leads to the least amount of conflict. Conflict actually can end up with the biggest reward. If you take very few risks, typically you won't hurt yourself, and you'll get a reward, but it'll be small. If you take risks, you could hurt yourself, but if you mitigate the risk, you can mitigate some of the damage, and if you take that risk and you're successful, then you get a bigger reward. And over the long haul, that's stronger and better. For example, I moved from the West Coast to the East Coast. My family was all on the West Coast, and I didn't really have any personal connections out in DC. So I got the job, and then I went onto Craigslist and applied for different apartments. I found this one group house within my budget with these guys where I had no idea who they were. They became some of my best friends in DC. So that was me taking the risk. I had the safe choice, which a lot of people do and I don't blame them, which was to just stay in my hometown and live with my parents and try to find a job. Or I could roll the dice. I could've fallen flat on my face, I could've hated the city I moved to, I may not have been able to find a job, or I could find a job and not make any money. But over time, if it all works out, you get rewarded.

Finally, don't second guess why you're in that room. If you got through the interview process and you got the job, you've already proven yourself to be worthy of doing the job. Now just prove that you can do the job and do it well. And if you do the job and you do it well, and you take those risks when necessary, you will likely be rewarded.

2.14 On Being Hungry: Gregor's Story

> *I hate to say this, but if you go to a potential employer, and they ask you about your prior job experience, telling them that you were a host or waiter isn't enough.... Employers would much rather you try to do a start-up that failed, because that shows a degree of ingenuity. Many companies are looking for risk-takers, and they're looking for somebody to challenge the status quo. And if they think you're docile, they think you're just not hungry enough.*

I finished high school, served for two years in the national army of my home country, then went off to university. I was actually two years behind my graduating class from high school, so I worked hard to get an internship my first summer. My friend's father was the CEO of this logistics company, so he was able to get us internships. But I knew what I was gunning for, and logistics was not quite it. I wanted to go into banking. My parents were able to help pass my resume around, and they got in touch with some bankers who took my resume and got it to their HR department. So then my second summer, I was interning in some data crunching for this international bank. Then my third summer, I applied to intern at all these big banks like Citi, HSBC, and Goldman. With these banks, they do all the screening online. Before you even meet someone, there's a psychometric test, an analytical test, and so forth, and they're pretty brutally honest that they only look for candidates with a 3.8 GPA from the top schools. So because my GPA wasn't that and I didn't go to an Ivy, I was struggling. It was very demoralizing to find the standards that they had set, knowing that I had no chance. But you know, I persevered, and in truth, that's sometimes what you have to do. I don't know if schools do enough to help students, and in truth, the onus is on the families and the students themselves. A lot of kids just don't realize that.

So I ended up emailing random asset managers and hedge funds that I found on Google. I was quite bold, I found something like 15 to 20 emails and just said, hi, I'm an economics student, and I'd love to do a summer internship with you. I did not get many replies. The ones who did were very kind but brutally honest, they told me that they typically hire people who have some experience. They don't have training programs, so they're just not interested if you have zero skills. So I assessed my options, and I ended up going back to the same bank I was at last summer. They actually contacted my former manager, who told me later that he gave me a glowing review. So I went back to that bank, and this time I went to a different country. At the end of that summer, I interviewed with the head of the business, and I was very lucky, they told me that people thought very highly of me and so they gave me a job offer to join them next summer. So the pressure of senior year was off! I had my job offer.

The job was a two-year training program as an international associate doing rotations. My starting salary was probably in the top 5 percent, I'm pretty sure of that. My first placement was in London, which is expensive, but I was well paid. I started in the middle office, which looked at settlements and confirmations with trades. Then I went to transaction banking, and I didn't want to stay there, but it's kind of the bread and butter of banking. Then I did market risk on the commodities team, which is where I really found things getting interesting. Our job was to basically analyze oil, aluminum, and gold and to track if the price of the asset goes the other way, based on historical analysis, then theoretically how much would we lose. We worked quite closely in conjunction with the regulators and a set of parameters on how much theoretically you should lose. It was very exciting for me. Sure, I could go into an advisory role and work on big transactions like this company buying that company, stuff that would be in the papers, but it just didn't suit my personality. I just can't sit there for hours on end and just keep doing spreadsheets and iterations to come up with the right price for an asset. I'm quite competitive, and I want to know what it's like to be in a position where I know I've lost a lot of money, or that I've made a lot of money, but also be in control of my own destiny.

Actually, my last rotation was supposed to be foreign exchange, but the commodities team had a crisis and they actually went to my manager and asked if they could have me back for the final rotation. But then, I was very disappointed, I actually did not get a job offer from the commodities team at the end of my rotation. It wasn't because I wasn't a good candidate. Rather, they had actually hired another guy to replace me who was more senior. He was somebody who had like four years of experience over me. So I was just there to help them fill in the gap until he arrived. That was a bit of a sucker blow. They had another position in Asia, which again I did not get accepted for, because they needed a Mandarin speaker. The one thing that did come out of it though was my manager. He ended up connecting me to the head of FX [foreign exchange] trading, and eventually, that led to my permanent position there. So yeah, sometimes things happen that aren't as planned. You've got to be ballsy, you've got to go and ask someone, can I have an interview? If you don't ask, you'll never know.

Long story short, I stayed with them for three years. Then I knew I needed to get out of my comfort zone. So my boss asked if I could move, and I said yes, and he sent me to New York. I did well, and I took on more and more work over the years, then I became a manager and got myself a recent graduate to help me out. And that's where I am now.

My advice to someone currently looking for their first job is … so a lot of my friends, they were super bright, super hardworking, smarter than me, and more hardworking than me. But when I looked at their resumes, a lot of their resumes would be babysitters or waiters. I hate to say this, but if you go to a potential employer, and they ask you about your prior job experience, telling them that you were a host or waiter isn't enough. The skill that you get from that doesn't help you in those situations. It's almost like employers would much rather you try to do a start-up that failed because that shows a degree of ingenuity. Many companies are looking for risk-takers, and they're looking for somebody to challenge the status quo. And if they think you're docile, they think you're just not hungry enough. I have somebody who works for me now, and I've been quite heavily involved in recruitment. Honestly, I really don't care about your GPA. If you make it through interviews with HR, you probably have good enough grades anyway. When it comes to me, I will have my own tests, and your grades on paper, as far as I'm concerned, at least with the American system, it's just whether or not you can regurgitate information.

Also, get yourself out there. Of course, don't be annoying, but the more people who know you and who you've networked with, it will help you in the end. Try to set learning outcomes or goals for yourself. For example, at the end of my three months, I want to be able to do this. When you leave college, people will be asking, what is your skill set? When you're in your job, after two years, they'll ask again what your skill set is. Having work experience doesn't really help, because work experience means you've sat there for five years. You need to show that you learned something. Are you able to analyze a balance sheet, or can you analyze countries, can you give me a breakdown of somebody's debt profile? These are the tangible skills that employers look for.

2.15 On Lifelong Government Careers: Sid's Story

I've stayed at this company all this time. It's a government job, so it has a lot of job security that a private company cannot provide. I've been through many recessions, and I've seen how engineers employed by private companies suffered through recessions, because during recession time, they

> may not have enough jobs for the company to employ them.... I saw the difficulties they encountered, and with my company, which is a state agency, my job was secure. That brought a sense of security both at work and at home.

I started by studying civil engineering. I was initially more interested in structure design and structure construction. But then I had a professor in undergrad who was really good in transportation engineering, and he made transportation engineering fun and exciting. He would always tell us about being on the board of this committee, and all the decisions they made. I found it really interesting, and eventually, he offered me a scholarship to do my master's degree in transportation engineering. Actually, I intended to go back to Malaysia after my bachelor's degree, and I hoped to work my way up to own my own company in construction. But because my professor offered me a scholarship to do the master's degree, I accepted the scholarship and stayed there to do my master's degree, then I got the job, and before long, I'm staying here in America for 30 years.

I started applying for jobs after the first year of my master's program. This was in the early 1990s, so we relied on publications like newspapers and magazines. There was a civil engineer magazine where the state transportation agency advertised for the position. I had to get the physical address, and then write to them to ask for the application form. Then I filled out the form and mailed it back to them, then waited to see if I got an interview. Everything is by mail, so the process is long and tedious. We did have phones back then, but getting ahold of somebody is difficult. You can only really talk to the HR department, not an engineer or anyone like that.

I only applied to that one job for the state transportation agency as a junior transportation engineer. It was just one phone interview. No in-person, no video, nothing else. I got the job, started in November while I was finishing my master's degree, and I stayed with the same agency for 30 years.

The job as a junior engineer begins with just checking others' calculations and making sure that they did everything right mathematically. Then it's followed by progressively more responsibilities, starting with simple tasks like alignment design, and then some minor projects to begin with. Then as I got more experience, eventually I started doing my own analysis, like highway capacity analysis. Then there were bigger projects like realigning a road. And then after that, we had to go to a rotation program, so I went to construction for nine months, where I learned different aspects of construction compaction requirements and all the specifications that contractors have to meet. Then after the rotation program, I became permanent, and I started to head up my own projects. I was actually part of the team with the project to create a brand-new freeway. So that was a four- or five-year process where I had my own project. As far as the pay, I began in range A, which is the lowest pay at the time. I made like $1,300 a month. And then after I got my master's degree in May, I got bumped to range D automatically, and my pay increased by a whole $1,000 a month.

I've stayed at this company all this time. It's a government job, so it has a lot of job security that a private company cannot provide. I've been through many recessions, and I've seen how engineers employed by private companies suffered through recessions, because during recession time, they may not have enough jobs for the company to employ them. So once the project was done, they were let go. I saw the difficulties they encountered, and with my company, which is a state agency, my job was secure. That brought a sense of security both at work and at home. As I became more seasoned in the job, I was assigned greater responsibilities, I rotated through various departments, and I became more well rounded as an engineer. Then I got a promotion, and I got to stay in this department that I really enjoyed. So now, I'm a senior transportation engineer and the chief for central region hydraulics.

I still remember in my first job, I had to work a lot harder than other employees. I had to bring work home to do, because the first impression is really important, especially in the first year or two. You want to establish your reputation as being a good employee and a good worker. So, to me, that is the most important thing for a junior engineer, to work harder than anybody else and pick up things quickly.

My advice to someone currently looking for their first job is ... you have to know the company, the core values, and the mission of the company. Do your research, don't go into the interview unprepared. You need to prepare really well for the interview to get your first job. And after you get your first job, do the best that you can. Put in the extra hours to establish a good reputation.

2.16 On Overpreparing in Your Job Search: Daniel's Story

[The job search] is super competitive. There's so many little things that matter. So you have to persist, but you also have to overprepare. Make sure your resume is flawless, make sure your application is flawless.

I've loved everything about school and education since I was a little kid. I challenged my teachers and they challenged me. Neither of my parents had the opportunity to go to college, but they provided every opportunity for me to go to college. A lot of our family friends were in education, so I grew up around assistant principals, principals, and teachers. I loved high school so much, I was involved in everything: multiple sports, choir, drama, you name it, I tried it out. I always thought that it would really be cool to be a high school principal someday.

I actually went to college initially as a political science major, because I had a lot of great experiences in mock trial in high school. But then I took a water safety instruction class, where I taught everyone from little kids to adults in their 50s how to swim. I really enjoyed this, and I was pretty good at it, so it got me to realize that I wanted to be a teacher. So I went to my advisor in college and asked if I could switch to a major in education and still finish in four years. They told me it'd be really tough, but I could do it if I took some summer classes, maxed my course load each semester, and did all my student teaching on top of that. So that's what I ended up doing. For my student teaching, I did some high school teaching in economics and coached volleyball, and I also taught swimming at a resort over the summers.

I finished my student teaching in April at the same time as graduating, so I started looking for jobs right away. Now, college did a great job preparing us. They told us to go and try to introduce ourselves to the school's secretary at the same time that you're applying. In those days, there were some job postings that you could look at, but there were not a lot, so you had to sort of search them out. I think EdJoin had just started, but still, all the applications were on paper. So I would research everything about every single school, the principal, and the programs they have, and I would write my letters specifically targeted for that specific school for that specific position. I would say I did my homework more than most, so even when I went in, I would go and ask for their informational packets to study the school. I went through several interviews. I remember one time, over the summer after I graduated, I actually drove down six and a half hours for a job interview at 1:30 in the afternoon and then turned around and went back the same day.

Obviously, I was frustrated a little bit during this time. I think the greatest challenge is that it's very rare to get direct feedback on why you weren't selected, especially when you make it through two or three rounds of interviews. I'm somebody who wants to continuously improve, and I played sports my entire life, so there was always a coach there giving me feedback. In most job interviews, you're lucky if you get a letter or response back after your interview. I worked in HR for four or five years of my career in schools before I became an assistant superintendent in the school district. Because I remembered what it felt like to work so hard to put in an application and then never even get a response from districts, even after multiple interviews, I prided myself in being someone who called every candidate back when we interviewed and emailed every candidate even if they weren't selected. So I would say that when I went through those challenges in the job search, the frustration of not receiving the level of communication I would like, it actually developed a skill set in me that I carried with me in my future career.

Now, other times, it made sense. At this one high school, one of my best buddies from college, we did our student teaching together, and we were the two finalists for the position. He got the job and I didn't. The funny thing is, the older I get after almost 25 years of experience now, I truly know that when I don't get a position, it's definitely meant to be or there's a reason for that. Just like when I ended up at the school I started teaching. Compared to the seven or eight places that I was a top finalist for or had interviewed for, this school was the best one for me. It just took me a few steps before I got that job offer there, and I had to go through those other interviews first.

So the job I got was actually at the school district I really wanted. When I first applied, I interviewed and they said that they didn't have a position for me. But then, maybe a week before school started, the principal at that school I wanted called me and asked me to interview for a job. It was very informal; the principal even specifically told me not to wear a tie. We talked a bit about my background and interests, and he told me that if they get enough kids enrolled, they'll have a job for me. A few days later, after the first day or two of school, he told me that they had enough kids enrolled, though they were still balancing the classes and building the schedule, but they had a job for me if I wanted it. So I took that job and started right at the beginning of September.

The job was so awesome. I felt prepared because half the classes I was scheduled to teach were the classes I had student-taught the previous fall. So I had all the curriculum, I had all the lessons, and I just needed to make them my own. I was perfectly prepared in my mind to open up my classroom. One challenge though was that they had me in basically seven different classrooms to share with other teachers because of space issues. Some people jokingly called me the "cart boy," because I had to lug all my materials around in a cart. Most of the teachers were great, but I was an unwanted visitor to one of them. So that was challenging, but I was also just happy to have the job, happy to cart my things around.

One of the things that's always been important to me is learning people's names. I tried this as much as I could at college and in high school growing up. One of the first things I decided to do was to really get to know the kids. So I did two activities that first day or first week. One was I took a picture of each of them. I developed these pictures then studied them over the weekend, and by Monday I would learn their names. It was 180 kids or something. This way, I let them know that I cared about them and wanted to know their names. The other thing that really stood out from that first week was also letting them know who I was. Being a history teacher, I liked archaeology and digging for artifacts, so I did an artifact bag. The students would bring their own artifact bag and share a little bit about themselves and bring in a few objects from home that meant something to them or represent them. I shared my own artifact bag as well. I think doing those two things that day really opened them up, even if it was things like "I'm a San Francisco Giants fan" and all those kids were either Dodgers or Angels fans, it sort of created a bond with them. I told them it was going to be tough, but it was going to be fun. The other thing I learned too from that first day is, after all my years of teaching at that school, I've never used a seating chart in my life. These little middle school kids, who were a little squirrely, were just shocked that they could sit wherever they wanted. I used that as a way to tell them that I'm going to let you spread your wings and fly. But I'm going to rein you back in if you can't follow our guidelines to stay within the boundaries. So for most of them, it was a privilege, and they all succeeded.

I cannot say enough that my college overprepared their teacher candidates to be successful. When I got in there on day one, I felt that everything they taught me had paid off, because I'm prepared to take over this class. It helped that all the teachers there were so friendly. I had just turned 22 a month before in August, and there was not a single teacher at this school that was under 40. I was the only new teacher that wasn't a transfer or somebody experienced. I was a novelty or something like that, I was fresh blood coming in. Here, I was no threat to the existing power dynamics, but I was a novelty of interest, and they all embraced me. Now over those five years I spent at that school, we had more retirements. After my first year, I finally got my own classroom, and then in the later years, we hired more new teachers. One of the greatest moments was when they nominated me for the Sallie Mae First Class Teacher of the Year award, which is a national award, and the district can only take one person a year for that. I was the one they selected. So that was really exciting to me because I got to spread my own wings and do what I thought was best for kids, but I was also able to share ideas with a lot of veterans.

I was at that first job for five years, and I taught English and honors history, advised the leadership class, and others. During my fifth year, a rival middle school called me and I ended up as their school's dean of students. I stayed there a few years, then moved to an assistant principal of athletics position at the high school where all the middle schoolers from my school would go. Then I moved over to assistant principal of instruction, then my family and I moved away from the area. I applied for assistant principal and principal positions all over the new area we were moving to, and I luckily got a middle school principal job at a school that needed a lot of reshuffling and reorganizing. Then I moved to a high school principal job, and finally, I'm now the assistant superintendent at a large urban school district. Even during this time, I had plenty of interviews that didn't work out and plenty of back and forth with other jobs where they called me but ended up not hiring me. That's why I always joke that things always work out for the best. Even though I applied for several jobs that I thought I wanted or was disappointed when I didn't get it, this was the one I was meant to be at. Things in my school district are pretty crazy right now with budget issues, but we're still better off than most. In between all of this, I taught doctoral classes for education leadership. I'm about to start my 24th year in K-12 education now.

My advice to someone currently looking for their first job is ... first, I'd tell them it's super competitive. There are so many little things that matter. So you have to persist, but you also have to overprepare. Make sure your resume is flawless, and make sure your application is flawless. I've seen people put a deceased reference, where I knew the person they put as a reference and knew that they were deceased. Be persistent, but be specific in what you want, even if you have to wait for it. If it's a teaching position, and you have three or four districts, pick your number one to be a substitute teacher. Get to know them, because if you don't get the job the first year, sub in that preferred number one district and work hard, get to know people, help with other events, and maybe get a long-term sub spot. Many times, if somebody is doing a great job for us in a temporary or sub position, quite often, they're the first ones we hire. Some people just think they should graduate college and get a job immediately. It doesn't always work that way, because there are a lot of people that want the same job. If you're not persistent, if you're not fully prepared in the way you present yourself, you're going to struggle. I have so many stories of colleagues that work with, where it took them a long time to get a principal job or an assistant principal job or Superintendent job, but the ones that persisted ultimately got a job, and in most cases, it was the perfect match for them.

Also, don't lash out in your disappointment. There have been times in my career when I was disappointed, and maybe I felt there were politics that played into why somebody got a job and I didn't. You have to learn to let those things go, and whatever you do, don't send emails about it. I always taught people, every reaction or decision, to wait a minute, an hour, a day, a week, a month, depending on what it was, unless it was a life or death decision. I think that's a good response to have, because sometimes I call people to give them feedback, and then they just argue. You never want to be that person, that's just the death of you in that district or with that employer if you argue and try to tell them why they should have selected you. I know, it's a normal feeling, but if people are prepared for that and respond respectfully, then something else will fall in their lap. Then they'll look back five years later in that process and say, I'm glad I didn't get that other job, this job was a perfect fit for me, but I didn't know that at the time.

Lastly, find a mentor that they can trust and vent to. Not only vent but also learn from. That's the one thing I really lucked out on. I had mentors my whole life from kindergarten through 12th grade who were educators. I could think of one friend who was a volleyball coach, and she had me be her assistant when I was still a student at the school. She later became the high school principal there, so I learned so much from her. Then I continued that sort of mentor relationship with other people either in the current job I was doing or the job I was aspiring to. I would say find one or two mentors that you respected or appreciated the most when you were in high school, and see if you can take them out for lunch and pick their brains. Once you get that first job, look around for mentors. There are people I can now call to ask about school finance, but then there are also former principals I can call about principals' stuff, and there are HR leaders I can call. Even when I was disappointed with a job or a job I didn't get, I always had a mentor who was helping me at the current level, but also going up to the next level. The principal at my first school who hired me was the first professional mentor I had in a real job, and he's still a close friend today. I talk to him probably every week. I think that would be my best advice, this isn't something that you should do alone. And even though I thought I was a trailblazer and doing great things in my first year of teaching, I couldn't have done it without that support structure and without those mentors.

2.17 On Changing Plans and Taking Risks: Taylor's Story

My career path felt quite windy at the time. I remember just having big pangs of insecurity in my early 20s about, "Am I doing the right thing? Is this the right path?" Actually, in retrospect, I don't see that as a negative thing. I really like the experience that I was exposed to a number of different aspects of a think tank of the non-profit world, and I think that's actually helped me gain experience to, pretty confidently, serve as an executive director.

The summer before my senior year of college, I participated in an internship program run by a nonprofit think tank organization. I really enjoyed the program. They also have a yearlong, full-time professional development program in which they place you at an organization for a year. So that was on my radar pretty early into my senior year. They opened up applications pretty early, so I quickly applied, I was accepted by the fall of my senior, and then I got a placement for my full-time job in the spring after graduation.

But in the meantime during senior year, there were a ton of jobs I applied to in lots of different roles. I applied for an events role, I applied for a student organizing role, I applied for another program manager role, policy analyst role, all at various nonprofits. I applied for at least four or five other jobs. Oh, a development role too. I was a 22-year-old, I was just looking for any sort of job. The way it worked back then was they would fly you to the city and you would just do a day of interviews, in-person interviews just back-to-back-to-back, which was pretty convenient. For many of them, I didn't get a formal rejection. They just follow up if they say yes.

I actually didn't intend to go down this career path at first, since I had majored in rhetoric. But in college, I started a little charity institute and organization, and so I got more politically minded, and that made me familiar with the whole free market, libertarian, think tank network.

I had worked for two summer internships before in various different nonprofit organizations. But I've got to say, I felt kind of unqualified going into this job I ended up getting because it required an economics background which I did not have, but they hired me anyway. My degree was in rhetoric, and it said on the listing, "Must have economics or political science background." But I just thought I'd try anyway, and they hired me. I asked them afterward why, and they said it was really because of my strong writing background.

So I started this job as a policy analyst at a nonprofit. At the time, they were pretty new but a rapidly growing organization. I think they had at least 100 people on staff. I felt excited but also a little hesitant. It was my first job out of college, I didn't know what to expect, and especially I was worried because they were more conservative whereas I was more a libertarian. But I quickly adapted to the job, and I really liked it. The first day was just, besides the jitters, lots of orientation and whatnot. But once I finally got to sit down with my two superiors, I really felt at home. They really made me feel comfortable. They felt very casual, at ease, in a professional way, of course, so I thought that was great. They really made a point to emphasize their availability, that they can be bugged at any time. My direct superior played, eventually over time, a strong mentorship role. She would explain everything in policy pretty thoroughly, giving constructive criticism of my work but in a careful way.

But there were certainly several cons as well, not so much for my department or my superiors, but more for the organization as a whole. It fluctuated in size quite a bit. After I joined, it really started to decline. There were mass layoffs near the end of my tenure, so a lot of people in my department but also in other departments that I had worked with were fired. It seemed like the management didn't really know what was going on. Fortunately, I was not laid off. I think I was the only policy analyst who was hired at the time who was not laid off, so that is an early accomplishment of my work that, in retrospect, I'm actually pretty proud of.

I stayed at this first job for about two years. Then I got an opportunity from a different nonprofit, actually, it was the organization I was involved with in college. They basically recruited me to come on for an editor role at a project they had just launched, which is the organization that I run now. So I was hired by this nonprofit about eight years ago, and I stayed on for two and a half years doing the editor work, but then also kind of doing more director of communications work with them. At one point, I was kind of the head of their global communications. That role kind of eventually evolved to them offering for me to take over this editing project I had been working on and make it my own nonprofit organization as the executive director.

Now, my career path felt quite windy at the time. I remember just having big pangs of insecurity in my early 20s about, "Am I doing the right thing? Is this the right path?" Actually, in retrospect, I don't see that as a negative thing. I really like the experience that I was exposed to several different aspects of a think tank of the nonprofit world, and I think that's actually helped me gain experience to, pretty confidently, serve as an executive director. But at the time, I did have some temporary regret, particularly when I left my first organization. I thought, "This is the organization I want for my life." And I left for the same pay rate too, so I didn't get any more money. But I just remember almost having a mild panic attack after I submitted my resignation letter. Looking back, in retrospect, it was absolutely the right decision, and it led me to the path that I'm on today.

My advice to someone currently looking for their first job is … the main takeaway would be that it's important to expose yourself to a variety of different roles at a variety of different organizations, even if you feel confident that a certain career path is what you want to do. Say you want to be a lawyer, then you should intern for summer work at a law firm or work as a paralegal for a year or so. I think it's important. Your early 20s are a good testing ground for a path to see if it's truly what you like to do. But also, if you don't really have a path for certain, it's a good experiment lab to taste-test different types of things.

So I'm glad that I had that wide breadth of experience in my early 20s, albeit on a junior level. But it really, eventually, helped me narrow down my path and then go confidently on that path. It really wasn't until my mid to late 20s when this opportunity for my own nonprofit came up that everything just kind of clicked and I felt confident in the path I was going. I've felt that confidence, that assuredness ever since then. This law professor I know once said, "Success is being prepared and having the courage to say yes when opportunity opens its door." When I was given this opportunity to start my own nonprofit organization, it was literally not something I had intended. It wasn't my idea. It was someone else's idea for me to do it. It did take me a good 24 to 48 hours to mull over, but I realized that this was a rare opportunity that only comes across once or twice in a lifetime, such a special opportunity that could really lead to major success, even though it is a risky bet. But looking back at my early career experience, I knew I was a good writer and I have a pretty good network. I had never fundraised a dollar before, but I just had a feeling that the combination of those connections could help me. Plus I was in my mid to late 20s, single, living in the city, and I could live pretty inexpensively, so I thought, "This is the best time of my life really to take such a risk" and so I did that.

2.18 On Recovering from Being Blind Sided: Tabia's Story

Theologically, I had some views that didn't align with this denomination that was looking at it. So what they said to me was that they felt like [my application] wasn't well fleshed ou.t.… I didn't really know how to navigate the process well. So it was a total blind side [when I didn't pass].

I worked several part-time jobs while getting my bachelor's degree and then a graduate degree before I finally started my first full-time job as a church pastor after graduate school. So to be a minister in my denomination, you have to go through an educational process, and then you have to go through a process with the church. I had wanted my process to line up like it does for most people, but for me, it didn't. And I was only looking at this specific denomination, which was a very closed circle because it was very clear to me that I wanted to be a minister in this specific denomination, I didn't want to look anywhere else. I will say that this process was extremely specific and rigorous for my denomination. I think I, or anyone else, wouldn't go through all of the testing and the process if it wasn't certain that the goal is to work in this denomination. You wouldn't put yourself through all of this if you weren't going to pursue this long term.

I was forming my own pastoral identity, so I had to write a statement of faith. I thought it was my statement of faith, so it's personal, and I assumed they'd just read it and then send you on. But theologically, I had some views that didn't align with this certain denomination that was looking at it. So what they said to me was that they felt like it wasn't well fleshed out, but what I think was true was that our views didn't really agree. I didn't really know how to navigate the process well. So it was a total blind side. I was expecting it to be a proforma interview. Instead, they said, "You don't pass, you didn't do what you were supposed to do, you have to redo this statement of faith, and you can't come back to us for another three to six months because that's how we schedule our process." They only considered candidates four times a year, so that's why the timing didn't work out.

So because of that, because I wasn't prepared to get my first job, which I've been preparing for this whole time since college, I was devastated. I thought, "Well, I don't really have much money. Am I going to go home and live with my parents after grad school? How is this going to work?" One of my professors was meeting with me, and I was explaining what had happened, plus I had just gotten dumped by my boyfriend. I was like, "What am I going to do now?" He said, "You're bilingual, you speak Spanish. Why don't you do this program? People keep asking for volunteers. It's with the church. You would be perfect for it. If you get out of town, you could use your skills and gifts while you're waiting to get through this process." So I ended up abroad while searching for my first ministry position. Today, that wouldn't be that weird, but back then, it was on Skype, and it was really exotic and different.

Now in our denomination, there's a matching system. Churches will put up their positions, and then ministers will put out their positions, and then the software will do the match. But for my entire career, including my first call, I've never participated in the match. You don't have to. I've always looked at the profiles and just self-submitted my own materials to the churches that I think are good fits. So that was the way I did it then, that's the way I still do it, and it's worked out well.

Each church does it a little differently, but most of them do an initial interview on the phone, and then they sometimes, depending on where you are geographically, will bring you in for a short interview or an hour-long video interview. Then if both parties want to continue moving forward, they usually bring you in for an entire weekend, and then after that, you'll have to get approval from a higher body to do what they call a neutral pulpit, which means you'll need to come in and preach at a church that's not the church that you're going to preach at. Then sometimes churches will have candidates where they'll bring in multiple people to do those, so it's not even a guarantee that you'll get the job after that. Then the congregation has to vote on you, which is usually proforma. But then after that, you get the job.

So it's a very emotional process, and it's a very long process. The more you invest in it, the harder it is, I think, for both the employer and the pastor to get through. I actually still am connected to some people on LinkedIn who were chairs of such committees, where either I opted out or they decided not to hire me just because you get to know people so well through the process. I went through that process with maybe four churches. About two of them either I or they decided that we don't want to move forward early in the process. One I got almost all the way to the end of the process, and then the church decided they didn't want to hire me, and then the fourth one was the one that was the fit.

Remember that pastoring is a very relationship-oriented job. I forgot to mention that they will sometimes have to do a psychological assessment as part of the interview, either before you go or when you're there. But they set you up with lots of people, so it's fairly draining. The chairs of the search committee, by the time you've interviewed, you've worked with them for many months. Usually, they've asked you for sermon tapes, they ask your information, they get to know you, they're vetting you, they've talked to your references. They know a lot about you, not just professionally, but personally because that's of interest to them in pastoring.

So finally, I ended up as the associate pastor at this church, which was in this big gothic-sized building. Remember, I was the associate. I wasn't the head boss. So it's like, "Well, welcome. Here you are." You say hello, and you meet the rest of the staff. But I remember sitting at this big desk with a paper and thinking like, "Okay, what am I supposed to do now? I'm not preaching on Sunday, what do I do? Who do I call?" It was a challenge, but I learned a lot. I was the second in command, so that was the job where I learned that I didn't want to stay there, that I wanted to be a senior pastor. I didn't like being bound by other people's vision of what they wanted to do, particularly somebody that I didn't really agree with.

So it's been about 12 years since then, and I've served at two different churches as the senior pastor now. Almost all of the skills I learned in my first job transfer because it's the same job. It's just more responsibility. Everything I learned in the first job was like a subset of the things that I've used now. I didn't learn everything I needed, but almost everything I learned applied in some way. It was almost like a student-teacher becoming the teacher in some ways because, in the first position, I would preach once a month, and then in the subsequent ones, I was the main person. Or, in the first job, I was watching the pastor moderate the board, but then I became the moderator in the other ones. In my first job after that job, I copied everything that I saw my first boss do, and in that job, I learned how to have my own style, and then in this job, I have my own style.

My advice to someone currently looking for their first job is ... for me, when you're first starting out, and you're very ambitious and high achieving, you maybe don't have a sense of perspective on how long your career is, so you are really impatient. Now that I'm midcareer, I'm like, "Wow, I was really anxious." Have patience if you can. It's hard because it's a long process. But trust your sense of call in the Spirit. That's something that we believe very deeply in. So if it's not a match, something else will be. Try to not take it personally, I think it's a good lesson to remember not to personalize the rejection. Now, honestly, if somebody had told me to be patient, I don't know if I would have even listened, but maybe I would have settled down a little bit about not getting to do everything I wanted to do. I've learned now to think, "Well, I'm not going to be here forever. I'll just enjoy the journey, and think about what I want to do instead of being anxious and restless about it." I think that's probably the biggest thing.

Also, I have always relied on mentors, people who know me well. That's also a very reformed principle in my own church, that your sense of call is confirmed by people that know you, so you can't just sit in the closet and wonder if you go to mentors or advisors, and my mentors and advisors have always said, "Oh, but you have so and so gifts."

2.19   On Saying Yes to Everything: Korey's Story

I originally moved from New York to California in order to be a part of the film industry. But there's no guaranteed income with that sort of career pursuit. Any sort of consistent part-time work you can get, it's kind of what you need to say yes to, especially if it's something that's life giving, you're good at, and pays the bills.

The whole thing was sort of an accident. I started attending the church in my senior year of college, and the only reason I did was because the prior worship leader invited me to be part of his worship team. I had been taking an improv class that year and the first rule of improv is to say yes. I felt like I wasn't saying yes to enough things, so I said "Yes" and started joining the team. A couple months later he left that position, and so the pastor asked me to take his worship leader position in the interim for the rest of my senior year. I got paid a stipend to do that every Sunday. But, more or less, that's how I got the job that was considered my full-time job that following year after graduation.

Actually, I got my degree in theater with an emphasis on acting, and I originally moved from New York to California to be a part of the film industry. But there's no guaranteed income with that sort of career pursuit. Any sort of consistent part-time work you can get, it's kind of what you need to say yes to, especially if it's life giving, you're good at, and pays the bills. So because of my history in ministry and the flexibility that that job would offer me, I said yes to it very, very easily. I knew I would need to take additional part-time work to supplement that job, but going into it, just knowing that that was the nature of the field, I had the mentality of, "This is what I need to do to reach my actual career goals."

That lifestyle of juggling so many different part-time jobs, on top of a full-time job, in different industries was both thrilling and fun. Because I'm a naturally creative person and like to do a lot of different things, I get a lot of energy out of it. Then some seasons it was totally exhausting and led to burnout. For one period of my life, I had 10 different streams of income at the same time and was barely making ends meet. During that time, prayer really helped me cope with the burnout. My faith was a huge part of that. Part of it was gaining wisdom and insight from others and really evaluating, "Okay, what jobs were actually helping in that particular season?" Some jobs were unrelated to the career path I wanted to be in, but they paid the bills. Some were related, but they ended up being a larger waste of time. Some things were neither. They didn't help the bills, they weren't a net gain at the end of the day, or they didn't have the maximized effort output that I needed.

I eventually left that full-time ministry job, but I learned a lot from it. Some aspects of the job shook my confidence a lot during those first few years, especially in how I handled my relationships with others. Now, I think having the time and perspective to look back and say, "Okay, I didn't handle those relationships particularly well in these areas; that's where I wish I could've grown better." I think it only comes really through experience and humility. I also learned how to lead. I learned how not to micromanage, how to set clear goals, and how to manage teams.

Now, it's been almost 10 years since I graduated, and I've had technically three full-time jobs and over 15 part-time jobs. I worked as an administrative assistant at my college, am now a middle school teacher, and I did entertainment shows for kids' parties, music gigs, photography, videography, editing, start-ups, live streaming, and a bunch of other things. It's been very random, but somehow, in hindsight, I can see them all kind of fitting together to where I am now. For example, I met a woman at my church who was making a movie, and she needed a personal assistant. I had worked a few years as an administrative assistant at my college, so I had lots of admin roles, which obviously were not related to theater at all. But I needed some more income, and I got the skills from that, essentially helping her in her personal career. The more her film picked up, she invited me to be part of that creative process, so I ended up being on set. I ended up with an associate producer role, having never worked on a film before. I was running the back lot, which I had never been on a film set before. When it came to the editing process, I had had some editing background with small kind of fun videos or an internship for a Young Life summer camp, but nothing to this degree.

When we got to the editing process for this movie, we weren't pleased with what we were shown initially, so I asked my boss if I could take a swing at it. She said "Yes" and because of that I became an editor on the film, got a job with that same production company, and have edited four feature films since then, three or four feature films since then, having no prior experience. So all this came from building a great relationship with that post-production boss. Because he personally really enjoyed working with me, the doors were just swung open for that opportunity to come. So just like most of my other jobs over the years, it was 80 percent relationship building and 20 percent competency in the needed skill set.

My advice to someone currently looking for their first job is ... unless your gut feels weird about a situation or opportunity, say yes to it. If your gut says it's weird or kind of off, just don't go near it. Also, treat people incredibly well. Don't try to promote yourself. Just be a good listener. Be someone who builds up others. Make yourself the best person to work with, because it makes it easier to hire you. Choose humility. Don't let your pride get in the way of opportunities just because you think they're beneath you or for whatever other odd reason.

Next, take the time to evaluate what is worth doing. Some things you'll need to say yes to because you gotta survive, you gotta eat. Some things you say yes to because it's an open door. Even if it won't necessarily feed you, it might open up future doors where you want to head down, and some things will bring you neither of those things, so don't waste your time or effort doing those things either. Even then, you never know. Be open and be flexible and humble.

Then, to somebody specifically in my industry, I'd say almost the exact same thing. But also, have really good friends who support you, who maybe necessarily don't do the same things you do. That's probably a helpful support system to ground you when things feel crazy.

2.20   On Coincidences: Adnan's Story

> *My entire career has been about all those sort of weird, random happenstance things that happen and these weird coincidences that lead to other jobs, other opportunities, including my personal life.*

I come from an immigrant family. My parents are the first generation in the US. I'm the first generation born here in the West. My parents were ethnically Indian, but three generations of my family grew up in East Africa, in Tanzania. My dad had a college degree from the University of East Africa, and his biggest regret is that, because of circumstances back in Africa, he never got his PhD. So it was always an emphasis growing up that I was going to go to graduate school. It wasn't really optional. It was just what was going to happen.

So I go to college, and I'm finishing my degree there. And the assumption is just that I'm going straight through to graduate school. I had taken all the exams with the LSAT [Law School Admission Test] and GRE [Graduate Record Examination] and was ready, but along the way, I ended up living in DC in my junior year to do an internship. My professor in the DC program really encouraged me to take some time off before graduate school. I initially ignored the advice. But later that year, I ended up meeting this professor who was visiting my college at the time, and he and I ran into each other often in the hallways. He invited me to chat with him, and it turns out that he was a former state governor and former presidential candidate. We sit in his office and chat, and I tell him about my life plans, and he literally interrupts me, saying "Son, I've been a lawyer for 20 years. Let me tell you one thing. You've got to take time off before you go to law school." And he went into this 30-minute speech about why I need to take time off.

I'm sort of reeling because I've heard this from my professor and this very well-known politician, but at the same time, I'm getting pressure from my family. It totally throws me off. I finally decided, actually, I'm not going to go to law school. I'm going to take time off. I'm going to take all this advice I've been given. But now I've got to figure out how to explain this to my father, who's not interested in this idea. In immigrant families, there's not really a debate, it's just sort of what you do. You've got to be a doctor, lawyer, banker, whatever. And you go to grad school. So the deal I made with my dad was, look, I want to take time off. But here's what I'll do to prove to you I'm going to go to law school. I'm going to buy the diploma frames, but I won't buy the nice ones, I'll buy this horrible ugly laminated frame. That way, every time I look at it, I'll know that I've got to go to graduate school. Then when I did get my law degree, I promised my dad I would get the nice diploma frame.

So that's what I did. I decided to work for a couple of years before going to law school. Now my original plan was just to move to DC and get a job working in politics or working on Capitol Hill. That's what I was told I had to do, move to DC without a job, then find one once I got there. But then a friend of mine knew I was sort of in the job market, and he knew I wanted to be in politics, so he forwarded me an email from a Republican political campaign that was hiring in the LA area. I figured I might as well apply, and I ended up getting the job as a field organizer for the campaign. Congressional campaigns are small, they have about four or five staff people. My job was to knock on doors or coordinate people knocking on doors, make phone calls, get signs up, and the like. I stayed with them for two years, doing the fieldwork but then also doing some work as the research director for the campaign.

We ended up losing that campaign. I also was going through a breakup at the time, which totally broke my heart, and so as soon as that campaign ended and I had lost, within two days I booked a flight to DC. I packed a bag of clothes and moved across the country with no job, no apartment, nothing. I stayed with a guy who I'd met while on the campaign who lived in DC, found a temporary apartment, and then got a job after about a month. Actually, the way I got the job was that I was looking at this guy's apartment to be his roommate, and although I didn't end up living with him, he actually recommended me for a basic computer support job on his team. This guy was the senior legislative assistant to a congressman at the time, he ended up becoming the legislative director and the chief of staff while I was there, and now he's a congressman himself. So my entire career has been about all those sorts of weird, random happenstance things that happen and these weird coincidences that lead to other jobs, other opportunities, including my personal life.

Actually, the weird coincidences go back even further. Back in my first job, on that campaign, we flew a lot of high-profile people in to do events. We had a cancellation from the Speaker of the House who was supposed to come in from DC, and so we had to scramble to find someone, and we ended up getting in touch with this famous actress. But our candidate really wanted people who had paid to see the Speaker of the House to be able to take a photo with him, so he called our DC office and got them to find a cardboard cutout of the Speaker of the House and ship it over to us in LA. The DC guys end up getting this cutout and shipping it over to us. Now, years later, I'm in DC and attending this fraternity event, and I meet this random person and we get to talking. Turns out, he was an assistant in our DC team and was the one who physically running out to find the cardboard cutout. We ended up becoming really good friends, and fast forward a few more years later, I had finished law school and was working for a Congressman, he ended up as the executive director for a state party campaign and ended up hiring me as the lawyer on site for the upcoming presidential election. We won the state for the first time in 20 years, and we ended up winning the presidential campaign. Along the way, I met yet another guy who ended up helping me get my job at the Justice Department and then the White House. All of this is connected to that original random event with the cardboard cutout. By the way, just for what it's worth, I keep everything. While the cardboard cutout itself was lost to history, I still have this one receipt in my storage that has the pickup receipt and instructions to get that cardboard cutout from the air freight shipping center.

Now, I'm the founder and the executive director of a national security think tank and an assistant professor of law. That job goes back to another friend, who I met back in law school, who was teaching here and got me hired. Plus, the dean of the law school was the one who helped me raise the money to start the think-tank, and it turns out that his dad was the congressman and was the boss of my very first boss in my job out in DC. Oh and this other guy, who was the old boss of the guy who shipped the cardboard cutout to him, ended up becoming the rector of the university. It all cycles back.

My advice to someone currently looking for their first job is … first, only do jobs that sound interesting and fun. Don't take jobs because you have to do it or because your parents told you or because you feel because it's what you've always assumed that you would do. Do the jobs that look cool and interesting and fun. Try to stay on a rough path toward something, but don't feel like you have to stay on the exact path. With everything I've done, there has been randomness to it. I've done things that looked fun and interesting, and they have led to bigger opportunities. They've all ended up on the right track.

Chances are that if you take a risk, you're likely to succeed at it. If you don't succeed at that risk and the risk doesn't pay off, you're likely to be able to be resilient. If you're the kind of person who's looking for this kind of advice, and you end up taking it, you're also probably the kind of person who, if you fail at something, will learn a lesson and get better as a result and make yourself better as a result. If you're that kind of person, then where everybody else sees risk and danger, you should see opportunity. So while everybody else is turning away and going towards the safe bet, you should turn towards the risk and run towards it, because you're likely to succeed at that. And if you don't succeed, you're likely to dust yourself and get up and be more successful as a result anyway.

Number two, when you do end up at these jobs, work as hard as you can, make your bosses look good, and don't worry about getting the credit for the job. What will end up happening is, if your boss looks good, they'll hire you for the next job, they'll promote you within, they'll give you opportunities, they'll give you more good work. That ends up playing itself out, maybe not in that job, but oftentimes in that job, but also in the next job and the job after that and the job after that. Somebody will call somebody. Every job I've gotten was because somebody made a phone call saying, "Hey, you've got to hire this guy." The other thing is, just be there. Particularly in a virtual world, I really mean being physically there. And the reason I say that is because nine times out of 10, the best job opportunities I've gotten, the most productive thing that I've ended up doing, was because I was there late, at the time when the boss was there, and they're like, I need somebody to work on this, who's around, can you do this?

Always say yes to every job opportunity. It doesn't matter what it is. Even if it sounds stupid like you've got to go to the airport to pick up a cardboard cutout. Who wants to do that? Just do the thing, because one, your boss will appreciate it, number two, they need it done, and number three, you don't know what's going to come out of it. So just be present. And if you're there and you do good work and the boss gives you an opportunity, they're going to give you the opportunity again and again and again and again.

So that's the advice I would give to people generally. Now, for people who have the baggage of coming from an immigrant family, I would say you've got to be able to push back against your parents. You need to tell them that they've raised you the right way, and given you the right values and structure, but they also need to trust you to make the right decision even if it's different than what they think you should do. If your parents have given you all the tools to succeed, then you aren't going to fall down. And assure them that you're not going to forget the lessons they taught me, the lessons you learned growing up in a third-world country. You will be successful because of the sacrifices your parents made.

Also, find somebody like me who can call them and give them that speech. I call people from my community all the time. I call their parents and be like, hey, let your kid go away to college. Don't make them stay and go to the university next door to you. In fact, force them to go away to college. Allow them to not go straight to grad school. Give them that room and freedom. Because at the end of the day, it's hard for a parent. I've got a 13-year-old. I've already told him I'm moving next door to him in the dorms. I say it jokingly, but I sort of mean it a little bit, because it's hard to let go. But the truth is, you have to believe that you've given them the tools to succeed. And oftentimes, it helps the parents to hear from somebody else who did those things and broke from the mold and was successful anyway.

2.21 On Finding a Path Internationally: Maara's Story

I was based abroad where every job as a nonnational was tied to visa. You can stay about eight months before graduation.... A lot of my friends had been looking for a lot longer because as soon as they graduated, nobody could sponsor them. If they didn't find something, they are out of the country in a month. There was a normative pressure of just being around them and constantly hearing them.

I got a job right out of college with the company I had done an internship with. My internship was a three-month summer internship in corporate responsibility, which was something that turned out to be a lot more interesting than I thought it would be. I ended up speaking to different parts of the company, and I found that HR was interesting because they touch upon every part of the employee experience in a way that nobody else does. So the job I got with the company was a graduate training position with the company's human resources department. Since I was fresh out of school, they believed I needed some time just to learn the ropes. They put me through a structured training program before I would be transitioned to a full-time performing role. It was a two-year training program.

At the time, I was based abroad and every job as a nonnational was tied to a visa. You can stay about eight months before graduation. Being a female, I had the option of being sponsored by my parents at least after graduation. That would allow me to stay in the country. It sounds quite patriarchal, but until I found either an employer or a husband who could sponsor me, I wouldn't be able to stay in the country. And at the time, I had no intention of getting married, so I focused on funding an employer. A lot of my male friends had been looking for a lot longer because as soon as they graduated, nobody could sponsor them. If they don't find something, they are out of the country in a month. There was a normative pressure of just being around them and constantly hearing them. It was a pressure of, "Oh my God. I'm going to be deported in April if I don't get this figured out."

In the country I was in, it's a pretty unique system. The market is always tight. There are always not enough employers and a lot of employees. There's just too many people who want jobs. Because of the visa system, it becomes an imbalance. Everyone wants to stay in the country. I just looked and applied literally wherever I could. I focused on pulling strings with as many people as I could. Otherwise, nobody would give you the time of day. Nobody would even call you and say, "Come in for an interview." Around the time that I got the job offer that I ultimately took up, I had this alternate job offer for a lower pay but something that was very interesting in the learning and development space where I'd be working with managers and leaders and coaching and training them. I didn't even think such a thing was possible. I considered myself insanely lucky to have two job offers in such a market. That's the long and short of it.

For the job I ended up getting, the process was actually really simple. I was called in for a conversation with a hiring manager who I was not very familiar with. About 10 minutes into having a casual conversation with me, she pulled out an offer letter. She was like, "Here you go." I went in really nervous, expecting a full interview, but it seemed to me they had made up their mind based off of my internship performance. It was more just to understand whether they and I were on the same page of what it was that I wanted in my career. Once that was established, there was no need to interview me.

I went into the job a little disbelieving because I was still a fresh grad. Being a fresh graduate, you generally feel amazed that somebody hired you. Given the context of the market and most of my friends still struggling to find jobs, it just felt unreal that I got it. I also had great managers. My team was very supportive. I'm sure we had our ups and downs that I'm probably glossing over right now. I remember we had pretty open boundaries about walking. This was in the times we used to work in the office full time. There was no telecommuting whatsoever. You had to be there all the time in each other's faces more or less. You had cubicles but you were still next to each other. There was just the banter of every morning coming in and somebody joking with the other person. There was trust in the team. Obviously, there were issues. Overall, I was never made to feel I was not part of it.

I also enjoyed learning from different mentors every three months. The pro was in learning about a bunch of different pathways, the con was having to quickly adapt to whatever way they wanted me to learn. For example, one of my rotations was in database. My mentor at that point was someone who sometimes gave us the impression that she did not want us to come to her for help. She wanted me to figure things out on my own. This was frustrating until I eventually found that there was a super user of the database from another time zone. He became my point of contact and eventually a lifelong partner for three years after that. That was nice.

So after I finished the two years of training, I worked for two years as an HR specialist for the company, which was basically a lot of continuous improvement projects. Since that point, I transitioned to a role in the US where I was an HR business partner for a year with the same company. I took a two-year sabbatical during which I pursued a master's degree. Currently, I'm working at a government agency in a state department of health on the West Coast, as an HR analyst. I'm back in HR working more specifically on employee engagement work.

One overarching theme of my career is that communication with your manager matters a lot. Obviously, every manager has different tolerances and boundaries for what is acceptable to bring to them and what isn't. Understanding those boundaries is super important. Maybe this is a stereotype of my generation, but I feel the need for feedback quite often. That feeds into the second point, which is whenever possible, ask for feedback. Obviously, it has to be meaningful. Don't spend a day working with someone and ask them for feedback. At the end of anything that happens, always take the time to reflect on it. You'll be surprised oftentimes by what people have to say to you both positive and constructive.

Lately, I've learned that sometimes perfection isn't everything. People often want you to give them something minimally valuable. They just want to see something as the barebones minimum. Sometimes they don't need to see perfection. Oftentimes, that's enough for them to understand where you're going in there. They don't need you to do anything more. I'm trying to deal with the discomfort of not producing perfect work.

My advice to someone currently looking for their first job is ... in some ways, I wouldn't want anyone to get inspired by my example because I think I just got lucky. Obviously, you can be smart, but everyone is smart. Everyone out there has their own capabilities. The only piece of advice I can give others is to not underestimate yourself. I did it back then. I remember my first team meeting with 10 to 12 others when I was introducing myself, and I said "I'm just a trainee." My manager called me out on that and said, "You are not just a trainee. You are a trainee who is going to bring a whole other mindset to our team, which we desperately need. You are going to be pipelined into being a future leader for us."

Also, maybe this is more the case in the country I was in than in the US, but networking matters. It's very annoying to have to say it and to have to constantly deal with it. I think if I had LinkedIn back in the day, I would have spent time making the most of LinkedIn. So try to get to know who are the people who are in the jobs you want. Understand what their experiences are like. Get to know as many people as you can. Just be patient with the process.

2.22 On the Challenges of Being a Person of Color in Finance: Afi's Story

I also realize that this industry is harder for young people, especially young black males like me. When you walk into a brokerage office, you don't expect to see a young early 20-something Black male talking to you. Some of the clients were hesitant, and sometimes I was met with resistance. There were some clients who would walk right past me when I tried to greet them as they entered the office, as if I wasn't there. I just had to learn how to brush it off and keep moving on.

I went to a large public university for my bachelor's in economics. I completed a yearlong internship with this large brokerage firm during my senior year, and then I joined them full time as a stockbroker trainee. Actually, I kind of stumbled upon the internship by chance. Our school had a career fair, where they normally have about 200 different employers come to talk to students looking for jobs and internships. They had this online portal where you can sort through all of the different employers. So I filtered to look for internships for economics majors, and the only one that came up was the company that I ended up working for. So I went to the career fair with some copies of my resume, looked around and talked to a few different places, and then stopped by the company's kiosk. That's all I did for searching for internships.

The internship itself was a year long. As I finished the internship, I was looking for full-time job openings at the location I was at in my local city. But the problem is that at the local branch, if someone doesn't leave or move on in a promotion, there's no opening there. So for there to be a job, someone had to leave, get fired, or get promoted. None of them worked out, so I ended up graduating without a job offer. I moved back home to another state and continued looking for jobs.

It took about a month, which I guess wasn't that long. I was full-time looking for jobs. I considered Teach for America, which actually they were paying slightly more than this brokerage firm surprisingly. However, I focused on looking at the branches that the brokerage firm was opening. I understood the company culture very well and I really believed in how they focus on educating people about finances and investing. So I wanted to stay with them. But I had to consider factors such as living at home with my parents, or commuting 40 miles, and so forth. I ended up finding a branch near home, so I could live with my parents, which helped with the costs. But for that month while I was searching, I was like, how am I going to make some money? I was expecting to go directly from the internship and then start working. I didn't think of taking a break.

One other thing, this was all around the time of the 2008–2009 economic crash. The times we're in now are a little bit reminiscent, like this disaster preparedness type of mentality. And looking back, those were actually the most exciting times to be an investor. Even to this day, a lot of what I experienced encouraged me in my career and influenced a lot of what I like to do on the side. I mean, it was hard, I remember certain days when we were so busy that we didn't even eat lunch.

Anyways, going into this first job, I was just so excited at the opportunity to make money, that, looking back, I probably could have negotiated better in terms of the pay. The commute was definitely difficult, driving 40 miles to work and 40 miles home. But luckily I knew the company from my internship, so a lot of the job was familiar. It was more about learning their client base, getting familiar with them, letting them get familiar with you, and becoming someone the clients could trust.

But they had this setup where you're paid a certain amount, then you study and get your licenses after about three or four months, then your pay increases. Without those licenses, I wouldn't be able to make transactions or speak on certain investment products. I passed the first license, and it was a hard exam that was about six hours long. I was never the best at taking exams, so I was just so happy to pass that. After I passed it, I had to take another short exam, only about 60 questions, but more from a legal perspective for my second license. It was so much harder, and I failed it the first time. Actually, a lot of companies will say if you fail a license test, they have to let you go because they have other people waiting for the position. This company was a little nicer. I studied again, took it 30 days later, and failed it again. My company said they liked me, so they gave me one last try to pass. So it was this dark cloud lingering over my head. But I was able to pass it on my third try, I think it was the day after Christmas that year, and it was the only thing I wanted because I was studying nonstop.

Looking back, I also realize that this industry is harder for young people, especially young black males like me. When you walk into a brokerage office, you don't expect to see a young early 20-something Black male talking to you. Some of the clients were hesitant, and sometimes I was met with resistance. Some clients would walk right past me when I tried to greet them as they entered the office as if I wasn't there. I just had to learn how to brush it off and keep moving on. But I definitely was in a place where I didn't belong. I've now worked in four different branches, and I've experienced it at every branch, even when I became a branch manager later on.

However, I had this one coworker who really helped me. He was this older, White gentleman, and he would always have my back. There was this one rough phone call I remember happening where the client was just so upset with the company and said some really bad words. I basically just hung up, I was upset over the situation, and this coworker stepped out to a liquor store and bought me a six-pack of beer and put it on my desk. It was so funny and out of the blue, a weird but nice gesture. It was the first of many times when he would be helpful and encouraging for me.

Anyways, so broadly, I went from stockbroker trainee to senior stockbroker to branch manager at two different locations. I got to the point after about nine years when I was ready to leave. I wrestled with going back to school for my MBA, and I experienced some failure there with not getting good scores on the GMAT [Graduate Management Admission Test]. Eventually, I stepped into government consulting, got some certifications in IT [information technology] and project management, and then I recently started my own company for financial education. I'm focusing on reaching people like myself who don't understand anything about the stock market. I want to create space for people to ask silly questions and be empowered to make better financial decisions and build wealth and help future generations.

My advice to someone currently looking for their first job is ... stay flexible. That's one of the reasons I was able to move up within that first company and be one of the younger branch managers in the company at the age of 26. I was one of those people where I just didn't say no. Need someone to cover a day at the other branch? I'd offer to go help. I wanted to learn. To me, once you learn something, no one can take that information from you. It also helped me start creating this network. I was creating a space for other people like me to become more comfortable in this industry.

I would also say to find ways to create value in your position. There was a time in my previous company when they didn't necessarily have someone who handled marketing. They didn't want to pay someone else to do it, so I volunteered. I didn't know what I was volunteering for, but I ended up running the awards program for the marketing awards. Later on, when I wanted to leave the company for more pay, they said no, we need you, because you're running that program for us. They retained me by beating the pay. Things like that, where I found ways to increase my value.

2.23 On Adapting to Nonlinearity: Tristan's Story

We didn't build this thing called life, because if we did, we would make rounded corners on everything. But instead, life is full of sharp edges. You're going to get cut, hurt, bloodied, and bruised physically and emotionally. We didn't make life, but we adapt to it.

My first job was in the military. It was a defining moment in my life because it was my first step away from the family restaurant that I worked in growing up. The restaurant was more a family responsibility than work, though I did put in much more than 30 hours a week of work for the restaurant. I started as young as eight years old, making pizza boxes in the back room whenever my parents couldn't get a babysitter, and I continued all through high school and college at the local state college. I enjoyed working in that environment and I enjoyed feeling a sense of pride in being part of the family, that team cohesive unit of everybody working together to make sure this thing is successful.

Anyway, I started looking into the military because of the opportunity to do something different. I needed to get away from the town I grew up in, I wanted to spread my wings. But at the same time, I didn't want to disappoint my family, because I was 21 years old and managing the restaurant for something like 80 hours a week. I was in small town America, so I walked into the recruiter's office located right next to the barbershop. It took a couple of weeks for me to work up the courage to go and knock on that door. I ended up speaking to a Marine Corps recruiter, and they had me do this simple test, and they said, "Wow, your test scores are great. We think you'd be an amazing cook."

Well, I told them that I was going to the military to get out of the restaurant business, not to stay in it. They were probably just filling slots on an Excel spreadsheet of who goes where. So they were pushing me into that role, and it was a little off-putting. I ended up talking to an Army recruiter next, and they said I'd be a great cook as well, or a communicator, or a radio person. None of that was appealing to me. I finally came to a point where I understood that I was just in research mode. With every conversation I had, every book that I would pry open, and every magazine that I would look at for military recruiting, I was starting to get a little bit clearer understanding of something completely foreign to me. That was difficult, but I had to do it, and that then opened the door, opened my eyes, and exposed me to other facets of the military.

Eventually, at some point, the idea of being a [Army] ranger came up. I talked to a recruiter about it, who told me that a ranger contract was almost impossible to get. I got sent to talk to this sergeant, and he gave me some insight and showed me what being a ranger was like through some videos, and I said I wanted to do that. The sergeant then looked up to see if there were any ranger contracts available, and he told me there weren't, so I got up to leave, and then he all of a sudden said that one opened up. Maybe he was playing me a little bit with a little bit of screening because he was trying to see if I was serious about signing up to be a ranger. And I did it, I pulled the trigger and signed up.

So looking back, that whole process was a desire, followed by research, followed by some uncomfortable moments. You've got to do these things. There's an element of networking. I hate that word because no matter how many hands you shake, it's about what they do or maybe what one of their friends does. It's talking to people and getting the word out; for me, because I spoke to my friend in university who had a brother in the

Special Forces, I never would have known that and he never would have introduced me to his brother if I didn't speak about it. Everyone has a personal calculus, right? There's a series of variables that put you in a position to make a decision, but the beginning and the end of that math problem is asking what you personally want. And my calculus at the time had some major movements that were going to change everything and have an impact on the restaurant and by proxy, my family. It was an arduous experience and one that changed my life forever, and it was the second most important decision in my life.

Anyway, I was thrilled by the time I made that decision to sign up. I was going to be doing something different. I had a desire to go overseas and support my country during the [Gulf War] crisis. I also wanted to see what was outside of this small town and outside of my state. I also looked forward to breaking away from the day-to-day. This was also a big deal for me because I was quite shy and introverted back then. It was like, wow, I'm doing something for myself. And I had no idea what was behind the door that I was opening. But I knew it was a door that I was opening myself, and that was an amazing experience.

So the next few steps involved everything from a mental aptitude test to buzzing my hair, and then my parents dropping me off at a hotel somewhere. It felt almost like a field trip. I didn't need to go make pizza boxes or cut cheese tomorrow. My parents were supportive. My mom was very emotional, but my dad had left home as a young kid also, so, he was more impressed that I was doing this by myself. Then I ended up in Louisiana, Basic training, in classic rows of white A-frame homes. It helped that I was used to the yelling in a pizza restaurant, so the discipline and being yelled at to go do push-ups was fine with me. Then after basic training, I went off to airborne school, and then finally ranger training. By this point, there are only about 20 of us left there.

They started us off with something called the Ranger Indoctrination Program. RIP, no joke. At this point, it was the first and only time in my entire military career that I was nervous. It was the first time where I questioned myself if I had what it takes. I was carrying these two big green duffle bags, they were very heavy and had to run a 6:30 mile. Some people have said it's hazing, which, sure, that may be part of it. But if you're a young person in the military, you're about to go jump on an airplane and fly somewhere across the world to go into combat where things are exceedingly chaotic. You won't have time to prepare, you'll be in reaction mode. The folks in charge have been around for a while, and they're helping us get trained so we can react correctly without thinking about it. Plus, it was a weeding-out process to figure out who could sustain that level of pressure.

A lot has happened since then. The number one change is that I'm not as introverted as I used to be. I also think elements of growth occur through exposure to people. From the other side of a cash register at the pizza shop to all my experiences in the military, I found myself constantly growing and absorbing. I never finished college, and I don't regret it. The experiences I had helped me grow up in a much richer way. My older brother tells me today, "Man, everything you've been through in life, like if your car runs out of gas and there's three feet of snow so you're walking five miles to the gas station ... that would be nothing for you." I can adapt. I think about it like I'm juggling bowling pins. If something happens, I can take a bowling pin out. We didn't build this thing called life, because if we did, we would make rounded corners on everything. But instead, life is full of sharp edges. You're going to get cut, hurt, bloodied, and bruised physically and emotionally. We didn't make life, but we adapted to it. We put things into place either directly from experience or through lessons learned. And I've learned that I can keep those sharp corners away from me to make better decisions.

My advice to someone currently looking for their first job is ... I have been out of the military for 10 years. If you look at everything I've done out of the military, nothing makes sense. There is no flowchart of career progression. There's no demonstrative attempt to create a "career." No one should ever enter the workforce with the priority of doing what they love as their priority path. Because it's an exceedingly difficult thing to do what you love in the first moments of your decades in front of you. A career I believe is an archaic term that is more from the 50s and 60s, in factories around America where you're going to be a manager. A career is, I think, better defined for people entering the workforce now out of universities as getting exposed to a particular industry to determine whether or not you like that industry, and as that moves forward, you can look back on it as a career.

2.24 On Setting Your Own Pace: Kyla's Story

It's okay to take breaks and to finish school at your own pace. For me, it was also trying to decide what I wanted to finish my degree in. It probably would have been quicker to finish it in education since I was so close. But I also thought, why pay to finish a degree that I've already determined I don't want to work in anymore? So do what feels right for you and just keep pushing through.

I started college right after high school. I think I tried to do engineering or something like that because it was what everyone told me to do. But after the basic freshman engineering class, I realized I didn't want to do that. I changed to education, and that was interesting at first, but I was doing education at an engineering school so I didn't make any connections with my classmates. Plus I went home every weekend for my part-time job, and the education program was very small and taught by a lot of foreign teachers that I had difficulty understanding. Their lectures were completely different from the textbook, and the test questions were different than the lectures, so nothing matched up or made sense. I found myself overburdened, plus I had a medical condition one semester, so I ended up just skipping a lot of classes and taking a break. I left college after about two years.

I was then working as a substitute teacher plus other part-time jobs. It just so happened that a full-time job came open, and I needed the benefits. So I applied through the district's website, and I went and did the interviews. I knew one of the interviewers since I was already a substitute teacher in that district. Actually, I knew other people in the administration as well, but I didn't use their names, I didn't want that to be why I got the job. I've always hated interviewing, I'm not very good at it. I'm not good at selling myself, I guess. So I just made sure that I answered the questions. They were a bit desperate to get people, so I ended up getting this job as a paraprofessional, an assistant special education teacher, in the district. For this job, you didn't need the degree that a teacher does, since you're just assisting. I just needed to help do anything they needed, even changing a diaper for some of the students. So for me, having taken care of children in my family before, I had done all those things.

The best part of the job was working with the kids. I loved that. The worst was that as time went on, there were some issues. I sometimes had problems where kids would throw things and hit each other, and I would send them to the office, but they would just be given candy and sent back with no consequences. I know it was special ed, and we had different circumstances, but we still wanted to try to improve behavior. It was difficult. My teacher and I would talk about these challenges, but some politics in administration made it difficult for us to talk to anyone else.

Eventually, I left that job and went to babysitting, and that's when I finally went back to college. Then I worked for a grocery chain, then eventually I got this job with the federal government. It finally feels like I'm a bit more on track. I finally have a job that pays enough to cover living expenses, and I got a security clearance so that opens up many more doors. I'm still learning a lot on the job, and this field is very new to me. I'm, in a way, naive compared to my coworkers regarding the business world and stuff like that, but so far it's going good.

My advice to someone currently looking for their first job is ... it's okay to take breaks and finish school at your own pace. For me, it was also trying to decide what I wanted to finish my degree in. It probably would have been quicker to finish it in education since I was so close. But I also thought, why pay to finish a degree that I've already determined I don't want to work in anymore? So do what feels right for you and just keep pushing through.

Talk to people as well. I talked with some of my family more than I did my parents. As much as I love my parents, they just didn't have the same experiences to relate to because they never went to college. I think that's where a lot of the pressure came from; they wanted me to have the degree. But I always talked things over with other people, asking for help or for advice from others.

Also, applying and interviewing can take up a lot of time, and you can get discouraged if you interview and then don't get it. I definitely recommend learning how to interview. I didn't have too much experience interviewing, and there were several times when I thought conversations went great for interviews and then I wouldn't get chosen. Keep applying though. For example, I had this offer from the government, but there was a pause in my security clearance process. So I ended up applying elsewhere, and I essentially got an offer from them, but that same day, I got a call that they were continuing with my clearance. So don't get discouraged, don't give up. It's okay to apply to different types of jobs, because I never knew for sure what I wanted to do with my life, and I still don't know 100 percent.

2.25 On Reflecting on Times of Desperation: Ray's Story

I got laid off due to COVID, and I was unemployed for almost a year. In many ways, it was like a repeat of the start of my career. It was desperation again. I had loans, rent due, and I needed food. I did the same shotgun approach, I applied for probably over 200 jobs and interviewed with at least 75 companies, and again, it was just this one job that gave me an offer.

By my senior year of college, my degree was going to be in advertising, and I think everyone hits the panic button as graduation approaches. My mom was very kind, she said I could move back home if I needed to. My dad was like, "Figure it out." So I just took the shotgun approach. I jumped on LinkedIn and Indeed, and I texted friends asking if they'd heard anything. Even two months into the summer, I was living in an apartment and paying rent with no income coming in, so I took any interview I could. The vast majority of the jobs that I was applying for would be marketing, assistant communications, and some executive assistant positions. Loans were coming due, rent was coming due, and I needed to feed myself, so I thought, "I'll take anything."

I didn't get a job until three months after I had graduated, as a marketing assistant at an environmental consulting company. Honestly, the reason why I took this job was desperation; they were the only offer I got. Even though the reasons why I joined that company weren't very noble or high-minded, and I wasn't even thrilled per se, it probably was one of the best first jobs I could have hoped for. I just remember distinctly, my first day, turning on my computer and having to turn around to my coworker behind me and ask, "How do I use Outlook?" I knew absolutely nothing, and that job taught me how to be a professional. It was an all-woman team, and the lady taught me from top to bottom, how to work, and how to work well. They taught me some technical marketing things that I will use in my next job, and they provided solid friendships and also professional references. Even now, years later, I use my first job references and skills to get here.

Since then, I moved to a different job, but then I got laid off due to COVID-19, and I was unemployed for almost a year. In many ways, it was like a repeat of the start of my career. It was desperation again. I had loans, and rent due, and I needed food. I did the same shotgun approach, I applied to probably over 200 jobs and interviewed with at least 75 companies, and again, it was just this one job that gave me an offer. Actually, it was connections that helped me. My roommate at the time worked at this university, and so I asked him if he knew anyone in the department, I was applying for that job, and the next day I got an interview request. But even then, it took about a month and a half before I actually got hired. Now I'm the communications coordinator for the housing office at a small liberal arts school on the West Coast. I'm also working on my master's degree to work with individuals with intellectual and developmental disabilities.

My advice to someone currently looking for their first job is … Looking back on my collegiate experience, it was great. I don't regret it. But I definitely had some of my peers who pursued hard, tangible skill sets, that they were able to immediately jump into their first job fairly easier and more quickly than I did. Whereas on my end, I had to do really intense legwork of trying to prove to a potential employer, "I can write well, I work well in teams," which is actually extremely valuable. It's hard to express in a 20-minute interview. So my first piece of advice is to learn a hard skill set.

My second piece of advice is to leverage your network. I didn't understand the value of networking at first. I grew up in a minority household, and it was very merit based. The kinds of conversations that we were having with each other were like, "You need to work hard, and you will get good outcomes because of your hard work." For us that meant getting As, doing extracurriculars, and things that I could put on a resume. Which is all good, but the reality is, and I hate this truism, it really is who you know. That bugged me for so long. But it really is merit based plus who you know. It's like, "You need to work hard and be able to prove that you can produce and execute, and you need someone to get you in the door so that you can actually do that." Take LinkedIn as an example. I used it as decoration, as frosting when it should have been the whole cake. I should have been reaching out to alumni. I should have been reaching out to parents and my friends who own companies. I should have been asking people who are established in their careers, "Would you be willing to sit down with me, just for coffee, give me a moment of your time, and share your wisdom?" I didn't do any of that going into my first job, and it showed.

Last thing, I would tell people that you can quit well. In my first job, I left because I was able to finish most of my work in four or six hours each day. I had created these core competencies that allowed me to just breeze through my work, and it left me with a lot of time on my hands, and it left me feeling bored. It left me feeling underutilized. A good manager would be able to see like, "Okay, I can utilize my worker for more." But that's not the totality of the picture because I didn't go out of my way to say, "Hey, you're not utilizing me. I still want to stay, and if you want me to stay, you should give me more work." But even then, when I quit, I really tried to quit well. I told my boss, "Here's why I'm leaving. There's absolutely no bad blood. I am so grateful for everything that you guys have given to me." After I left, I still kept in touch. I still updated them. One Christmas, I sent the entire marketing office a box of food. It was so funny because that second job was a total bust. A waste of time, but not really, because it taught me what I don't want. And again, even now, I'm still using for my professional references the people I met in my first job.

2.26 On Throwing the Plan Out the Window: Dana's Story

Throw the plan out the window. You know, the plan they tell you that you should be done with college at 22, have a family at 30, and so forth. It creates so much anxiety and stress when you don't achieve that, and it's different for every person.

My first full-time job was at a retail store after I graduated high school. At the time I was wait-listed for university, and I needed something to do because I was still living with my family. I only applied for one other job, a cleaning job going into offices and cleaning restrooms and counters. It was really quick to get this retail job. I walked in, did an interview, and then they hired me. This was before the internet, so you just walk around and fill out paperwork, I didn't even have a resume.

My job responsibilities were just to help the customer, restock items, and later on some duties in taking money to the bank. It wasn't always easy. I remember one time the big boss from the bigger store down the street came in, and they pushed me into a shelf and said, "That's not clean." It was a short few months though, because then I got married to someone in the military and moved. It's interesting though, I found that I was always the awkward kid in the adult work environment. I still am. I think that's why I ultimately chose to work with kids now as a children's teacher. It's just so hard to work with adults, especially in an office space.

So after moving, I worked part time in a child development center as a teaching assistant, then I ended up working at a public university as a lead children's teacher and have been here for decades. I ended up getting my college degree along the way, after over 10 years, mostly because I had to redo my GED [general educational development] and had to raise my kids as a single parent.

My advice to someone currently looking for their first job is ... no matter what the job is, treat it like it's the presidency. Give it your all to learn everything that you can and every aspect of the business. One day, maybe everyone is out sick, and you're the one who can do the job, and you'll get promoted. So be open to learning everything and be curious. Oh, and be on time.

Also, throw the plan out the window. You know, the plan they tell you is that you should be done with college at 22, have a family at 30, and so forth. It creates so much anxiety and stress when you don't achieve that, and it's different for every person. The assistant director here is two years younger than me and is finishing their PhD, and I was so upset with myself for not being where they're at. But then they helped me just bask in the moment of what I've achieved with my bachelor's. We definitely had some hard times, being a single parent going to school and working. We had no internet at times when I couldn't afford the bill, so I would take my kids to the library and do work there. So things change, but it's your life and your path, and you need to be happy and love yourself.

2.27 On Proving Your Worth: Colton's Story

> *[My first job] was scary because I was just thinking, 'These guys took a chance on me.' I didn't have a major in computer science. When you are in that position where someone clearly takes a chance on you, you want to make sure that you do it for whoever stuck their neck out on the line for you. I wanted them to understand that I thanked them for that, and I took it seriously, and I wouldn't let them down. I treated every project like it was my last. I put more hours in, and I stayed late, and I never missed a day of work.*

I applied for several jobs as I finished college. Before I graduated, I was going through this long interview process with an initial interview, a screening exam, and a final interview. I had gone through several other interview processes with several jobs. But I just needed a job, and it was important to me to go ahead and get one. Because once I finished my degree, my time would be up. It would be time to go and do something. So I took the interviews very seriously, I was very dialed in to make sure that I would have a job by the time I graduated.

It's interesting because I majored in Russian, and I wanted to get into government. But I've always been very good with computers and IT. So I ended up applying for a job with a now-defunct electronics retail chain. I didn't want to get to a position where I was shaving in my parent's basement because I didn't have a job. I actually never moved home. I went from my graduation to moving into an apartment in a new city. My parents helped me move there, and we all crashed in a one-bedroom, 500-square-foot apartment for a night.

When I showed up on the first day of work, it was so surreal. It was scary because I was just thinking, "These guys took a chance on me." I didn't have a major in computer science. When you are in that position where someone clearly takes a chance on you, you want to make sure that you do it for whoever stuck their neck out on the line for you. I wanted them to understand that I thanked them for that, and I took it seriously, and I wouldn't let them down. I treated every project like it was my last. I put more hours in, and I stayed late, and I never missed a day of work.

I primarily did Y2K work when everybody feared that the world was going to come to an end because it was a two-digit year. I did a lot of programming for that in very old languages, COBOL, RPGs, control language, and fun stuff like that. It was exactly what I needed for my first job because I learned how to be a professional. I worked in a team to do stuff rather than flying solo. I hadn't done that before as far as in a professional environment.

A lot of what I gained from that job was the people who took me in and taught me more about how to work in a professional environment and especially how to work on a team. I learned how people needed to be treated. I remember this one person who I had some conflicts with because we had different working styles. I thought I was getting it, and I wasn't. She was getting frustrated, and I was getting frustrated because she was getting frustrated. But we learned to sit down and talk it out and figure it out.

I stayed for about a year. Then I took another job closer to home. I was still a kid, but I knew now that I had learned a level of professionalism at that job and I had grown. Since then, I've always been working. Ironically, I've always been in IT. I'm the CEO of a business analytics consulting firm now. I take analytics knowledge and apply it to various clients from health care to wineries to food banks to casinos. I actually had to rebuild my company from scratch due to COVID. I almost lost everything, but I was able to rebound and stay steady, and now everything's really starting to take off to another level. One more thing, I'm a Person of Color, and I own my own company. Twenty years ago, this probably would never have happened.

My advice to someone currently looking for their first job is ... sometimes people's first jobs don't really paint their professional picture later in life. They don't define it. I beg to differ. I think you can always take something from your first job and apply it to who you are as a person or who you are as a professional.

The mentality that I would have to learn something new is something that I still use each day. I tweak it because I'm obviously more experienced and I can tweak it more. But I also go in there and I say, "Well, this is what I learned from my first job and it still holds true, how to be a professional, how to respond to people, how to technically write." These are very basic skills that I don't see in many people today. Especially the writing part; it's really frustrating watching when people give me something and it's not up to the quality that it should be. I try to do a lot of teaching without being condescending because I'm not perfect. I try to show them how I look for things and make it seem like a discovery process rather than me dictating what it is that they should be doing.

2.28 On Staying Open to New Directions: Thomas' Story

I'm learning to be myself in this career. I tried to use the higher education lingo, and I don't do that now. I have side hustles doing yard and lawn care in case it doesn't work out. It's been a beautiful thing because I have my full-time job and I have my side hustle. It's the best of both worlds.

Technically I was in the Marine Corps for a few years before and during college. People ask if that counts as a job. Actually, I say it's a way of life. It's a cliche to say that, but for me to sit here and try to describe the Marine Corps to someone, I don't think that I would be doing it justice because it was very subjective and very specific to me. I'd start throwing out acronyms and then have to explain the acronyms and I'd start cursing because that's what you do in the Marine Corps.

So my first "normal" job was my role within a large public university as a student services coordinator. I always referred to it as my first real big-boy civilian job. I was ecstatic to get it. Coming out of my undergrad studies, I was in what I call a dark space. I had completed this degree in environmental and sustainability studies and I was looking for work geared toward that area, but I just couldn't find anything within the state. Even though it wasn't that long, just a few months, it felt like forever. I was looking all over for jobs, and I couldn't find anything. Here I was, a husband, a father, with a college degree and experience in the Marine Corps, and I was stuck working a part-time job in a local store. There's nothing wrong with that, but I really needed a career, something that I could really talk about and be proud of.

Then, I had a friend at the university ask if I'd be interested in working in her office, and I never really thought about that before. Five years ago if you had asked me what working in higher education was like, I couldn't tell you. It was a big moment for me to realize that there are jobs and careers that exist in higher education.

I found the job ad and read through it, and I thought I would be a solid candidate. But I wanted to make sure, and also I was scared about competition because it said a master's degree preferred not required. So I tapped into my networking skills. I went and spoke with people who I knew in the college to gather as much information as I could. I reached out to professors, talked with the office ahead of time, and learned about this curriculum development grant that I'd be helping with, I had to put forth a lot of effort to get that job. I did so much prep work that I felt overly prepared to the point of being nauseous. I remember taking that elevator up to the fourth floor for my interview and I thought I was going to puke by the time it got to the fourth floor. It was bad. I also remember that I focused all my energy on this one job. I tend to get tunnel vision a lot, very rarely is there a plan B or C because I think backup plans allow me to go easy on myself, which I never want to do.

Well, I got the job, and I immediately fell in love with the work. On my first day, I was so excited that I had made it, I had a steady source of income. I wore my nice collared shirt with khakis, went to the administration building and got my faculty staff ID, read the welcome email carefully, and got ready to learn. But the thing that really shocked me, the most salient memory of day one, was having lunch in the conference room with faculty and staff members because I had never been in an intimate or casual situation with them before. I heard them talk candidly about grading papers and the more papers they grade, the drunker they get. It humanized the other side of higher education for me.

Actually, for the longest time, higher education was something that people told me I couldn't do. They would say, "You would be really good in construction, or working outside with your hands." To me, it was always implied that I was not good enough for college. My cousins are good enough for college but I'm not. I never excelled in school, and I never saw it as an option for me. But then when I was presented as an option by starting in community college, I realized I could do it. That led me to my bachelor's, then getting this job, and since then getting my master's in higher education administration.

It's not always easy though. I have friends who work in aviation, plumbing, and HVAC [heating, ventilation, and air conditioning], and they're making a lot of money, a lot more than me. And I enjoy the kind of work that they're doing. So I'm in this position now where I'm in admissions trying to essentially sell higher education to prospective students. It's difficult at times because I don't always know if this is the right path for these students. But I'm learning to be myself in this career. I tried to use the higher education lingo, and I don't do that now. I have side hustles doing yard and lawn care in case it doesn't work out. It's been a beautiful thing because I have my full-time job and I have my side hustle. It's the best of both worlds. This past summer, I could be having this conversation with you and then the following day, just sweating my rear end off with my headphones in.

My advice to someone currently looking for their first job is … for students looking for their first job, you need to develop the ability to leverage people. You have to have conversations with people. Look for the jobs you're interested in, look for people on LinkedIn in those jobs, and look at their paths. There's very rarely a linear path especially if you're looking at jobs that are not STEM-focused. It's wide open, and don't be afraid of that, don't get tunnel vision like me to focus too much on any one path.

Don't feel dead set on having to have the end-all-be-all job right after earning your bachelor's degree. Everything you do, whether it's your dream job or not, is an experience that can build into other opportunities. I have these conversations in my job with students who say they want to go to graduate school right after college. But why? What's the purpose? Maybe you should take some time off first. Maybe you should look at these jobs that are out there that might not be exactly what you want to do, but still, you're building experiences that can lead to these opportunities. Maybe you'll come to realize you don't need a master's degree or maybe the master's degree you were looking for isn't the right one.

2.29 On Pivoting from Your Original Career Path: Mika's Story

After five years, I got a job in a counseling center. People were shocked, surprised, and disappointed. They had lost their minority faculty member. But I was happy. I think I may have even taken a pay cut… Over the years, that's led to where I am now, in a leadership position overseeing multiple student affairs departments ranging from disability services to counseling to social work. I've been here 10 years, and I've never stayed anywhere for 10 years.

Honestly, my first job that wasn't an internship or part of a degree program was as a college professor in my late twenties. I was finishing up grad school in the Midwest. This was over 20 years ago, so I don't remember exactly how I found the job. But I remember applying to a few different jobs, and there was this program that was for minority students and People of Color to do a one-year visiting postdoc at various liberal arts colleges. I had done a couple of interviews at other schools, but then this liberal arts college called me through the program, they said they didn't have a one-year postdoc available, but they did have a tenure-track position in my field. They invited me out to interview. It was the dead of winter when I was in grad school, and I was flying out to the West Coast, which was very different. I ended up getting that job, which was really interesting since the program I originally applied for was the one-year postdoc, but it ended up leading to this tenure-track position.

I became an assistant professor of psychology at a small liberal arts institution teaching classes in minority studies and basic psychology. I did a fun class on psychotherapy in film as well. I had advisees, did research, and got my license to be a practicing psychologist. But I was so young, this was so long ago. Back then, I didn't even qualify for the retirement benefits. All of my colleagues were older; most people didn't go straight from undergrad to PhD to tenure-track faculty. I didn't even know how to dress, people would mistake me for a student.

I distinctly remember feeling like these colleagues were not the people I would normally hang out with. They've got families and older children whereas I was young and single. What do I have in common with any of them? Now to some degree, they tried to mentor me. But I don't think I was getting great advice, especially on where to publish or how to improve, and I ended up leaving after a few years. Plus, I was never passionate about research. I enjoyed teaching and mentoring students. So I started planting seeds to do something else, getting my license, and doing some clinical work.

After five years, I got a job in a counseling center. People were shocked, surprised, and disappointed. They had lost their minority faculty member. But I was happy. I think I may have even taken a pay cut. After a year, I got a call from a former colleague asking if I'd consider working in student affairs. I said I didn't know what that was, but she said, "Of course you do. You would call us when you would have a problem with students, and you would participate in the programs we had. You know who we are and what we do, and we think you'd be perfect for this job." So I ended up taking on some work there as well, and at some point, I was working like four different jobs between student services, private practice, teaching, and others. Over the years, that's led to where I am now, in a leadership position overseeing multiple student affairs departments ranging from disability services to counseling to social work. I've been here 10 years, and I've never stayed anywhere for 10 years.

My advice to someone currently looking for their first job is ... I've been on both ends now, looking for jobs and as the hiring manager for jobs. Unfortunately, I just don't hear of a lot of people who blindly apply for things and find themselves in lovely positions. Generally, people tend to have more success if they're a part of some network like they know somebody who knows somebody on the hiring committee. I think things shouldn't be that way. You should just be able to launch your career on your own merits, but you really do have to be networked. I remember for my current job when I was switching institutions, I knew a colleague at that school, and they got me out to interview, they went to my job talk, and they even texted me insights about what subjects to discuss with my interviewers based on the behind-the-scenes feedback they were getting. I probably would have gotten the job without this person's insider intel. It's hard for me because I'm an introvert and I don't naturally walk into places and love meeting people and love networking. I dislike that, but it really is important to go to conferences and make a connection with people. You never know how many degrees of separation there are between you and the job that you want and the person who could actually help you. It's a small world in certain industries. That's the advice I would give.

The other clear distinction for me is someone who can reflect on a mistake, own up to it, and identify what they learned and how they may have corrected it. I will hire that person any day over somebody who cannot reflect on their own contributions to an error. So when people interview, I think it's really important to be able to articulate where they made their mistake. Now I know this person will never make that mistake again. Don't just use the interview time to showcase all of your strengths. I always ask folks, "Tell me about your most difficult day at work or a mistake that you made and what you learned from that." I get really lovely thoughtful answers and those are the people that I want to hire.

2.30 On Faking It Until You Make It: Darius' Story

Go in with confidence. Sell yourself. If you don't believe in yourself, how are they going to believe in you to do a job? If they're going to hire you to do something, you want to make sure you can do it to the best of your ability. So go out there and show them what you got. If you don't know it, fake it till you make it.

I finished my college degree in IT, and I was looking for a lab that would help pay for my graduate school program. In college, I was in the robotics club and we won a few robotics competitions. I had this portfolio of custom-designed robots from animatronics to layman tasks for lab research. I got connected with this institute through a lab I worked in during college, and I became friends with some of the professors and program directors at this institute. When graduation came about, it was all word of mouth. I had a professor send my resume out to them, and I ended up meeting with some people at the institute to show them my robotics portfolio, and they were really interested. Maybe I was overconfident, but that was really the only opportunity I focused on. Oh, except on the side, I briefly tried to create my own custom-order robotics company. I put that aside once I got a part-time job at the institute and went to graduate school.

I did my master's in modeling and simulation while working part time at the research and training institute. As I was finishing, the conversations were pretty informal. My boss came up and asked if I was interested in working full time after graduation, and I said yes, and then there was some discussion about benefits and salary, then the paperwork, but that's it. Honestly, not that much changed. Actually, the one interesting thing looking back is that I realized I couldn't take as many risks. You see, I played rugby for 10 years, and I once hurt my shoulder pretty badly. I realized that when I went full time, I had to be more careful, because if I got hurt like that again while full time, my work would suffer and people at work who were counting on me wouldn't appreciate that. It was actually a tough decision for me, to pull out of being so invested in rugby. Still is, I think about it every day. I was part of my college's national championship team. It was a decade of my life that was a blast and a fun time. But I don't know. Maybe in the future, I'll go back to it.

Anyways, so this first job was pretty much the same work from part time to full time. Everything I do is pretty much mechanical or electrical engineering and some form of research, simulation, and training. We're not small but we're not super large, so everyone has their own specialty. So, when a project comes up, you're front and center on this project because that's your task, that's your specialty. It's pretty cool to share that and be happy for other people. That's something I really enjoy doing for myself and seeing other people do.

I'm still at this job, six years later. That's kind of a long time, because we're a research lab, so people are coming and going pretty often. People help out a bit during undergrad or stick around just to get their degrees. So I've grown a lot of friendships and have had a few friendships go as well. And overall, I've enjoyed the experience. I started pursuing a second master's while still working full time, this time in systems engineering.

My advice to someone currently looking for their first job is … go in with confidence. Sell yourself. If you don't believe in yourself, how are they going to believe in you to do a job? If they're going to hire you to do something, you want to make sure you can do it to the best of your ability. So go out there and show them what you got. If you don't know it, fake it till you make it. In research, if I don't know something, I'm always willing to say I'll figure it out even if it's not in my field or my specialty. There's a funny quote above one of my bosses' desks. It says – if we knew what we were doing, it wouldn't be called research.

More specifically, I had a friend who graduated with just a mechanical engineering degree. I say "just," because for me, my background in IT and robotics meant I had engineering as well as programming experience. Wherever you go, it's always a benefit to have some sort of programming skill. It sets you apart from other engineers. I've talked to engineers who couldn't relate when we were discussing binary or coding or programming languages. Having that little bit of extra knowledge moves your resume to the side of the table in the good pile. That'd be my advice. Broaden your skills.

2.31 On Starting a Career Later in Life: Tori's Story

I took a very long and circuitous route and I'm thinking that most people would not take as long as I did to sort of land in a job. I had many part-time jobs along the way, but my first real full-time job wasn't until I landed as a research assistant at a small specialized medical university on the East Coast.

I took a very long and circuitous route and I'm thinking that most people would not take as long as I did to sort of land in a job. I had many part-time jobs along the way, but my first real full-time job wasn't until I landed as a research assistant at a small specialized medical university on the East Coast. So I went to college, then medical school for my MD, then a master's in public health (MPH) degree, but then I basically dropped out of the workforce to raise twins because I had my twins. My husband was in the Navy, so I followed him around his Navy stations and raised the kids. Over a decade later, my husband was a professor at the specialized medical university, and I was there supporting him because he was wheelchair bound and undergoing treatment. I sat in on some classes, and he encouraged me to go get my second MPH degree. That's when I started part time as a research assistant, and I went to full time around the same time when my husband passed away. This was almost 30 years ago.

I had an MD and an MPH when I went into the research assistant position, so they used me for a lot more than an incoming new research assistant. But I also had been outside of the workforce for 13 years. I spent all of that time as a full-time mom, so my connections were mostly other women in similar positions.

Interestingly, fairly soon after I arrived there, I was doing some research for a faculty member, and the opportunity arose for me to actually apply for a tenure-track faculty position. Well, some people thought I had no business going for a tenure-track faculty position. I hadn't ever been in teaching or doing my own research. But I got the job, and at the time that I joined, it was six years to make tenure or you would have to leave. So there was quite a bit of pressure for me to perform in all three areas of teaching, research, and service.

I was able to do it. But that's kind of just in my nature to go like gangbusters. I have never shied away. Back in high school, I was the first female class president in my sophomore year and then my junior year. And then my senior year, I was the first female student body president at my high school and it was a big high school on the West Coast. So I never have shied away from just jumping in. Actually, I was just named in a book of women physician pioneers. I didn't know I was a pioneer, but evidently, I was.

My advice to someone currently looking for their first job is … people have to think about what kind of job they really would like and would enjoy and want to spend time doing. It's just not worth spending time working in a job in an area that you don't like or that you have no interest in. That's really sad to me. I know that some people have to in order to support families and make ends meet, but if you can find something that you really enjoy and love doing, that's where you start.

2.32 On Leaving a Hostile Work Environment: Allen's Story

> *If you have somebody in your organization kind of butting heads with you, most likely it's not going to stop. There's certain things you can do to put it off, but only for so long. I'm not the type to say retreat or leave, but sometimes it's better for your own mental sanity. Being able to take your skills and knowing how to apply them in not just your organization but any organization is really, really important.*

I was in my mid-20s after graduating college, a little older than my cohort due to being in school an extra year or so. I had some internship experiences and looked a little bit older, but I was still in that early career stage. So I started searching around October after I had left a summer internship. I had a bit of savings that could keep me going for about six months.

I had some computer science experience, and I was great with SQL and some Python and R. I thought maybe data analysis would work, so I sent out a bunch of resumes in that area. It took several months. Eventually, I got an interview through this one job I applied to on Indeed. It was pretty quick. I did one initial interview with the head of the department and the IT manager, and they seemed to really like me, then I did a second interview with a basic literacy test, then I got the job offer. It was pretty casual. I remember there was even a typo in my job offer email.

My job initially was mostly doing internal uploads for data. But things started spiraling from there. When I first came in, they didn't have a desk for me, I had to sit at a workstation that they also used to assemble laptops to distribute across the company. Definitely not ergonomic, I had some weird neck pain after working there by the end of each day. I could deal with that, but it turned out there was also some emotional discomfort. It was more so over time. Certain things would be brought up that would leave a weird feeling. I would try to ask a question but never get an actual answer. Later on, I learned that they actually were trying to get me to replace my boss because they didn't like how she operated.

So, it really was one person in the organization who was a pain point, and that person also had total control and knowledge over this IT area that the company needed to run. It made for a hostile environment. There were days when my boss would lean over people's desks, yelling at them. One time I did something wrong with a data dashboard, and she was yelling at me, but I went ahead and deployed it. That's when I got my first-ever anxiety attack, I passed out and fell out of my chair.

I learned from all of this that organizations really need to make sure if young people are coming on board, they need to be put into the hands of managers who actually really care and have a heart. If you don't have the right managers in place, you will end up with an organization that can't spur any growth on a lower level with new people coming in. It's crazy with the labor shortage and people retiring, how much we need people to pass down that information to the younger generation and then for them to be able to take up the mantle. There needs to be a big, big switch in how that's handled.

Eventually, I got to the point where I was talking to a therapist, and I was planning on leaving at the end of the year. They told me, "Why are you waiting? You're in constant distress, and you're throwing up every morning going to work." I had a lot of friends that identified the same issues, so that helped. Even my girlfriend at the time, who's now my wife, said, "You're not yourself at all." And that's kind of when I knew I had to make some changes. I walked into work the next day, wrote a resignation letter, gave it to my boss's boss, and that was it. What's funny about it is as I was leaving, other people in the group were apparently making bets on how long I'd last.

So after that, I was fortunate enough that I had a friend who was at a different company, and I was able to get a referral. He knew I had the skills for the role. I've been here for a while now, and I feel very, very valued. It's crazy to think about the difference between these two organizations.

My advice to someone currently looking for their first job is ... if you have somebody in your organization kind of butting heads with you, most likely it's not going to stop. There are certain things you can do to put it off, but only for so long. I'm not the type to say retreat or leave, but sometimes it's better for your own mental sanity. Being able to take your skills and knowing how to apply them in not just your organization but any organization is really, really important. Let's say something happens in the organization, and you don't want to stick around. You have options. So always keep the door open.

Sometimes when things are chaotic and wild, it's hard for you to personally identify things. So, that's why it's always important to have someone that can help. Not necessarily a therapist. It can be friends. If they're very good friends, they'll help actually identify those things. But make sure to talk to people about things that you might be dealing with, because that's the only way that things can change.

2.33 On Starting at the Bottom of the Ladder: Dex's Story

> *I realized that there's nothing wrong with an honest day's work. Somebody has to go pick up that trash, clean out the toilets, and service the AC units. That's work, that's a job for a reason, and it was a big complex with like 200 doors. I was the lowest run on the ladder in the team, so when something needed to be done and nobody else wanted to do it, it came down to me.*

After college, I moved back to Florida and moved in with my parents. This was not long after the recession, so it was a weird time to be looking for jobs. I woke up every day and applied to like five jobs a day until I got a job. I started by focusing on jobs relevant to my bachelor's degree in English, but there weren't a lot of jobs in that area, and so I just got really frustrated. It was a lot of rejection. You know, the classic meme where you apply for an entry-level position but you actually need two years of experience. And then some jobs were 100 percent commission that was door-to-door sales type of stuff, which I didn't want to do. So eventually I saw this job as a full-time groundskeeper for an apartment complex, and since I didn't want to be that 22-year-old living at home with no job, I took it.

There was some irony there. I had part-time jobs starting in high school and all through college, and I felt a certain level of independence, making my own money and working. There was an irony that I had graduated and officially became a "qualified adult," only to then struggle with not finding a job and not having that independence, and having to be supported by my parents. So that was the most frustrating part.

I realized that there's nothing wrong with an honest day's work. Somebody has to go pick up that trash, clean out the toilets, and service the AC units. That's work, that's a job for a reason, and it was a big complex with like 200 doors. I was the lowest run on the ladder in the team, so when something needed to be done and nobody else wanted to do it, it came down to me. For example, that meant every day getting a five-gallon bucket and one of those little pincher things to pick up cigarette butts and fast-food wrappers and everything like that all around the complex.

Yes, the job was easy in the sense that I didn't need any qualifications for it. I had a pulse, a brain, and two arms and two legs. I think that's really all that was required and even some of that could have been debatable. But like I said, there's nothing wrong with an honest day's work, so I never actually felt like that work was below me or anything like that. Sure, it sucked doing it for a year and a half while I kept searching for other jobs. But I never felt more righteous than the position or anything. Plus, in my part-time jobs, I've done plenty of menial tasks, like my seasonal jobs in restaurants, so I was used to it.

Also, there were other duties that I learned along the way by being that extra person to assist. For example, installing appliances and fixing things in apartments in between tenants, doing some resurfacing, and replacing light fixtures and outlets. It wasn't complicated, but I learned how to do it. Plus my teammates were nice. They were super authentic and genuine, straightforward, and it was clear how to work with them. I think that every experience is valuable in one way or another. So I don't regret that job.

Anyway, since then, I finally got a job in sales and marketing, which I thought was more relevant to what I wanted to do. Then I did some grant writing work, then worked my way up in communications and marketing, mostly in the construction industry. Now I'm a director of marketing for a professional sports league.

My advice to someone currently looking for their first job is ... be patient. I don't regret my first job, but maybe if I could have changed something, I would have been a little bit more patient with my job search. That first job certainly did not directly advance my current career in communications and marketing. But I've learned to try to identify opportunities that are more in line with what I wanted to get out of a career, then deliberately pursue those instead. I think of each of my steps since my first job as steps on a ladder. Well, my first job was a step to get to the ladder in the first place, then I started climbing on it from there. And that first step towards the ladder was a big puddle that was full of spoiled milk and all that. But it still was important in that it got me to where I'm going. So take one step forward each time, learn as much as you can, and you'll get to where you need to go.

2.34 On Being Employee Number Seven: Sheri's Story

When I started, the team was really small; I was employee number seven and I was their first researcher. Plus, I was remote, so I basically didn't interact with anyone for a long time in a meaningful way until later when the company grew. I think what was tricky with onboarding was that there wasn't a robust research portfolio at that point in time; they were still trying to figure out what to do with me as their first PhD hire. It was actually a few weeks of me not really knowing what I was supposed to do.

I was finishing up my PhD in my early 30s, and I had been working as a part-time graduate research assistant for the government. My faculty member passed my name along to a friend of hers who started a nonprofit in another state and was looking for remote employees. This was before COVID, so people weren't really sure about remote work yet. However, this faculty member knew that I preferred to work remotely because I traveled a lot, and she offered to connect me to her friend for a job.

It was super informal. The nonprofit director reached out and asked to chat, he told me more about what he was doing, and he asked me questions about my interests. It was like a three-hour conversation. I remember I was walking around my bedroom doing laundry while talking to him. But we had this instant rapport, and he was able to share all his ideas, and I talked to him about how I could help bring those ideas into reality. He had me send in my CV and some materials I had previously designed, which was this big travel guide for my local city. Then they set up an interview with the other four executive leaders at this new nonprofit, which actually I had to take while hot spotting my phone in the car because I was stuck in traffic on the way home from a gig. The interview went long, and it got dark, I was parked in the car trying to turn on the lights so they could see me; it wasn't ideal. But actually, I later found out that one of the reasons they thought I'd be good for the job was because they saw, from how I handled the interview while sitting on the side of the road, that I was someone who could think quickly on my feet and go with the flow. Anyway, they offered me the job after that, and I started about a month later. The whole process was like a month and a half since I initially got connected with them.

When I started, the team was really small; I was employee number seven and I was their first researcher. Plus, I was remote, so I basically didn't interact with anyone for a long time in a meaningful way until later when the company grew. I think what was tricky with onboarding was that there wasn't a robust research portfolio then; they were still trying to figure out what to do with me as their first PhD hire. It was actually a few weeks of me not really knowing what I was supposed to do. I once texted the founder that I needed to step out for a moment, and he said, "I can't stress enough how much I don't care." He emphasized that it was a deliverable-based schedule, I do what I need to do with my time, as long as I get more work done.

Over time though, I think I found my "professional home" there. Eventually, I found myself in a role where I pressed them to think about translating work to practitioner settings. I asked questions about how we could use language and design products that don't look like they're for a publication, but rather are something that our mom, brothers, or neighbors would want to read. I pushed them to be more creative, more thoughtful, and more design focused on how we produced and disseminated communications about our projects.

My advice to someone currently looking for their first job is ... I tried a lot of things, and I also did a lot of information interviews in different spaces. I found the question that mattered to me was, "What does being creative look like in your space?" When I found places where people didn't know how to be creative, I realized it wasn't the place for me. My recommendation would be to find the question to help you figure out what you want to spend your time doing for 40 hours a week, and then shop that question around. However, it would be unlikely to find a professional home for your first job. The thing or advice I would give to students or to other people is that your first job won't necessarily be your home, but it is a place where you can understand your worth, and your qualifications, and get the language to describe who you are and what you bring to the table. I have a traditional academic job that came from other traditional academic training, and I spent a significant amount of time in my early 20s as a bartender, as a waitress, and owning a restaurant. While I don't count those things as my first job in my career, I certainly think that those experiences also contextualize why I'm better at my job now or understand or appreciate this work now. Someone else might not think bartending or serving are skills that you can use at a job where you need a PhD, but there are significant one-on-one interpersonal skills from bartending that I use every day in my job.

2.35   On Being a Lifelong Learner: Warren's Story

Especially in consulting, it's vital to have this ability to talk about anything intelligently, even if you don't know what you're talking about. You need to be able to find resources quickly, whether that's stuff online or track down other people in our company that have done something similar. It's all about being a continual learner.

I went to college for a computer engineering degree. I did a co-op for nine months with a company doing research and development in their software testing department, then I interned there over the summer for three months, then I finished my last semester of school and started working at the company full-time in December. So I had a job offer lined up as I finished my last semester, which was really nice.

I originally got connected with the company through a recruiter at a school fair. He was very charismatic compared to a lot of the other recruiters there who were very dry and very corporate. The company wasn't big, and he talked about how they focused on finding skilled people and promoting a good culture rather than some huge management structure. At the time, I wasn't quite sure exactly what I wanted to do, and that just sounded really appealing.

I do remember applying to like 50 different internships and co-ops during college. That same recruiter then emailed me and invited me for an in-person interview. I drove an hour and a half from home to their office, I was there for three hours interviewing with a couple of different people, then I heard back a couple weeks later that I got the co-op position. It was really simple and straightforward, I think I was their first co-op and it was a small company like I said. It was very different than this other company I applied to, where I was one of thirty different candidates for an internship, and they had us all in groups of five doing panel interviews. That was super intimidating compared to this.

The job itself focused on testing products and going through small iterations to automate and improve things. Since it was a small company, there were a lot more opportunities to expand my own network. I was constantly working on something different. It's like, we'd get a new client that needs X, Y, and Z. We haven't really done that before, but now you have to learn it and be able to help. Plus, even if I got stuck on a project that I wasn't crazy about, it was short term and I'd have a new project soon. There actually wasn't much difference between the co-op, the internship, and the full-time job. Which was good, they didn't have me getting coffee or anything, they literally told me that they'd treat me like a regular full-time employee the whole time. Which of course meant that the first few weeks, I felt very in over my head. But fortunately, I had a lot of help, and there were experienced people working with me, alongside two other new full-time employees, so I wasn't the only new person.

I will say one downside is that consulting really depends on the clients. So there was an eight-month period where I barely had anything to do, and it was pretty boring. I ended up reading a lot of process documentation. But then I landed an exciting new client, and that's how it goes. The other thing is that because it was such a flat organizational structure, there wasn't much room to grow. At bigger companies, you'd have jobs like engineer 1, then 2, then 3, then senior engineer. We didn't have as many layers.

So after about six years, I left for another company, but then I actually came back after a year. So now I'm back at the same company I started with but with a slightly higher title. My job itself actually still isn't all that different.

My advice to someone currently looking for their first job is … always be willing to learn something new. Jump in and be the first person or one of the first people to say, "Hey, I'll take that on," even if you have no idea what you're doing.

Especially in consulting, it's vital to have this ability to talk about anything intelligently, even if you don't know what you're talking about. You need to be able to find resources quickly, whether that's stuff online or track down other people in our company that have done something similar. It's all about being a continual learner.

I've heard people say before that the value of college is not so much about whatever your major is or whatever you actually learn in college. It's about learning how to learn, and I've found that to be true. I'm sure some degrees differ. But for me, in terms of what I majored in during college, a very small percentage of that really applies to what I'm doing now. But it gave me a framework for how to find answers and track down information.

Lastly, don't get discouraged if whatever you're looking at seems like it's not panning out. A lot of times, you don't get it right the first time. Just try to get as many different experiences as possible. Don't pigeonhole yourself into one specific technique, computer science language, hardware platform, etc. Be willing to jump between different languages and different platforms. Just always be open to new opportunities.

2.36 On Faith through Disabilities: Gerald's Story

This was back before the Americans with Disabilities Act, so although most managers weren't going to blatantly say, 'Oh, you can't see, we don't want you,' that's what ended up happening. They would be polite about it, but I ended up applying to over 200 job applications and got rejected from every single one.... That's when the depression came in. I'm struggling to process this in my mind. I believe in God, and I believe that God created me with a disability, and I want to contribute meaningfully to society. But I'm just sitting there on a bench idly.

I got my bachelor's degree in computer science a long, long time ago. But after college, due to a tough economy and some personal health challenges, I went seven years without finding a full-time job. It was dreadful. I thought I'd be very employable, I had internship experiences with big companies, I knew the programming languages that were popular back then, and I had good qualifications. But the main issue was my health. I ended up losing my eyesight over time; I went from 20/20 vision in high school to having no acuity, just a little residual light perception, by the time I was wrapping up college. I made it through college using cassette tapes and some recent technology in primitive speech synthesizers. I remember I had this one particularly supportive professor. Instead of sending me to disability support services for my calculus exam, he sat down for hours with me and read the exam out loud, then patiently waited for me to respond. He still tested me, of course. But he told me he didn't want me to suffer from someone in disability services, who didn't know all these symbols, trying to give me a test without the proper vernacular and say something like "What's this squiggly line from 0 to 1" instead of saying that it's the integral of dy-dx from 0 to 1. So it was people like him who helped me get through college, and he along with many of my other professors wrote amazing letters of recommendation for me.

But then reality hit. This was back before the Americans with Disabilities Act, so although most managers weren't going to blatantly say, "Oh, you can't see, we don't want you," that's what ended up happening. They would be polite about it, but I ended up applying to over 200 job applications and got rejected from every single one. I mean, I had some interviews. I did this one interview with a technology company where the recruiters asked me some math questions and gave me a pen and paper to figure out the answer, I told them I couldn't use it because of my eyesight, but I was able to figure out the solution in my head. That gained their respect. But then they flew me up to their headquarters for the next interview, and their software was all in a graphical user interface that had no accessibility options for people who were blind. There was no legal obligation or duty for them to accommodate my disability. So when it came down to it, they said, "Thank you, you seem intelligent, but you can't work on our systems, sorry."

That's when the depression came in. I'm struggling to process this in my mind. I believe in God, and I believe that God created me with a disability, and I want to contribute meaningfully to society. But I'm just sitting there on a bench, idly, while my wife is working, and I'm trying to find a way to stay productive. I got angry, and I took it out on other people. But over the years, I learned how to deal with it. I learned to find more and more friends who would be allies to help me carry the burden. I learned also it wasn't always just about working harder and trying harder. I had to change my plans.

So eventually, with some government help, I was able to go to law school instead. I had tried taking the LSAT, and I got exceptionally high scores, so I was surprised and took that as a sign that maybe I should consider this path. I got my JD [Juris Doctor] and passed the bar, and I thought I might be a prosecuting attorney. Then it was back to the job search. I did an internship, got a couple of law review articles published, had good credentials, and just submitted to all sorts of jobs.

The one that worked out was actually the patent office. I actually applied right after law school, and I didn't hear back for two years. By that time I was doing some part-time work for a fellow attorney, and I got this letter from the mail. The miracle here is that by this time, I had moved three times and was in a different state. That letter was certified mail and said "do not forward," and yet somehow it ended up getting forwarded three times to end up in my mailbox. The letter asked if I was still interested in the job and told me I had 30 days to reply. Well, by then I had passed the 30-day mark. But I called back anyway, and they told me

I had great credentials with a STEM background plus a legal degree, I was perfect for the job examining applications for STEM patents. They actually just offered me the position on the phone, right then and there.

Here's the funniest part. I had disclosed in my cover letter about my visual disability. Now, it was two years later, and they had lost that cover letter. So when they offered the job to me, they didn't know about it until I asked about accommodations. That took them by surprise, and then they tried to backtrack the offer. But thankfully, I had gone to law school, and I had already put in writing that they had offered me the position and I had accepted. So that's how I got my first job, finally, in my early 30s almost a decade after graduating college and two years after graduating law school.

So the takeaway is that with life, the journey is very circuitous. There are valleys and through the valley of the shadow of death, it can be almost overwhelming. That's why it's so good to have people on your side who are not going to give up on you. I got to say, I'm so grateful for my family who helped me get through all of this.

My advice to someone currently looking for their first job is … I wish I could just succinctly say, "Here's the formula." That doesn't exist. The reality is that the unemployment rate among individuals with disabilities – I like to say, talent with disabilities – is something like triple that of the ordinary. But my only advice is to not do it alone. Have connections. Not just job networking connections, but relational people who can nourish you and refresh you.

2.37 On Managing Your Expectations: Ronan's Story

You're probably not going to end up where you think you would, and that's not a bad thing. There's this statement that we use in America that's very toxic and dangerous to our mental health statement. Everybody has heard somebody say it: 'I love my job. I love what I do.'

My undergraduate degree is in communications with a focus on journalism. When I completed undergrad, I was looking for positions writing for newspapers. I had a few bites, and a few interviews, but I eventually hit that point where I've got to find a job and it is what it is. At the time, my university was about an hour and a half from my parents, and my dad had been diagnosed with cancer while I was an undergrad. So given that, and given that I had no job, I moved back in with my parents after finishing undergrad.

I also had a passion for disc golf, so I kept looking for jobs in journalism or in disc golf. But I realized eventually that those two things weren't going to happen. So I broadened my search to any job that could sustain me, but allow me to play disc golf on the weekends. My logic was, if I'm going to be miserable during the work week, I might as well not be miserable on the weekend.

By coincidence, I had a friend of mine who played disc golf who worked at the credit union that I ended up getting employed at. She knew I was looking for jobs and said she'd make a few calls for me. She helped me get a part-time job as a teller at her credit union, and then a few months later, by around January after I graduated, I went full-time. That being said, even while I was part time, I was still constantly looking for journalism jobs. But I was pretty happy, I had some extra time during those part-time months with my dad, who ended up passing away a few years later. As I look back, I'm thankful that I had that time because we had some really cool experiences that I had because I lived there with him. Money-wise, it wasn't very much pay, but it kept me going, I was just surviving, so to speak.

So I stayed in that role for about eight months, and then I was promoted to a loan processor at that credit union. The original job didn't require a bachelor's degree, and I had one, so they eventually offered me a higher position, and that basically started my financial career accidentally. I guess I realized that even though I kept an eye on writing jobs for journalism, it wasn't going to work out. And I realized that I was good at finance, I did well in math, even though this job was something that I did not want to do at all. But since it was easy, even though I didn't want to do it, I stuck with it, since it gave me the ability to play disc golf every weekend and to spend time with my dad.

It's interesting to me how there are random moments in my life that I'll never forget. I remember meeting with a career counselor my senior year in undergrad, and he asked the standard, "What do you want to do?" question. I remember responding, "I don't want a job where you work when people don't work." That's always stuck with me. If somebody offered me $500,000 a year to be a real estate agent, I don't think I would do it. I wanted, and still want, a normal 8 to 5 weekday hours job.

Funnily enough, now, almost 20 years later, I'm the operations and logistics manager for a professional disc golf group. We have a professional tour and major championships, and my team is in charge of all the operations and logistics for these events. What happened was, after about eight years at the bank, I just hit a mental breaking point and quit one day.

I'll never forget that my boss, the senior vice president at this point, asked where I was going, and I said I had no job lined up. From there, I had this random job in college financial aid for another eight years or so. I basically kept doing really good work with numbers, which again I never really wanted to do, to the point that I was getting job offers without applying for finance roles.

But I kept up my hobby of disc golf during all this time. I competed in the US Open and multiple world championships while in these finance jobs. Then I had a neck injury that really messed up my ability to play, and so I started directing events. It was my way of continuing my life in this world that I love, even when I couldn't play as much. Eventually, I got to running tour events and major championships. This eventually led to just about a year ago, when a job opened up at the disc golf group, and it blew my mind. It was a brand-new position, and it was perfect for combining my passions with this numbers-driven skill set I had built over my career.

I didn't get the job at first. It really crushed me. I thought it was finally my chance at a dream job, and again it slipped away. But three months later, they called me back, and they said that they didn't have a specific position or a salary, but they knew that they needed me. So they said they'll figure out the details, as long as I agreed to work with them. At this point, I was a high-level director in financial aid, and they were asking me to come on as some kind of manager role. Plus, they had extra money because of the boost in the popularity of disc golf recently, but that didn't mean it would be sustainable long-term. But I realized worst-case scenario, I do this job for a few months, then everything crashes, then I can still go back to financial aid. So I took this job, and I've been here for about a year now.

My advice to someone currently looking for their first job is ... you're probably not going to end up where you think you would, and that's not a bad thing. There's this statement that we use in America that's very toxic and dangerous to our mental health statement. Everybody has heard somebody say it: "I love my job. I love what I do."

The logical part of my brain laughs at that. Whenever I hear somebody say that, I always think, "Well, if they weren't paying you, would you do it?" And if the answer is no, then you don't love it. I think that there's this concept that you have to wake up every single day, that you're excited to go to work, and you just can't wait. And that's not true. It's so easy to sit here and listen to a successful story like mine, but then forget that I was making $22,000 sitting at a teller's desk almost 20 years ago, miserable and bored out of my mind.

But on the other hand, you also shouldn't go to bed Sunday night and dread the fact that tomorrow's Monday. You also shouldn't hate every minute of what you're doing. So you've got to find that middle ground. Even now, I have found this job that I truly do love and would do for free if I was financially able to. But it's still a job. It's still work. I still have to do things I don't like doing. Right now, I'm having to read through 50- to 60-page-long proposals. I don't want to do that. It's still a job, right?

On a different note, one piece of advice I have is to be solution-minded in your work. Don't be afraid to challenge things professionally, and don't be afraid to dive into processes. I used to say this to my team all the time, "Let's just dive into how we do this. And worst case, at the other end of it, we find out we're doing it the best way."

Lastly, I've had to fire people. I've been fired. It's not the end of the world. It is what it is when it happens. And that doesn't mean you're a failure, it just means you weren't really a great fit for what that company was offering.

2.38 On Making the Most Out of Your Degree: Nolan's Story

> *Be intentional with your experiences while in a degree program. One, build the language and be able to translate that for people who didn't study the same subject or field as you. Two, when you're going through your program, you're also creating your professional brand. Take that very seriously, because having a brand will assist in developing your future profession.*

I did some summer work during high school, then worked in residence life part time through college and my master's program. Then after graduating with my master's degree in psychology, my first full-time, regular job was at a state Job Corps as a career training. I was working with second English language students on their career development as a coach and career specialist.

Luckily, I wasn't really stressing about finding a job. I had my graduate assistantship work that I could keep going with as I finished up my degree. So I did some casual searching, and I originally found the job on Indeed. I was not looking for anything specific besides career development. I put in my resume and used the algorithm of jobs that were in the area overall, and this one popped up. They seemed inclined to have me interview. I was coming in with work experience, even though part time, in higher education and working with students on career development, so I think that helped. The interview was in person, weirdly to say, during COVID. I got the offer letter a few days after that interview.

I enjoyed the work tremendously. It utilized some of my skills with student development while also giving me the chance to work on special projects to engage my skills from my master's program. I did that job for about a year, then weirdly enough, someone found me on LinkedIn and saw my work history and some presentations I had done, and we ended up having some informational interviews. I was interested in their work within a PhD program in my field, and they were interested in what I did. I think I did like three informational interviews with them. At that moment, I had a mentor tell me that I should just go ahead and ask for what I wanted. So I asked this team, who was at a different university, if they had any openings for a consultant position. They said they actually did, and within a few months, I got the formal offer to join their team as a talent strategy consultant, which is where I'm at now.

I love my job. I currently work with faculty and staff and their leadership development, while also bringing my expertise within talent acquisition, leadership talent development, talent performance management, and instructional design, which we work on in the supervisory development program overall. Now, I always say that, sometimes, the work that you do won't fit all the buckets that bring you joy. So, I do consult on the side and I do have a consulting business.

My advice to someone currently looking for their first job is ... be intentional with your experiences while in a degree program. One, build the language and be able to translate that for people who didn't study the same subject or field as you. Two, when you're going through your program, you're also creating your professional brand. Take that very seriously, because having a brand will assist in developing your future profession. Even when you're in school, start thinking about your brand, and craft your LinkedIn accordingly.

Also, don't forget to utilize those that you help and assist, such as those that you volunteer with, by requesting letters or introductions. Individuals do not know what you need until you ask. Sometimes, they are able to give you all that you need. But if you don't utilize your resources, then you won't be able to know what's available.

If you're applying for jobs, I always say, go and copy the job listing, and then copy your resume and put that side by side, and then compare the two and see what's compatible and what's not. Searching for a job is a full-time job. So, network, network, network, but also put in the work as well to tailor your resume and tailor your cover letter as well.

I think mentorship was very essential in the roles that I have been in. For example, all of the faculty members were my mentors because I would spend extra time and learn from them and also collaborate with them on special projects. Also, most of the mentors that I accumulated over time grew through organic curiosity overall, where I would reach out to people just to hear about their experiences. I actively searched for them and asked them questions.

2.39 On Working Hard in Any Position: Zara's Story

I actually loved the job [as a cheesemonger]. The work was very interesting because I got to learn a lot about cheese. It was mostly self-directed learning. There wasn't really encouragement to do that, but there were books hanging around.... Within like six months, they had me doing the manager's duties like inventory, and there were people who were 50 and 60 years old that hadn't been asked to do that stuff yet. So, I felt like a good worker.

My first full-time job was as a cheesemonger at a fancy grocery store when I was 16. I had been searching for a full-time job for a few months. But my resume was basically just some volunteer work and extracurriculars, so I didn't know how someone with no work experience was supposed to get a job. It definitely felt like the cards were stacked against me. I remember having my parents help me edit my cover letter, which was just a default template, but with one sentence or so customized to be specific to the job I was applying for. I applied to jobs like a hostess and a salon. I wasn't interested in retail, so I looked for food service as the easiest first job to get.

Most of the places, I just never heard back. Very few places sent an actual rejection. Which of course is very frustrating, it kind of leaves you in the lurch and feeling like you have all these possible futures. For me at least if I apply somewhere, I actually really invest in imagining myself there. So having that many unknowns is always very stressful. Eventually, I got an email asking me to interview with a kitchen manager for this cheesemonger job. It was a very short process, but I guess in retrospect, it was a really entry-level job so they weren't looking for much.

On my first day of work, I was really nervous. I knew I looked young, but I suddenly became very aware of my appearance in a way that I hadn't before. I was really nervous about the uniform, I wanted to be prepared with the right shoes and clothes and all of that. I paid very close attention to the rules, trying to orient myself to the new landscape.

I actually loved the job. The work was very interesting because I got to learn a lot about cheese. It was mostly self-directed learning. There wasn't really encouragement to do that, but books were hanging around. And in the job, a lot of it was people coming in and wanting recommendations, and so you'd have to try the hundreds of different cheeses to be able to give a good recommendation. I grew up eating fancy cheese, and so it kind of felt like, "Oh, I actually have something to say here. I can have some sense of personal purpose or creativity." The people I worked with were really nice. Within like six months, they had me doing the manager's duties like inventory, and some people were 50 and 60 years old who hadn't been asked to do that stuff yet. So, I felt like a good worker.

That being said, there were a lot of issues with my manager around hours, and I didn't really have a sense of how bad it was at the time. There were several times she would ask me to clock out because I hit 40 hours, but then I had to stay behind to still help with cleaning up. At the time, I was aware that it wasn't cool, but I also didn't want to be confrontational about it and I liked my job. It wasn't a big deal, but I definitely worked for free or worked overtime without getting paid for it. There were also a lot of issues with me having to repeatedly remind her that I was a high schooler and that there were times I really couldn't come in because I was in school, even though I was working full time.

I met all sorts of people. There were retired people, young people, food professionals, middle aged, and more. I was definitely the youngest. But it was kind of this island of misfit toys. Artists, angry people, shy people, creative people. Yeah, I probably should've spoken up about the overtime issue. But in general, it was a good experience.

Since then, it's been 16 years and I've had, let's see, 10 different jobs? Lots of part-time jobs in food, and some art school, then I found a passion for understanding the psychology of retail teams, so I went to graduate school, and now I'm working as an organizational development and coaching specialist for a large government agency.

One thing that has stuck with me since my first job is the idea of humility. I wanted to appear really professional in my first job, but I didn't do anything to express what I knew. I just listened. I think that's a mistake that people make to try and overcompensate to preserve their image or something. I also learned so many other things on my first job: Follow through. Responsibility. Being on time. Being able to have an opinion about something. Self-confidence. Incorporating your own flavor into the work.

My advice to someone currently looking for their first job is ... the quality of your experience is pretty much up to you. It's not up to your boss or anyone else around you. You can choose to be curious or not. I would also say, if we are in situations where we can't necessarily see the relationship between what we're doing and what we want to be doing in the future, we can still be building common skills like responsibility, curiosity, attentiveness, or organization. These basic skills are the same across most jobs. Even if it is not the dream job, it's really worthwhile to put everything into it, because it'll pay off down the road to be better than you were.

2.40 On Selling Out: Irena's Story

I struggle with this idea of pursuing your passion, which I think people are told over and over again. For kids who aren't financially secure, like I was, that's hard to do, and it makes us feel bad. Yeah, my passion may be to go teach, but I need to make money to pay off my loans or to help me family out . . . remember I totally felt like a sellout, taking that consulting job. So my advice here is that it's good to have a passion, but maybe that passion is something you do on the side. It's like how I taught lower-income kids on the side and at night, while I had the more stable, well-paying job during the day.

I majored in business administration in undergrad, about 20 years ago, and we were just starting to learn technology and information systems. I did an internship with a tech company in Asia, and I was able to talk about that when I was looking for jobs as an example of how I was scrappy and proactive, able to find an internship in a different country overseas. Now, I actually didn't really want a job in the business world, but I was an immigrant and my parents were really focused on me getting a financially secure job. We were political refugees, and I moved here when I was young. My parents had college degrees, but they took a significant step back in their careers when moving here and switched to blue-collar work. So we had a very working-class upbringing, plus my father died unexpectedly when I was a teen, and we had no family or financial safety net to rely on. So my mom made it very clear, I had to go to a good business program and get a good financially stable job. I was actually interested in religious studies at the time, and I remember my mom wouldn't let me major in it.

I didn't have a high enough GPA to qualify for the big consulting jobs, so I had to think outside of the box. I was a finalist for some rotation programs but didn't get either of them. I remember for one of them, at a bank, I went into the bathroom during my final interview and called my parents and said I couldn't do it, everything was just so corporate and sterile, and I hated it.

So I ended up looking for entrepreneurial companies. I went to some job fairs both at my school and in my hometown, and I met someone at one of those large insurance companies. They told me I'd be great at insurance sales, and they talked about how I would use my network to sell insurance. I didn't know what that meant at the time, I didn't realize it sounded like a pyramid scheme, I just thought that someone wanted to hire me and so I was going to take the job. At this point, I was about to go on a vacation after graduation, but I guess I had submitted a resume for a start-up company job at some point, and they called me right before I was planning to leave. They rushed me through the process; I literally drove overnight to get to an interview before I flew out overseas on vacation the next day. But it ended up working out because that's the job that I got. Sure it paid $30,000 at the time, but I thought that was amazing, so I left for vacation knowing I was coming back to an actual job.

The job was still in sales, but more high class. Every day, I called like 50 or 75 people in these high-up C-suite positions, trying to get them to schedule a call with my boss so he could sell them this technology product. My coworkers were cool, they were in their 30s or late 20s, and I looked up to them. Plus we worked in a downtown city and would go out for lunch and hang out outside of work. But the work was very monotonous, and it made me realize that I hated talking on the phone to other people. I only ended up staying a few months, because I knew my interests were elsewhere.

After that, I ended up switching to a friend of a friend's new company, also working in sales, selling this product at airport kiosks. I did that for a couple of months because I was waiting for my application to go through to work at this global government agency, which I actually wanted to do long term. So I knew this was a short-term job, it was just while I was waiting for my application to go through.

Funnily enough, I got accepted to the government agency, and I was about to be deployed to Eastern Europe, but that caused this big conflict with my family where my mom was adamantly opposed to it. She said we fought so hard to get you out of that part of the world, why in the world do you want to go back? It just so happened that around that time I met a friend who knew someone who worked in international consulting. They managed to get me an interview, and then I got the job, which was so remarkable since like I said, my college GPA was never good enough for these consulting firms. Now this was a hard decision, between the international consulting firm and the global government agency. I told myself I would never work for corporate America, but my mom really wanted me to do the consulting job, and that was really important to me. So I took the job, and that was the start of my actual career.

It's worth noting that the job was not as glamorous as I'd hoped. I never got deployed overseas. My job was basically to support other subject matter experts who were overseas, setting up their visas, figuring out how to pay them, and booking flights, it was all very administrative. I actually started doing some teaching on the side, helping students in high school with standardized testing, and I actually really enjoyed that, but I didn't want to do teaching full time. I also liked spreadsheets, and I lived in a city where you kind of need an advanced degree to move up in your career. So eventually I found myself getting a master's degree in international education development with a focus on finance and planning, which was kind of perfect for me. Long story short, I ended up staying in the program to get a PhD, and now I'm a professor, which is not something I ever imagined doing. But through a series of things that happened, including getting married and getting fired from a job, I realized that I wanted to basically work for myself. That's why I went to the PhD, for the autonomy; I never intended to stay in academia. But I ended up falling in love with that autonomous lifestyle, and here I am teaching humanities as a university professor.

My advice to someone currently looking for their first job is … I struggle with this idea of pursuing your passion, which I think people are told over and over again. For kids who aren't financially secure, like I was, that's hard to do, and it makes us feel bad. Yeah, my passion may be to go teach, but I need to make money to pay off my loans or to help my family out. Especially for women, where I think we're socialized to think that we're supposed to help people, which leads to this conflict between wanting to make money and wanting to help people. I remember I totally felt like a sellout, taking that consulting job. So my advice here is that it's good to have a passion, but maybe that passion is something you do on the side. It's like how I taught lower-income kids on the side and at night, while I had a more stable, well-paying job during the day.

Also, your first job is just your first job. It is not the job you will end up in permanently, so don't freak out about it. It's a stepping stone into the next thing; you can have many jobs and change your career many times. There's this particular emphasis right now on kids that they need to have these highly coveted prestigious internships during the summers. But the kinds of things that I did during the summers, like being a camp counselor, may not be prestigious but one of the hardest jobs I ever had. It was an amazing opportunity to exercise leadership to take care of real people, and that's something that you don't get to learn in the corporate workplace. So my advice is to use the summer to try out different things. It may not be the thing that your parents want to do, and sometimes that's ok.

2.41 On the Challenges of Sexism at Work: Macie's Story

I think I could've done well with more training and more responsibilities, but sadly I think there was some sexism where I was specifically not given opportunities because of my gender.... Now that I'm older, I know there were some issues with that company. Looking back, it would've probably been better if I had moved on sooner and looked elsewhere.

My first job would be as an intern at a small local communications media company. I was in my late teens when I started the job, and I worked full time during the summer and kept the job part-time throughout high school and college. At the time, I really wanted to be a lifeguard, but my birthday was a few days too late for the cutoff. I also had a passion for movies and filmmaking, so my mom set me up with this interview with the owner of a media community that she had known for decades. I was basically offering free labor with how little they paid me, so they immediately gave me the job.

It was an entry-level position. I was stuffing envelopes and putting together CDs and DVDs. But at that point in my life, I didn't have much experience doing things with my parents nearby, so going to work for hours with semi-strangers was a significant change. I remember being very careful about what I wore, especially going out to buy business-appropriate clothes. My supervisor was incredibly warm and friendly, and she helped train me on things like editing software. Eventually, I started editing the video footage they had of, for example, a conference that they would copy to a DVD to mail out. These skills were really helpful, and actually, I remember when I got my next job, my new boss told me that she was able to bring me in at a much higher salary bracket because of my skill set.

There were still some challenges though. I don't think the management at my first job recognized my full potential. I think I could've done well with more training and more responsibilities, but sadly I think there was some sexism where I was specifically not given opportunities because of my gender. There were also some financial issues, so there was a lot of turnover, and there weren't many employees to begin with. Now that I'm older, I know there were some issues with that company. Looking back, it would've probably been better if I had moved on sooner and looked elsewhere.

I stayed at that company all through high school and college, where I studied graphic design and American literature. Then through this other connection, as I finished my degree, I joined this start-up company, bringing my skill set in graphic design and video and audio editing. Sadly due to some other issues, that job ended up being quite boring at times, so I left and started freelancing. Then I found this full-time job at a magazine company, which was incredibly busy and high stress. Now, it's 15 years since that first job, and I switched to a different magazine company and am now the art director. And I've been promoted several times at each place I worked along the way.

My advice to someone currently looking for their first job is ... your first job doesn't have to be perfect for you to get valuable experience and skills out of it. Don't sit on the sidelines because you are new or inexperienced. Show initiative and tell people about the things that you want to do. Bring up again and again, if you see an opportunity to do one of those things that you want to do, because everyone benefits when you're willing to do something extra because you like it. You might be waiting a very long time if you're waiting for an invitation to do the thing that you want to do. If you don't know how to do something, ask how to do it or look it up because almost everything is on YouTube, and everyone loves a self-starter.

2.42 On Loyalty to a Company: Esther's Story

Years ago, loyalty meant a lot. You stayed with the company, you weren't always out job shopping or looking for shortcuts. Nowadays people just go from one job to another, always looking for more money, so you don't see the loyalty to a company that you used to see. Back then, we stayed with a company, and they treated us well, and we gave back 100 percent.

I had just graduated high school, and I knew the things I excelled in: organizational skills, typing, writing shorthand, and so forth. I also worked part time as a receptionist. I knew I didn't want to go to college, and I wanted to work in an office environment. I just wanted to be a secretary, that was it, so I applied for those types of jobs. It's been about 50 years, so it's hard to remember, but I think I just applied to this position through the normal US government and my qualifications met the minimum expectations. I remember doing a couple of interviews with a commander and an admiral. So I started as an administrative assistant, I think a GS-5, for the armed forces.

That job opened up quite a few doors. I was very junior, but I was very responsible and was given tasks that most people my age would never have done. For example, when the admiral was in the hospital and his secretary was unavailable, I would take a government car to the hospital and take transcriptions from him. I also worked for two captains and a commander. So it was a lot of responsibility for someone as junior as I was. I loved it, especially the prestige of working at the Pentagon. I felt like I had arrived.

It was still difficult at times. The military men I worked with were decades older with so much experience, and they used words I had never heard before. I felt uneducated and inadequate at times like that. It was scary when I would get sent in to fill in for a seasoned veteran secretary, but it eventually helped with my confidence.

I only stayed at that job for about a year, because I got married to someone in the military, and then we moved states. I did a variety of other jobs from there, ranging from working in military bases, working as a cashier just for some extra cash, to working for vice presidents of companies. These were executive assistant jobs. Now my husband and I are retired.

My advice to someone currently looking for their first job is … the most important thing is work ethic. Probably most of the sick leave that I was ever given was unused. I took off for real medical issues, but I would not just call off because of an insignificant thing. I was always there, and they could count on me to be there early and to be there late, whatever they needed. Actually, there was one job where I was the assistant for a vice president, when they made me a salaried position, but I worked super long hours, and I guess later there was a lawsuit where I should not have been made salaried, and I received a substantial settlement because I kept such good records. I didn't even ask for the settlement, but I got it, that's how much overtime I put in to support the vice president. So work ethic is the most important, and I see that missing today in a lot of areas.

Loyalty too. I think those years are gone, but years ago, loyalty meant a lot. You stayed with the company, you weren't always out job shopping or looking for shortcuts. Nowadays people just go from one job to another, always looking for more money, so you don't see the loyalty to a company that you used to see. Back then, we stayed with a company, and they treated us well, and we gave back 100 percent. So in my opinion that's the most important thing.

2.43 On Bouncing Back: Aba's Story

> *I became a staff sergeant within my four years in that branch of the military, then I realized that I wanted to be an office in intelligence work overseas. But then the war ended, and when I tried to go for the position in intelligence that I wanted, some other people got it, so I was rotated out. I was upset about that, but there was nothing I could do because the war was over.*

I had some part-time jobs growing up, painting houses and working in a restaurant. But when I was finishing high school, I was told that I was going to get drafted, so I went into military service, and that was probably my first real job. Now the story here is that I was from the hood, I wore black leather jackets with long hair, and I ran with motorcycle gangs. We were Native American Indians, and we had some relatives in Canada. When I got the word that my draft number was coming up, my family was getting ready to send me up to Canada. I decided instead to enlist, and my family didn't like that answer.

Anyway, I was just a recruit, and they sent me overseas for a war, and I stayed for about two and a half years overseas, mostly as a fuel specialist. The job was mostly just to fuel one vehicle after another. There were some times when I would refuel spy vehicles, so I had to have the highest security clearance. Now, I hate saying this, but I'll say it here, I've always felt overqualified for everything I did. Dishwashing, car washing, and in the military, refueling vehicles; I always felt overqualified because I was able to learn what to do within a very short time. I read everything I could. I passed all the tests. That's how I gained rank so quickly. The people around me where I worked always said that. They would stay in their rank for three years, whereas I stayed for eight months in that initial rank.

I became a staff sergeant within my four years in that branch of the military, and then I realized that I wanted to be an office in intelligence work overseas. But then the war ended, and when I tried to go for the position in intelligence that I wanted, some other people got it, so I was rotated out. I was upset about that, but there was nothing I could do because the war was over. They didn't need anyone to refuel the vehicles anymore.

So I came back to the US and went to college. I lived in a trailer, worked as a bouncer at a bar, and did some gambling. Eventually, I became a private investigator, and I've been doing that for almost 50 years now. I'm also a process server for my own company. So I've been self-employed for both jobs for almost 50 years now. There was a moment early on when I thought about going to law school, back when I was still starting my company. I remember I got a call from someone in Alaska, and they asked me to fly up the next day because I could be getting a $3 million contract with my new company. So it was be poor and go to law school, or have a $3 million contract. So I went with the latter and never looked back.

My advice to someone currently looking for their first job is ... for those looking to go into the military, if you're smart, and you know what you're doing, go to college first, then become an officer. It's a different view of the service when you're an officer, and you can do more things. I could have gone to college, but I didn't like school, and I didn't get the best grades because I ditched school. If I had gone to college and gotten into the military as an officer, I would've stayed in the service for a long time.

2.44 On Inventing a Role: Sia's Story

[My boss] had an admin assistant, but he needed somebody to help him with his day-to-day work.... We invented my role as we went along. I made it very clear what I did not want to do. It was actually a great working relationship that gave me a lot of experience, gave me a lot of trust, and really allowed me to broaden my skill sets and taste a lot of different kinds of work that the agency had to offer.

I did some waitressing all through my college and master's programs, which was helpful experience. However, my first full-time, permanent job was as a strategic coordination officer for the director general of a government agency. He had an admin assistant, but he needed somebody to help him with his day-to-day work. He had people who reported to him with staff under them, but in terms of managing his own workload, he needed an extra hand. We invented my role as we went along. I made it very clear what I did not want to do. It was actually a great working relationship that gave me a lot of experience, gave me a lot of trust, and really allowed me to broaden my skill sets and taste a lot of different kinds of work that the agency had to offer, which was actually quite instrumental in the way that my career developed after that.

I was in a place where most of the jobs were government work, and I knew that's what I wanted to do. A lot of people had the idea that getting into government was really hard. I probably applied to 20 to 40 jobs. I had a big running file folder of all the applications I had applied to. I actually had a few people who were really great at mentoring me on how to apply for jobs, particularly government jobs. I think it's quite different than the private sector. But it was really helpful because I prepped interviews with them. So once I got into the interview, I interviewed really well. Because I worked in the service industry for so long, I have a good rapport with people. I took everyone super seriously and never made any assumptions like, "Oh, I got this in the bag." I always made sure that all of my responses had multiple examples. They were all noted down. It was my first foray into the job market. That's how I was told to prepare, so that's how I prepared. That's how I prepared for every job.

At the same time, a lot of the jobs I saw posted were looking for a few years of experience, even on entry-level jobs. It was humbling at first. However, I learned to position my research assistant work and some other part-time contract jobs I had related to my master's coursework to sell my experience as meeting that criteria. In my area, the government agencies were a little anal about making sure candidates had X years of experience. You can't just say you have it, you need to tell them exactly your background and prove it. Cover letters were like five or six pages. It was irritating, but it was the process for jobs.

The job was like any other job. I came in with 20 percent nerves, 60 percent excitement, and 20 percent focus and observing. Now I was bored to tears when I first started. There was coordinating a couple meetings, which irritated me because I knew there was an admin. I really forced my boss to distinguish what my role was from the admin, which I don't think he had even really thought through. So we developed my job because he could see that I was bored and I needed more. It emboldened me to progress a lot faster than I would have. So my boss just started dropping me these massive files. She'd be like, "Okay, well, we're doing an organizational reorg. So, why don't you help us write this operational plan?" I was like, "Sure." I don't know what that is, so I was googling on the side.

That led to the job becoming amazing. I would get these random files and tasks, like writing treasury report submissions. I had no background in doing it, but I was so bored that my boss just gave it to me to try, and I would learn how to do it and show him a draft and ask what to do next. I don't know how easy it would be for everybody to do what I did, to be honest. It came down to personality and trust between me and my boss.

Eventually, after three years, I moved from that first position into a midlevel position, where I actually ran some of the initiatives myself. That was a tremendous stepping stone for me. I did that job for about three years also. Then I was offered an opportunity to go back to my hometown and become the associate scientific director of a government research institute. It actually has nothing to do with my master's in criminology, but it is administrative in that I run the institute. I've been doing that for the past four years. Actually, it's not exactly what I want it to be. That's ok. I gave it my best, and I had frank conversations with my boss like my other bosses. My boss knows I'm going to look for new jobs because this one isn't fulfilling me.

My advice to someone currently looking for their first job is … it depends on the HR process or the hiring process of the organization you're applying to because the government was quite rigid in structure. Picking your boss is paramount as well. Make sure the person that you are reporting to is the kind of person who will develop you. You're going to have boring stuff to do. Just bite your tongue and suck it up. Get it done quickly, get it done well so that they can see that you're "uber-qualified." Quite frankly, I think a lot of us are, because I don't think the roles are evolving quickly enough for our capacity. Just keep that context in mind, and see what kind of skills you can bring to the table to advance the roles within your organization. Pick your boss and never go for a salary. Even if you're paid a lot, if your boss sucks, you'll be frustrated all the time. Your work won't be fun. Just don't subject yourself to that. There are too many places to work, and there's too much work to be done.

2.45   On Start-Up After Start-Up: Dario's Story

Our company got bought out by a huge multinational conglomerate, and then the vice president of this other company invited me to join him. That happened again and again, so I just jumped from start-up to start-up. Then about 20 years ago, I retired from the start-up world and we moved across the country.

I finished my college degree in something called business and industry. It was a split major in business and then whatever you wanted to go into in industry. This was over 50 years ago, and I chose design drafting. So I got a job through this agency that would place you with companies that needed people, and after 90 days, you can become a regular full-time hire. I ended up at a start-up company, which always means that you do a little more than what your job description says because you do whatever is necessary. So I did some drafting, some prototyping, and other duties which kept it fun and interesting.

I stayed there for about 10 years, working my way up to become the manager of their engineering services. That included everything from the initial design of projects, mechanical designs, and the drafting area, to the prototyping area and the document control area. So it encompassed quite a bit. Then our company got bought out by a huge multinational conglomerate, and then the vice president of this other company invited me to join him. That happened again and again, so I just jumped from start-up to start-up. Then about 20 years ago, I retired from the start-up world and we moved across the country. I stayed home for about five years, just did stuff around the house, and then I got a little antsy to do something. I ended up teaching at a high school on building trades for a year, then there was an opening at the health department as a sanitation inspector, and I figured what the heck, I'll try it out. I actually didn't want the job full time, but they asked me to do it, so I did that for three years, then I managed to find a part-time version of the job, which I did for a decade before retiring.

That last job was interesting. It had nothing to do with my education. But they had eight weeks of training and things like that with the health department and other agencies. We did things like inspecting restaurants, complaints from the public, animal bite encounters, and some crazy things. I actually really liked it, in fact, I think I liked it better than my start-up jobs.

My advice to someone currently looking for their first job is ... well, job hunting nowadays is a lot different than fifty years ago. I know a lot of things are done online and I would venture to guess that there's a lot of inquiries through Facebook and social media. But I would tell people to work hard, for one thing. Hopefully, things are the same as before, but if you work hard and stay at it, I think good things will come.

2.46 On Breaking Traditional Expectations: Angela's Story

> *It's going to suck for a few years. But then, when you're in your mid 40s, you'll be so glad that you took the time to make your life your own. You lose many years of being afraid, crying, struggling, and feeling tremendous self-doubt, because your parents tell you this story: 'If you don't do these things, you're going to be homeless and hungry.' So be patient with yourself and trust that you'll figure it out. Hopefully, my story helps people say, 'Okay, it can work out.'*

I grew up as your classic tiger mom kid, really highly pressured, with really strict ideas about what was expected and what wasn't. My parents meant well. They just wanted security for me. They came from a place where they had memories of very hungry people in their childhood. Like many immigrants, they wanted to make sure that I never went hungry. So from the beginning, it was like, "Our daughter's going to go to a top school. She's going to be a Supreme Court Justice." It didn't even occur to them that I was an individual who might have preferences. You know how Asian culture can be. You have a role to play, and the family is more important. I was also the firstborn, so they put everything on me. I was taking college courses in math. I was winning violin competitions left and right. I was just your classic high-achieving Asian kid. But I wasn't very happy. There were a lot of big emotions. I'm a very emotional person, and I'm not good at just bottling things up and going along. I spent a lot of nights crying my eyes out and feeling really unhappy, suicidally unhappy, trapped. In my twenties, I got a lot of therapy, and that really helped. I highly recommend therapy. It's hard when you're 20 to admit that you need that because mental health has a stigma. It was hard to do that. For me, it felt like I had to detach from my parents, which is a huge deal. Fortunately, I have a really supportive partner who really understands attachment and has been there for me 300 percent. I don't think I could have done it without him, frankly. My parents can be quite modern and Western in some ways now, but it took a while to get there.

Anyway, I was recruited by Stanford for math. I was pushed by my mom to do a lot of math, which I didn't even really like, but I was really good at it. I went to Stanford, but I did not major in math. I started out majoring in earth sciences. Then I ended up dropping out for a time because I really wasn't terribly motivated by what I was learning then. Then I started working on a degree in product design, which included a lot of hands-on work, which was much more my kind of thing. I probably should have worked for a cabinetmaker or a wood shop of some kind, because that's really what I loved doing.

But then right out of school I moved several times with my partner, and we got married and had kids and I homeschooled them. I never ended up working in the field. For the next 20 years, I did a lot of pottery and other artwork, and I had a lot of odd jobs from playing gigs on the violin to reconfiguring light fixtures for more efficiency. It was scary, kind of like just walking off a cliff. I just left this path in life that I've always known that's totally secure, and I have no idea what's going to happen. It's not like someone said, "Don't worry, in 20 years you'll be a horticulturist." I didn't know this, so it's really scary.

But I knew I wanted to parent in a very specific way, very differently from how I was raised. I did that. I have four daughters, they're homeschooled, and we don't have a curriculum. We don't sit down and do school. What most parents do on weekends, that's what we do every day. We just live together. We cook together. We do projects together. They have their own interests. I support them, take them to the library, find them mentors, things like that, lots of hands-on learning from the whole world. It's just really different and very much with an eye to who they are as individuals, very much caring that they are really excited about every day of their lives. My husband is also from a very ambitious immigrant family. He also went through pressure to be a lawyer or doctor, and he didn't want that for our kids, either. That took a lot of energy and effort to raise them in that way. I got to do that. I wouldn't change a thing about that.

A few years ago, I had been doing a lot of gardening, and someone came to my house to buy plants, because I was selling extra plants that I don't need and want. She looked around my garden and told me about this gig that she does in raising other people's plants. I started working with her, and since then I've taken that up pretty much full time. So the work that I really love fell in my lap. I get paid quite a good amount to garden for other people. These people are loaded, and they want things a specific way, so I get to work with plants by myself. I really enjoy the solitude. So I've been doing that for the past few years, my first actual full-time job while I've continued homeschooling.

One other thing, I've come into contact now with many professional horticulturalists, and I asked one of them if I should go back to school. He said absolutely not, to just go with him to work at the private botanic gardens he worked at. So I love that I never even went to horticulture school, and I could have full-time work. That's one of the reasons I homeschool my girls. It's because I envision a future like that for them, as well. They already have work where people appreciate them. It's not full time, it's not always paid, but they have skills, and people appreciate them. I hope that as their interests develop, they just keep doing that work and someone goes, "Hey, I have this position, and it's only half time," and so on and so forth. That's my dream for all young people, that they could just do what they wanted every day, and someone would see value in them and say, "Hey, I have work that needs doing. Do you want to come do it?"

So I guess, at age 45, after 20 years of intensive parenting and self-training in horticulture, my "career" has begun!

My advice to someone currently looking for their first job is ... from my perspective now, a 20-year-old is just beginning their adult life. But it's going to stink. It's going to suck for a few years. But then, when you're in your mid 40s, you'll be so glad that you took the time to make your life your own. You lose many years of being afraid, crying, struggling, and feeling tremendous self-doubt because your parents tell you this story: "If you don't do these things, you're going to be homeless and hungry." So be patient with yourself and trust that you'll figure it out. Hopefully, my story helps people say, "Okay, it can work out."

Also, travel to go see different things. For me, it was a really big deal at one point to go to the Virgin Islands and find a part-time job waiting tables, just to prove that I could support myself and not starve. I even saved some money. Go travel, just to try things and prove that you can do it. I have read stories about young people who try a different job every month, just to try a bunch of things. I think that's fabulous advice. This is a long-standing interest of mine. I wish that people would create resources to support young people in these ways, like websites with companies that are willing to let you try for a month, and businesses that need help for a month, because I just feel like young people are fed this story like, "You've got to pick something, and you've got to stick with it." I wish there was a built-in gap year in the middle of college where people said, "Okay, you have to go. You have to go spend a year trying 12 different professions." I think young people would just make much better choices. They would know themselves better, and what they love to do, and they wouldn't have as much fear over their future.

I think the world really is learning that college is only one of the paths in life. You see that a lot of the people Google hires don't have degrees. You've seen lots of developments recently where I think people are realizing that we can be more flexible. One state just removed the requirement of a college degree from all of their government jobs, because they realize that people can have those skills without going to college. That's really encouraging that there can be more diversity and appreciation that skilled people can come from lots of different places. I hope to see more of that.

From someone who's in their mid 40s and made it through: Trust yourself. You're not crazy. You're not the only one going through it. And it's your life, it's yours to live. Trust yourself, trust your instincts, trust your intuitions. Be patient with yourself, try new things, and you will figure it out. Find mentors who believe in you, and lean on your friends who believe in you.

2.47 On Figuring It Out through Trial and Error: Glenn's Story

It may be impossible to know what you want to do when you're 20 years old. It's simply too early. You haven't got the experiences and the impressions that would allow you to make an informed choice of your career goals. So, throw yourself out there and do as many different things as possible in order to facilitate the possibility that you might discover what you like and dislike.

I was 15 years old, and my first full-time job was working in a factory that made integrated circuits. Back then, jobs were just advertised in newspapers, and it was quite common for even young people to seek and get a job. I was thrilled when I began my first job because it was a new kind of freedom. I enjoyed meeting new people, and I also had my own money. But it was a very strict job where you had to stamp a timecard in the morning at an exact time, either 7:06 or 7:12. It was useful in that it was the first time that I had to follow times and protocols. Plus I learned how to relate to my boss and to negotiate with others. But it soon became pretty boring. So, I felt I wanted really to do something else after about a year.

The next few jobs came to me organically through other people that I met. For example, I met people who asked me to install burglar alarms in people's houses as a job. I also repaired all kinds of electronics, which I knew how to do since it was a big interest of mine since I was about seven years old. I also worked as a cinema machinist, which was also from word of mouth, and then a series of similar jobs that mostly had to do with me driving around in a car and fixing things.

I started my own business. I bought two workshops where the general public could just pop in and leave their electronic devices to be repaired. I did that for maybe two or three years. I got bored of that. I moved out of the city and into the countryside, but I continued to fix things as a way of supporting myself. I also tried a career as a musician. I toured a bit with different bands. But of course, it was impossible to make a living out of that. You really have to line up with some musician or band who is really commercially successful to make any money. Doesn't matter how well you play. Or you can be a studio session musician, but I wasn't good enough for that or I didn't have the right connections.

So I eventually gave that up. By this time, I was in my late 20s. That's when I felt that maybe it would be fun to study. Since I had never finished high school or gone to college, I had to take the examinations to be eligible for college. So I did that for a summer, and then I went to college to study music for a couple of years. It turned out that it wasn't as interesting as I thought because I was more interested in the human side of playing an instrument or appreciating listening to music, rather than the rather dry stuff that musicology could offer in terms of reading music, sheet music, and analyzing harmonics.

But then we had a lecture from a guest professor who was a psychologist who studied behaviors and experiences related to music. He suggested that I take the introductory course in psychology in my spare time, which would be in the evenings. So I did that in parallel with the musicology coursework, and eventually, I took some other psychology courses on weekends. And soon enough, I applied to the PhD program in psychology.

The PhD program took me a very long time because I was really interested in everything too much, I tried to do a few impossible things it turned out, and a few things that didn't lead to very much. I also met one of the most important figures in my academic life, someone who was also interested in studying music from a multidisciplinary perspective. I applied for a grant with him as a co-applicant, and that led to two years of funding and 10 publications.

And then, I was unemployed. I had no job to go to after that. I applied to quite a few assistant professor jobs. But my merits were too weak. It turned out that most people who applied for a teaching position in those days had already worked quite some time in academia as adjunct professors. I was unemployed for one and a half years, but eventually, I found a faculty job abroad. It took an awful long time for various formal reasons. But eventually, I was offered the job, which entailed four years of pay for doing my own research. Then after four years, I got a permanent teaching position. Since then, it's been about 10 years, and I've been promoted to full professor.

My advice to someone currently looking for their first job is … well, the world is quite complex and quite formalized. I would advise you to inform yourself about the formal requirements as early as possible. I didn't do anything of that. I acted very foolishly. It took a very long time to get where I happened to end up. But on the other hand, I didn't have a master plan. So, I had no idea that I would end up in this kind of position.

But if you know where you want to be in five years or 10 years, I really recommend people to find out what is it that would make it possible for you to get there. What do education programs require? What do the employers require? What is the typical profile of the person who actually becomes employed?

But also the informal stuff matters. I tell my children to find the kind of people that have the kinds of jobs that they're interested in and ask about their experiences. What worked, what didn't work? What obstacles did they face, and how might they have avoided those?

In some cases, it may be impossible to know what you want to do when you're 20 years old. It's simply too early. You haven't got the experiences and the impressions that would allow you to make an informed choice of your career goals. So, throw yourself out there and do as many different things as possible to facilitate the possibility that you might discover what you like and dislike. To become the person you could be or want to be, it's very important to try out many different things and actually bang your head against whatever it is that's out there. You can't sit in your basement and reason and think out who you are or what you can become. You need to try it for yourself.

2.48 On Finding Value in Less-Than-Ideal Circumstances: Kara's Story

I struggled a lot with the feelings of the sense that I was manipulating people into a purchase. My manager really leaned into that side of it, verging into what I considered as too much manipulation.... But I ended up getting promoted in just two months, which was, in part, due to my work ethic and my drive. That actually set me up very well for my next couple of jobs.

I was finishing up my bachelor's in psychology. I had done an internship as an editor for the on-campus literary journal, then a couple of part-time jobs such as working as a team member at a clothing store and working as an ice cream server. I started looking for jobs during my last year in college. I applied to probably over 100 positions, primarily in HR since that's what I wanted to do. Failing that, I looked for anything that was clerical that I could maybe pivot into the HR space. It was very frustrating, and I had a lot of anxiety, because I had student loans and I was very stressed out about my ability to support myself, and I didn't want to move back home with my parents. I wanted that independence that I had gained in college. I wanted the pride of being able to say, "Yes, I achieved what college set out for me to achieve." So it was very frustrating, and I felt like a failure, not being able to find something that was in the specific area that I studied for.

Eventually, I found this one advertisement that was an HR internship, so I applied for it, but during the phone screening, they told me it was an unpaid internship. Then they said that they had a paid position available in sales if I'd like to be considered. I said sure. I ended up getting the job and starting right after graduation. But it was essentially door-to-door sales for this cable company. So even then, taking on this sales job was a letdown.

I feel like my first day was almost my interview day. The way that they processed their selection was that they had you do a full-day trial. So my first day, I went door-to-door with somebody who was already in the position, and I listened to the sales pitch. One of my tests was then to give the sales pitch to the next door that we talked to talk to. The job was definitely out of my comfort zone. I consider myself an introvert, so literally, cold-calling people and doing door-to-door sales was very terrifying for me. It was scary, and it was anxiety-inducing to feel, "Oh, this isn't me, but I have to put on this face to succeed in this job."

I gained more confidence over time, and I think I was able to walk that line a little bit better, saying "Yes, I'm an introvert, but I can put on this facade of being a little bit extroverted, and this can be my work person as opposed to my life persona." I was good at being persuasive and taking some of the buyer's perspective, asking questions like, "What are the issues that you have with your current cable company?" Then say, "Oh, it's been so frustrating," and bring in a little bit of empathy to the conversation. At the same time, I struggled a lot with the feeling of the sense that I was manipulating people into a purchase. My manager really leaned into that side of it, verging into what I considered too much manipulation. So we didn't always see eye to eye, since he valued outcomes and sales and targets above all other things.

But I ended up getting promoted in just two months, which was, in part, due to my work ethic and my drive. That actually set me up very well for my next couple of jobs. Because I was promoted quickly and because we had so much turnover, I quickly was able to get involved in interviews and training of the more junior coworkers that I had as team members. That was more in line with what I wanted. It was probably only about 10 percent of my time that I was doing that, but on paper, it looked very good to say, "Yes, I was promoted, I had responsibility over these more junior team members, I was involved in interviewing." It also set me up well for graduate school later on, where I could then take that experience and apply it to what I was learning in grad school. But at the time, it just didn't feel like I was a good fit.

I still ended up leaving after five months, and I took a very untraditional career path. My second job was as a freelance editor since I had some writing experience in undergrad. I did that for a year, then worked as a library associate, which is basically just a librarian but without a master's degree in library science. Then I went to graduate school for psychology, did a couple of internships, and then worked in a consulting firm for federal clients for a while. Finally, now I'm a senior consultant in people analytics for a different firm.

My advice to someone currently looking for their first job is ... the encouragement I would offer is that you are much more employable when you're already employed. Don't let it get you down too much because you feel forced into something that is not what you wanted. There will be good coming out of it regardless of how miserable the experience is, regardless of how let down you feel. You can always leverage pieces of what you're doing into the future. So even though at the time I felt, "Wow, this really is so far from what I wanted, how am I ever going to take this and leverage it into what I want to be doing?" I found later on that there were many, many different aspects that I could hold up and say, "Here is something relevant to what you're doing that I've done in my past. Here's some experience I have that I can translate into value for you."

2.49   On Resilience: Nathan's Story

The bottom line is that you just got to be persistent. Failure is an ordinary and expected outcome in any endeavor. You can't sit there and be brokenhearted every time that somebody says, 'You suck, and you're never going to get to where you are.' You have to become resilient.

I worked at a fast-food place a few days a week through college. I was probably overqualified for the job, but I needed money, and it was something that I could just show up and then leave. Then after college, I was preparing to apply for medical school, and I needed a job so I started looking at server positions at nicer restaurants. I just showed up at different restaurants and interviewed at something ridiculous like 45 places. Most of them just completely blew me off. But there was one or two that finally gave me a shot. They did this thing called training shifts to see how I would do. I sucked at it because I'd never done it, and everyone else had had experience serving. I was all nervous and fumbling all over the place. Most people did a few training shifts, I think I set a record with 11 training shifts. Thankfully, they just continued to let me do it, but finally, after a month I got the hang of it.

That first month was really tough. I realized later that there are different kinds of server jobs. There are places that you work at that are corporate; if you sneeze in the wrong direction, they'll just fire you. This was a place like that. I saw poor people who were working there for a decade, then someone would give them a bad review when they had a bad day, and they'd get fired. I didn't like that. Thank goodness I got into medical school about a year later, and I was able to put in my two weeks' notice. I thought I'd just take it easy and do nothing until medical school started, but one of the guys there, who I got along with, ended up going to another restaurant and said that I could go work with him. So I bartended a bit, and then they offered me a general manager position. It wasn't a bad job, and it paid decently. But I called the guy and was all nervous, trying to tell him somehow that I couldn't do it, I wanted to go to medical school. He was like, "Are you out of your mind? Of course, you have to go to medical school. Don't worry about this stuff." I think I got lucky because he was a guy who really had his head screwed on straight. So off I went to medical school, and my next job after that was residency, and now a physician.

My advice to someone currently looking for their first job is … I'm not smart, believe it or not. That has nothing to do with my success. I'm of ordinary intellect. From an early age, I had ADHD [attention deficit hyperactivity disorder] and dyslexia. Nothing came to me easily, and I thought I was stupid. Thank God I had a tutor who taught me, "Hey, you could do this. You just got to realize you work differently."

The bottom line is that you just have to be persistent. Failure is an ordinary and expected outcome in any endeavor. You can't sit there and be broken-hearted every time somebody says, "You suck, and you're never going to get to where you are." You have to become resilient. I think that's why I was able to walk into those restaurants and they'd ask me about my serving experience (I had none) and my references (I had none), but I told them they should hire me because I work freaking hard. That was it, that was the key for me.

The 20s are the hardest period because you're still figuring out who you are. If you went to college, you're just la-la land in many ways. It has no bearing on objective reality in any way. It's almost impossible to think positively about your career future in your 20s because you don't really know that's the truth until you have experience.

The final thing is so many people say, "Follow your dreams," and then when people follow their dreams, they say, "That's just unrealistic." Part of that is true. If you critically look at yourself and, for example, maybe you got a D average in high school and you want to do something that requires you to be an academic, eventually you do have to get real with yourself. But pretty much everything is possible as long as you work towards it.

If whatever I'm doing is not enough, I have to work harder to make that happen.

2.50 On Focusing on the Here and Now: Mason's Story

Whatever you're doing, do it well. Sometimes there's a temptation to think, 'I'm doing A, but I really wanting to be doing B over here. So, I'm going to focus on what I want to do.' That has its place, but the opportunities to move to the next step are directly correlated with how well you do your current job. If you do your work well, it opens up opportunities.

I had some internships and summer jobs while in college, and then I did a one-year master's degree in history abroad. I started looking for jobs, took some temporary work, and then finally got my first full-time job as an intelligence officer with a national agency almost a year after graduating.

Since high school, I have been interested in national and international affairs. I can trace that to high school teachers in history, the TV show *The West Wing*, and also just the current events I grew up with. In college, I majored in history, and I had a historian who was my senior thesis advisor and a diplomat-turned-professor who had these amazing stories and was an inspiring man. Taking classes with him felt like peering under the hood of how the world works. I did internships in DC and for Congress, and I worked for news outlets over the summer. I remember emailing my congresswoman for my district, just asking directly for an internship, and I got an unpaid internship. I think they pay interns now, which is great. I actually helped her write some speeches, and she was very complimentary about them, which meant the world to me as a 19-year-old. We would go to talks around DC, and we got to be in the hearings and see where the sausage was made, so to speak.

Eventually, one of my advisors suggested that I should do a shorter master's program abroad since it's harder in the US to get a PhD and a job in history. That helped me figure out that I didn't want to do the PhD, I just wanted to be more active, I wanted to change the world. So I started looking for jobs, and I spent several months in "preemployment," as my mother called it. The idea that I was just taxiing down the runway before taking off. All of a sudden, the structure fell away, and I had to figure out what I wanted to do. I had skills and interests, but they were broad. I was actually a bit torn between some journalism jobs I applied to and going back to DC. I would spend a week living on friends' couches in DC, clustering my interviews to do them during that week when I was there. I probably applied to well over 100 jobs. The digital revolution was just starting, so many of those were still paper applications. But sometimes the hardest decisions are made for you; in this case, I had accepted a temporary job in DC before I heard back from some of the journalism jobs I applied to.

What happened was that I came across an ad from a senior fellow at a think tank looking for temporary short-term help working on a book. I interviewed with him and ended up getting the temporary job, which wasn't a permanent career job, it was just for a specific project. So I was still anxious, still applying to as many jobs as I could. It just so happened that I went to a book signing, and I bumped into some people I knew from college. One of them was working at a national security agency and asked what I was up to, and I explained my temporary job and how I was looking into getting into government. A few days later, she called me, told me she was leaving for law school, and asked if I wanted to interview for her job. Coincidentally, I had been sending my resume all around, and it had gotten passed through a friend of a friend to the same national agency, totally independent of this college friend I met at the book signing. So when she recommended to the hiring team to interview me, they were already about to reach out to me, so it felt like kismet. I went through the several month-long process of interviewing and getting my clearances, and then I finally started in the summer about a year after I had finished my master's degree. That began my career in the intelligence community, which lasted for five years until I went to law school.

One takeaway that I learned from my jobs was the importance of being able to digest a lot of information and boil it down to some comprehensible summary, then be able to regurgitate it in a written or spoken product for others. I had a job as a special assistant to a chief of staff, and I learned how to manage up, while also managing down. People came to me and tried to get information or try to pass memos. I had to be able to work well with the staff to not be imperious and instead be helpful and conciliatory, while at the same time protecting my principal's time, which is often his or her most valuable resource. Of course, among other things, I learned a ton about the actual workings of the intelligence community of the national security apparatus. I had spent a year abroad researching British-American diplomacy from the 1970s, and all of a sudden, I was inside the room where some of these decisions were being made.

Eventually, I realized that I was always dealing with law, executive orders, and policy. I also felt like there were people that I admired and wished to emulate who were lawyers, even in the intelligence community. Finally, I knew I had to get better at some things like writing and analysis. So law school seemed like the right idea. I went, I enjoyed it, I graduated, I clerked for some federal judges, and now I'm a lawyer at a large law firm.

My advice to someone currently looking for their first job is … whatever you're doing, do it well. Sometimes there's a temptation to think, "I'm doing A, but I really want to be doing B over here. So, I'm going to focus on what I want to do." That has its place, but the opportunities to move to the next step are directly correlated with how well you do your current job. If you do your work well, it opens up opportunities.

Also, be nice to people. That doesn't mean being saccharine. But if you treat people genuinely with respect, it opens up opportunities. If you do the opposite, it closes opportunities. Maya Angelou, the poet and writer, had a wonderful saying: "People might not remember what you said, they might not remember what you did, but they'll always remember how you made them feel." If you make people feel bad, that will rebound to your detriment.

Finally, take advantage of opportunities. I felt very lucky that I had these opportunities come along, and I jumped at them. I think that is a valuable lesson for anyone in any field.

2.51 On Patiently Waiting for Your Moment: Jed's Story

What I really wanted to do was to farm full time, because I grew up on a family farm, I sold eggs starting at 10 years old from my own chickens, and I helped my family farm at local farmers' markets. But I was trying to figure out how to do that. I had a flair for writing, I won a number of essay contests in high school, and I was involved in the local news all through high school. So I decided that in order to be able to come back to farming full-time, I would go into journalism, make a living out of it, then retire back to the farm.

What I really wanted to do was to farm full time, because I grew up on a family farm, I sold eggs starting at 10 years old from my own chickens, and I helped my family farm at local farmers' markets. But I was trying to figure out how to do that. I had a flair for writing, I won several essay contests in high school, and I was involved in the local news all through high school. So I decided that to be able to come back to farming full time, I would go into journalism, make a living out of it, and then retire back to the farm. I went to college majoring in English, and I did all sorts of extracurriculars like debate, public speaking, and theater to sharpen my skills in communication.

Near the end of high school, I was working part time as the night receptionist for our local newspaper. They liked me; I was very reputable and dependable. So when I went to college, they told me that as soon as I could come back, they would hire me. That was great because it meant after college I could come back home and live on the farm, work at this local newspaper, and have my foot in both worlds. So literally when I graduated, I gave them a call, and they said they were ready for me, and I walked right into that position.

I was the investigative reporter at this local newspaper. I loved the chase of sleuthing a story and getting the scoop. I was one of five investigative reporters, but I was the only one who loved doing research, I loved finding out the background stuff. I quickly became the person who would listen to moles. People would call me if there was a problem, and I would look into it. I developed a reputation as the go-to person to find a newsworthy story. I was actually able to influence some things like the resignation of a commonwealth's attorney who was a crook, expose a service authority chairman, and more. That's what I enjoyed. I enjoyed the true power and purity of the press bringing the light of truth onto an issue and actually creating a better place to live in.

What I didn't like was having stories spiked. That means I would have a story, and it goes up through the chain of command, but then the publisher says we can't publish it because the guy we're writing about is a big donor or advertiser. That happened to me more than once. That was frustrating since I, as a young person low on the totem pole, wasn't privy to all of this information and who the big advertisers were and who was buddies with whom. One of my dreams, to this day, would be to start a newspaper with no advertising and only focused on hardcore investigative reporting on a local level. Not state or national, but local things that really matter to the people living in your area. The corruption even at the local level is beyond what you and I could fathom. All kinds of backdoor deals on where to put in a sewer line to increase real estate, where you get a tax break for doing something, it's mind-boggling. I've even done the business plan for a newspaper like this, if I can find the right person to launch it.

Anyway, at this point, I'm married and we're living in an attic apartment for $300 a month. We didn't have a television, we used a wood stove, we grew all our own food, and we were saving as much money as possible for a child on the way and our dreams of running a farm full time. We stocked away half our paychecks for two and a half years, then we realized that we had enough to live on for a year without earning any more money. So I handed in my two-week notice at the newspaper and came back to the farm full time, fully expecting that we'd run through the little one-year nest egg and would probably have to go back to work. But I realized that, because I worked hard and wasn't afraid to do any job from washing dishes to pushing concrete, I could go back in a year and get a job, I knew I was employable.

We took the jump, and everybody said we were foolish to give up our nice paycheck. And yes, it was tight. We ran through our nest egg, but in two years, rather than one. I also did some small odd jobs for people, building fences and planting trees, so that helped us limp along. In the meantime, I'm working the farm full time, I'm marketing and selling and putting together a business plan for how we can heal the world with grass-based livestock. I started presenting it at local clubs and networks, and we actually started to build up a customer base selling everything directly. About the end of the third year, we realized that we were actually going to make it. We had hit positive cash flow.

It was unbelievable. I'll tell you this: my dad was an accountant, and he did a lot of farm accounting for other farmers. He could never tell me who they were, but he was able to tell me that even in year four, our finances were stronger than many of the big farmers who drove flashy trucks and tractors. It's because we were so frugal early on, the big farmers owed tons of money to the bank, but we didn't owe anything.

It's now been almost 50 years, and we have grown to a $4.5 million business employing more than 20 people full time. My dad died only about five years after we started at the farm. But one of the things he did before he passed was that he brought me in and helped me cast a vision, an optimistic vision, for the future. We made a list of all the different jobs that our farm could support. Remember, at the time, we had only just hit positive cash flow. But my dad was thinking so far in advance. I still have that yellow piece of paper from that conversation, when we sat down and wrote out all the jobs and enterprises that could come from this farm. Today, we are certainly doing all of that and even more. We lease properties, we have an apprenticeship program, we have a massive customer base and more.

It's interesting, when I came back to the farm full time, most people thought that I was going to squander my communication talent. I haven't. That talent has enabled me to do marketing, messaging, writing newsletters, and creating patron loyalty through communicating our story. I was able to combine that gift for communication with my love for farming.

In fact, I've written 15 books, and I just finished another one a couple of weeks ago.

My advice to someone currently looking for their first job is ... a lot of people are good at things that they don't really like. Eighty percent of Americans don't like their job. So how can you be fulfilled? A lot of times, what you're good at is not necessarily what you love to do, and a lot of times, what you know a lot about is not necessarily what you like to do.

One of my best examples is one of our apprentices who's stayed with us for over 10 years. She came to us in her mid 30s with a master's degree in mathematics and working at a Fortune 500 company. Well, she was just no longer interested in sitting at a cubicle all day punching numbers, and she had started this little community garden plot in her condo area. So she found us online, joined us as an apprentice, and now she's still with us over a decade earlier.

Myself, I still remember my last meeting with my high school guidance counselor. I told her I wanted to farm. She didn't like that idea at all. "What? You're in the National Honor Society. You're on the debate team. You won all these essay contests.... What a waste of brains."

Most of our apprentices are in their late 20s. They've started their careers, but they realized that it wasn't what they wanted to do with their lives. So they come here and find that working with their hands, doing something visceral is what fulfills them. I tell people to think back to when they were 10 years old. At 10 years old, you're like a little adult. You're old enough to know what you like to do, but you're not old enough to have any responsibilities yet. It's actually that beautiful time when you've become you, you know who you are, but you don't have to perform. That is the purest form of you that there is. So if you can go back and recreate yourself as a 10-year-old, who is that person? See, here's the problem. As we mature, our dreams and our fantasies start to change and morph into other people's expectations. So suddenly, that pure you gets veered off on other people's agenda, and people often don't realize that until they're in their mid 30s, when they say, "Oh my goodness. Is this really what I want to do the rest of my life?"

Just like the girl I was talking about, she's good at math. So what does society say? Well, go do something in IT. You're good at math. It turns out, she's also really good at leatherworking, making jewelry, making soap, making animal-based skin creams, and giving tours. She's very well spoken, so she does all of our tours here.

My encouragement is to always go back to your 10-year-old self. What floated your boat? What were you reading? What were you interested in?

What were your hobbies? Chances are your 10-year-old self has a more pure understanding of you than your 30-year-old self.

2.52 On Negotiating Your Salary: Ray's Story

One of the things I learned the hard way is that your starting salary determines your salary increases moving forward. If you start off underpaid, then everything else will be stacked on that. Always look at the starting salary very carefully and negotiate it.

I finished high school, and I was taking classes at the junior college, and I needed a job. I needed to be able to pay for school, car, entertainment, and savings to transfer to a four-year university at some point. So I found a job as a grocery store clerk a few miles away from my house. I wasn't terribly ambitious when I was looking, I just asked around and found that my friend's mom was the accountant for the grocery store, so she got me a 10-minute interview and I got the job on the spot. I don't think I applied for any other jobs. It was all really fast, within a few weeks.

The job was fun for me because it was something new. I had worked a bit at my dad's architectural office in the past, so this one was a lot more hands-on, face-to-face customer service, and labor. It was a good environment, I got to know some regulars, and they pretty quickly had me working the cash register because I was pretty good at counting cash. I learned how to stock, how to price, how to clean, how to manage inventory, and everything else. Within a few months, I was opening and closing the store.

Then I went off to the four-year university, and I kept the job as a weekend job. I got my degree in English, did some temp work with attorney headhunters and a law firm in basic office admin roles, then I went to law school and interned with government agencies. After law school, I floundered a bit, because I was tired and was still trying to get jobs locally. I had a few stints with various companies, but eventually, I moved states and got a job with a start-up tech company as general counsel. Then I ended up at a major shipping company in operational management for something like 18 years, before ending up the past 10 years as a process improvement manager for a healthcare firm. My current job isn't directly related to law. But my experience in reading legislation helps. I can actually read the directives coming from state agencies and help translate them for my team.

I learned some things that still carry over to today. One, the work environment is important. I've been in good and bad work environments, and I could see the impact it had on people. In bad work environments,

I learned to try to alleviate that through being open and generous, trying to talk about personal things, and being flexible. You never know what you're going to learn that you may need later in life. For example, I learned how to pack and load grocery bags at the grocery store. Interestingly, that translated to my work in a shipping company, because I understood the basics of package management and could communicate to our packaging team in a way that others couldn't.

My advice to someone currently looking for their first job is … any experience you get is a good experience. For any job you get right out of high school, don't look at it as your career. Yeah, you're stuck in a job right now. Your current time may be unhappy or not preferred, hopefully not miserable, but there could be a payoff later on. It could be temporary; things change, and your life goals can change. When I was with that grocery store, there was one individual whose whole life had been working in that grocery store. He became bitter and angry, and he didn't feel like he had any other options. Don't forget that things can in fact change. Moreover, these are skill sets you can take to another job and find another career for yourself.

Also, you have to learn to negotiate for yourself. One of the things I learned the hard way is that your starting salary determines your salary increases moving forward. If you start off underpaid, then everything else will be stacked on that. Always look at the starting salary very carefully and negotiate it.

2.53 On Standing Up for Yourself: Clara's Story

Over time, I learned what I wanted and didn't want in a job. My doctor was very meticulous and not very forgiving of mistakes, so that made it a little bit difficult. Looking back, they probably should have hired someone with some more experience than me.… So I ended up leaving that job not long later. I told them that I felt like I wasn't the right fit for the position and that they needed someone with more experience. The doctor actually asked me to call them personally, and I told them that, because I didn't want to burn any bridges. If I have one regret, I wish I would have stuck up for myself more.

My first job was as a medical assistant at a dermatology practice. I had been looking for jobs for a few months as I graduated college. The problem was that in my area, medical assistants were starting to require certifications, and I didn't have mine at the time. Plus, it was my first job in the field that I wanted to be in, and I had never really talked to a patient before, so it was a little scary and unnerving. I definitely felt like I was at a disadvantage.

I knew I wanted a career in health care, but I wasn't sure exactly where to go from there. You actually don't need a college degree to be a medical assistant; many of them just require certification. But for me, I had my bachelor's in biology, and I wanted to go on to future schooling like PA [physician assistant] school, but I was looking for hands-on clinical experience. I had my basic life support experience, like CPR [cardiopulmonary resuscitation] and AED [automated external defibrillator], but I was missing the hands-on experience, the patient care experience hours. At the same time, a lot of the job was just taking notes for the provider, so from that perspective, I felt overqualified.

I actually tried reaching out to some athletic trainers I knew from college, to see if they had any student positions. I was starting to feel that pressure to get a job. But I eventually got some movement from online websites like Indeed, and I got some interviews. Actually, a lot of it was in-person shadowing, which I didn't quite expect, but they wanted to see how I acted in the environment with a patient. I remember one job I shadowed at was for a plastic surgeon's office. I'm relieved I didn't get that job, I wasn't ready for the surgery culture.

Eventually, this dermatology practice I landed at, I found on Indeed and they brought me in for interviews. It was a very small practice, so I did the interview with the doctor and the PA working there, and then I was called back to shadow pretty much later that day. It was a quick turnaround, and I got the job offer by the end of the day.

On my first day, I was terrified. My family wasn't in the same state, and we were in the middle of a pandemic, so I wasn't sure what to expect. I didn't have the professional protective equipment, and this particular office was trying to bring people in in person to stay open still. At one point, early on, we were making masks out of my boss's old lab coat. We didn't have the hospital supplies that other places had. Plus there was a lot to learn, and the other medical assistant was leaving in two days, so I only had two days of training. It was my first time sending in prescriptions, for example, and I had to learn all the clinical terms and how to talk to patients, and then also help them navigate the uncertainty of the pandemic. Yeah, terrified is a good word for how I felt.

Over time, I learned what I wanted and didn't want in a job. My doctor was very meticulous and not very forgiving of mistakes, so that made it a little bit difficult. Looking back, they probably should have hired someone with some more experience than me. I was even assisting with some procedures and transcribing patient histories, on top of more basic administrative work like scheduling appointments. It was kind of three positions in one, with very little training, and then the PA ended up working remotely, so that made it worse. It taught me what not to look for in a job.

I ended up leaving that job not long later. I told them that I felt like I wasn't the right fit for the position and that they needed someone with more experience. The doctor actually asked me to call them personally, and I told them that, because I didn't want to burn any bridges. If I have one regret, I wish I would have stuck up for myself more. I didn't know that I could have at the time, because that was my first job in the field. After now having jobs with better employers, I wish I was able to tell the doctor more directly that the workplace was not good. But now, I've switched to being a medical assistant at a different practice. I have my certification now, and I have experience, I got a pay raise, and it's just overall a much better workplace.

My advice to someone currently looking for their first job is ... don't be afraid to be direct and stick up for what you need. Especially as younger people go into their field of choice, maybe they want to get recommendation letters from these providers or move on from there in the company, so it's hard and sometimes feels like you don't have a voice. But don't be afraid to say what you need, because what you need is valid too. There are other positions out there, and there are plenty of companies hiring.

Also, it's important to mention the mental health aspect of a job in health care, especially during a pandemic. I think that that was something that no one was expecting. I was not on the front line by any means, but even just hearing a cough when you know you're not protected, was nerve wracking. People were being put on ventilators, but there was no treatment that we knew of. So you really need to be aware of that mental health component because you're caring for other people. You really need to make sure that you feel balanced mentally before you can care for other people. Because otherwise, you may feel like it's no use. A lot of the time, students who want to go on to do more things, so they think they have to stick through it in order. Not always. There are many ways you can get to where you want to be. So it's important to remember to care for your own mental health along that journey.

2.54 On Being Pushed Harder Than Expected: Klein's Story

If you're starting a new job, and your boss is pushing you pretty hard and you don't know why, it may actually be a good thing. That instructor from my vocational program was hard on me when I was in high school.

On Being Pushed Harder Than Expected: Klein's Story

I didn't understand it at first. I thought he was picking on me. But he then told me later in life that he thought I had a lot of potential, and he was pushing me harder than the other students in order to bring that out of me.

In my last two years of high school, I went to the local vocational center and participated in a carpentry program. I got along really well with the instructor, and he actually hired me to do some work for him over the summers. When I was graduating high school, I had planned on going to college, but this instructor introduced me to the owner of a building construction company and told them that I was this young man with a ton of potential. They offered me a job right away, and I took it.

I don't think they even gave me a job description. Basically, I was doing the grunt work. It was a small company, so no one had formal titles, so I was just doing hands-on work leveling foundation or other stuff. Then about a month later, the owner asked if I was interested in managing some house-building projects. It was kind of funny because I had no idea what he meant by that, but he said that they thought I was capable and they would give me some guidance and direction, so I said I'll do my best.

I really liked the people I worked with. It was a family business, and the son was in the process of taking over, they taught me a tremendous amount about the industry. They gave me opportunities when I really didn't know much at all. It was a lot of on-the-job training, and they were patient with me. At the same time, the con was probably that there weren't many opportunities, since it was a small family business that they were going to keep in the family. Of course, I still respect them to this day, they're still in business, but I was very career minded and wanted to climb the corporate ladder so to speak.

So fast forward about four years, and I was the superintendent by this point. I managed all the subcontractors and the suppliers to get materials for the job, and I managed the process of getting a home built. We built maybe 100 homes a year. Then during that time there, I met some other contractors, one of whom worked with this national HVAC company that was expanding rapidly. I wasn't really looking to switch jobs, but they invited me to come interview, and so I did, and that eventually led to a job offer as a field manager for them. I did that for several more years, and we had some really good successes, and that brought some attention to me since I was responsible for all the construction in that division. That led to promotions, including one that meant I had to pack up our entire family to move across states to a bigger role.

Eventually, almost 20 years later, I was in a place where I would end up having to travel quite a bit for work, and my kids were not in high school. I didn't want to travel or move again, so I took this huge leap of faith and said that I was done, I didn't know exactly what I was going to do next, but I was leaving the company. They actually gave me a very generous severance package, which they didn't need to do since I was the one who quit, but they were a great company. So I took some time off, then I decided to start my own construction company a little over a decade ago, and I've been doing that ever since. Nowadays I do it semiretired because I have other people running the day-to-day company for me.

My advice to someone currently looking for their first job is … spend a lot of time networking with people who are in your industry and people who are influential in your industry. Tell them, "You're someone I respect, you have been successful in your career in this industry that I'm interested in." Maybe even be bold enough to ask them to be your mentor. Looking back, there were definitely some people who I respected and admired, and if I had just asked them to be my mentor, they would've probably done that. But overall, there's no greater resource than to be in front of these types of people, interact with them, ask questions, get direction, and have them invest in your career.

Also, if you're starting a new job, and your boss is pushing you pretty hard and you don't know why, it may actually be a good thing. That instructor from my vocational program was hard on me when I was in high school. I didn't understand it at first. I thought he was picking on me. But he then told me later in life that he thought I had a lot of potential, and he was pushing me harder than the other students to bring that out of me. So now, I look back on that and have a great appreciation for it. So maybe your boss is doing that for you, maybe even ask them if that's why they're so hard on you.

2.55 On Widening Your Job Search: Devon's Story

Looking back, I probably could've done an internship, or volunteered at a hospital, or something to help me get a medical job.

I had some summer jobs and part-time jobs starting in high school and through college, like working as a parking attendant for an event center, doing some work with my dad who's an electrician, landscaping work for a doctor, clerking for a family practice, and being a personal trainer. My parents were helping me through college, so I thought it was my responsibility to bring in some money by working. After graduating, I kept up my personal trainer job for about six months, working at a national chain gym, until I landed my first big boy job out of school as a clinical allergy specialist.

I remember I found that job online, and this was back when online job postings were still getting started. I was working the personal trainer job and started my job search over the summer after graduation. We were still recovering from an economic recession, so there were a lot of challenges where entry-level jobs were looking for people with prior experience. Looking back, I probably could've done an internship or volunteered at a hospital, or something to help me get a medical job. But I didn't really have those opportunities, so that probably extended my job search.

So for that job I got, I basically was doing skin tests to help people figure out what they were allergic to. It was interesting because it helped me realize that I didn't exactly want to practice medicine. But I still wanted to work with patients somehow. It was difficult because most clinic jobs working with patients required special training or credentials, which I didn't have. What was cool was that they provided training. They flew all the new trainees to their headquarters for a week, and here I was just out of college, and that was a cool experience.

I stayed in the job for three years, mostly to pay off my student loans, and then I saved up money to go back to graduate school to study molecular biotechnology. I had realized by that point that I enjoyed the discovery frontier, sort of like the research component, which is what led me to a biotech program. Now, I'm in a doctoral program in neuroscience and I'm a graduate research assistant. Most of my research intersects with bioengineering.

My advice to someone currently looking for their first job is … networking is so important. There are tools now to facilitate that, like LinkedIn and other places. Creating your digital profile is now so important to increase your reach, and it's easy enough to do. We live in a digital world now, and I would definitely recommend creating your digital presence. From there, talk with your classmates, colleagues, and other people you know. Finally, don't overlook opportunities if they don't seem like a direct fit. It may be a step on the ladder for you, and it could help you broaden your search. Keep an open mind.

2.56 On Relying on Your Network: Rafaela's Story

Your network is what you're going to fall back on when times get tough. When that museum I worked at closed after just six months, my network at the presidential library helped keep me afloat by giving me a job, temporarily, because they knew I was searching for higher education jobs.... I know with networking, it often feels like you are just making connections that would one day have a benefit and a payout to you, which feels very transactional. But if you don't approach it that way, if you go into it thinking that you're just making friends, that's better.

About a month after I graduated college, I met with a family member who said their company needed an events assistant, and they offered me my first full-time job. By this point, I had been searching for several months, mostly looking online. I was mostly applying for higher education jobs, which is what I was interested in. I had actually interviewed for a job at my alma mater, but I didn't get it. I think I had several first-round interviews for several jobs, but none of them led to an offer. So this first job offer was very informal, it was never even posted officially on a website. I sat down for an informal interview, mostly to discuss my interests and my availability. I worked there for about six months, while still searching for higher education jobs. It was a good job, but it was challenging working for the family. They really wanted me to stay there, but I was looking for something different.

Then eventually I got connected through a college friend with a nonprofit presidential library, and they were looking for an event administrative assistant. I had actually interned with the library during college, and my old internship coordinator got back in touch with me and asked if I was interested. I interviewed with them, which was more standard questions and several rounds of interviews, and I got the job after a couple of weeks. Even though this was with a presidential library and not higher education, which is what I was hoping for, it still kind of aligned with my goals to learn about the event industry and work with nonprofits.

Here, there was one great person and I really wanted to be mentored by them, but they left shortly after I started. Then the person who was brought in, I butted heads with them a lot, and they were my direct supervisor. I ended up getting mentorship from a peer on the same team, but they had several years of experience, and that was fantastic. I learned a lot about planning, logistics, professional life working in an office setting, how to advocate for myself, how to set boundaries, knowing my own bandwidth, and so much more.

I stayed there for a few years, then I went to another museum that ended up closing after just six months, which was very providential because it was a bit of a toxic culture. That actually propelled me to start applying for jobs in higher education again, which is where I really wanted to be. Then eventually I got a job as an assistant director of alumni affairs for a private university nearby. I asked around for connections from the presidential library where I had worked, and one of them kindly put a good word in for me, which brought my application to the top of the pile. Actually, during my interview, they offered me the job right away. I stayed in that role for three years, then I got promoted to my current job, which is the director of alumni affairs. I oversee an event planning team across the country and put on all sorts of alumni events.

My advice to someone currently looking for their first job is ... your network is what you're going to fall back on when times get tough. When the museum I worked at closed after just six months, my network at the presidential library helped keep me afloat by giving me a job, temporarily, because they knew I was searching for higher education jobs. So, meeting people and making actual friendships is what's going to keep you afloat. Those friends know what's available at their company, they know if their hiring manager is going to be looking for someone soon, and they know if their friend is leaving their role. They'll put in a good word for you. I know with networking, it often feels like you are just making connections that would one day have a benefit and a payout to you, which feels very transactional. But if you don't approach it that way, if you go into it thinking that you're just making friends, that's better. That's how my partner and I met. Our mutual friend groups bonded over different networking events. That way, when I lost the museum job after six months, it didn't feel transactional for me to ask around for help, it was very organic. That's a true network. It takes a lot of time.

Also, try things that might seem daunting or intimidating. I often found trying things I found out I didn't like doing was just as helpful as doing the things that I knew I did like to do because then I could cross those off my list. It helped me learn what my limits and boundaries were.

For your job search, there's a lot to learn. I don't think I was properly set up, in terms of how to tailor your resume and cover letter. Now that I'm a hiring manager, I really know when someone puts effort into their application. My mentor in the presidential library was the one who really helped me hone and craft my resume and cover letter. Things like starting every sentence on your resume with an action word, that it doesn't always have to be listed chronologically, that I can take out some experiences in favor of putting in relevant work or even volunteer experience. I found that these were game changers, and it really set me apart when I was applying for higher education jobs the second time around. So I don't think I took enough advantage of things like the career center when I was in college, and I wish I did. So go visit your career center, get one-on-one help with your resume, and practice interviewing. Or find people in the field and shadow them and do mock interviews with them. Sometimes I found that hiring managers were really willing to give real feedback on your application or your interview.

2.57 On the Immigrant Experience in the US: Domenico's Story

> *I thought my career was going to be music when I came here, so I was not expecting this.... It was very traumatizing, working in this job doing hard manual labor for 10 hours a day, which I had never done before.*
> Note: This interview was conducted in Spanish and translated into English by a native Spanish speaker.

I came to the US in the early 2000s the summer after college. My girlfriend at the time was in the US and we were in a long-distance relationship, so I managed to get a visa to come into the US. I spent a few days looking for a job, and my family members quickly found one for me with someone they knew who did painting. Many Latinos know someone who is looking for a painter or a landscaper or something like that.

They asked me if I had painted before, and obviously, I exaggerated a little because I needed the job. But I had painted with some family members on concrete when I was growing up. I don't know if that counts as qualifications, but that was my experience going into the job. In some sense, I was overqualified with my college degree, but I lacked experience. But I also spoke the most English out of everyone who worked on that team.

Actually, I studied music in college. So I was thinking I could find a job on a radio station, or playing music at a church. So it was a little surprising to me that I ended up as a painter. I had this dream for music, and I was told it was possible, and because it was possible, I thought it was going to happen, but that's not the way it went.

On my first day, I was just told that I'd be picked up at 6 AM. The day before, I bought some paint clothes from a thrift store. That's all there was to it. They picked me up and told me to get in the van. It was very weird. It was dark out and cold, I was poorly dressed, I didn't know anyone there, and it was very intimidating. They took me to a Naval base and gave me a putty knife – which I had never seen before – and they had me scrape the bars on the windows with it. So I did that all day long, freezing because it was winter and next to the winter. They quickly realized that I couldn't paint like they thought I could, so they just had me do easy assistant jobs carrying things for them.

I thought my career was going to be in music when I came here, so I was not expecting this. I wasn't really familiar with the immigrant experience. I was lucky that I had a visa and came from an upper-class family back home, but I still didn't have permission to work in the places I wanted to. So it was very traumatizing, working in this job doing hard manual labor for 10 hours a day, which I had never done before. It was very risky, there was no insurance, and we didn't have seatbelts or helmets or any safety equipment. But looking back, it was a good experience in that it helped me sympathize with immigrants. I'm grateful I found a company like this one that would give someone like me work. I actually wish I could have learned more while on the job. Now, I'm buying a house, and I'm not very handy.

Since then, I have done some work in catering, landscaping, and close to 10 other odd jobs. About 10 years later, I became a pastor at a small church here, and I've been doing that for the past 10 years or so. That first job didn't really have anything to do with my current job in a practical sense, since I'm not painting houses or gardening. But much of what I'm doing now is working with people, many of whom are immigrants. So my early experiences have helped me a lot with understanding some dynamics when pastoring people, and understanding firsthand some of the injustices and abuse that people lived through.

My advice to someone currently looking for their first job is ... one, keep at it even though it's tough. You can come out ahead, and there are many examples of that. Two, maybe speak up a little more. Even as I'm saying it, I know it's difficult because if you're undocumented, you have rights but it's scary. I wish I had known better. You don't need to put up with things that you shouldn't put up with. You don't need to avoid complaining about things you should complain about just because you're scared and don't want to lose your job. We're human beings also, and we should be treated with dignity and respect.

2.58 On Being a Serial Entrepreneur: Claudia's Story

I've basically created my own career. Everything was mostly in the creative field, but it also still ties back to my farm. I've been writing a weekly garden column for the newspaper for over 15 years. I have two

> books out on gardening, one of them is a New York Times bestseller, and it's all from the hands-on learning I did as a kid. My book deals came from meeting someone on a plane. I'm on my 10th book now. I started a charity and a radio show that's now in its 25th year. All my work with the charity is as a volunteer, it's my way of giving back. Oh, I still have the egg business, even now 40 years later.

I'm a serial entrepreneur. I actually started my own business at the age of eight. My entire family were immigrants, and nobody had ever gone to college. I was in second grade, and I heard about something called college and I was very interested, and my family told me that I had to find a way to pay for it because they didn't have the money. So I figured, I'll raise eggs. I grew up on a farm, so I raised chickens and sold eggs. My parents helped a little, but the business was all mine. I did all the bookwork, bought all the feed, cleaned all the coops at 4 in the morning, and once I could drive, I drove everywhere delivering all my eggs. I had 2,000 chickens at one point. I won state championships for my chickens and my eggs between the ages of 12 and 18, beating out all the others who were actual adults. Sure, sometimes it was rough. I had to do all my farm work before I went to school, then again in the evening, then homework. But for me, the most important thing was going to college, so I took meticulous records and made sure that I was saving enough money to go to college. By the time I was in high school, it was a full-time job for me, and I saved up enough money by the age of 18 to pay for my own college education. After I graduated high school, I had to make my own money for everything: food, shelter, clothes, school, and books.

I worked all through college while taking a full course load, getting a degree in history. I kept up my egg business, and I worked elsewhere in translations (I could translate fluently in Dutch), at a health food store, and with our alumni organization. Sometime during college, I met a pretty famous Hollywood TV star, and he said he needed someone who looked like me, very healthy, for a vitamin commercial. I had actually never taken a vitamin in my life, but it was my first introduction to Hollywood, and I've been part of the Hollywood union for over 40 years now. Oh, I also studied abroad in France, I was a teenage ambassador to another country abroad, and I learned to speak something like seven different languages.

Eventually, I realized that I loved to travel but didn't have money for it, so I got a job with an airline so that I could travel. That led to me becoming a travel specialist, writing tours for places all around the world. My history degree actually helped here, since I had learned the history of all these places, and I was a good researcher and good at reading. Along the way, I got into some modeling, since I had done that commercial, and I was told that I needed an agent. So I called the first agent I could find in the phone book, the most renowned talent agency in my city at the time, of course, they were probably thinking that I was some ridiculous person, so they just told me to send in headshots and a resume. I didn't actually know what that meant, so I sent in these pictures of me doing crazy things like skydiving and jumping off cliffs. Then I went in for an interview, and they liked my energy, so they set me up with a photographer, and that led over time to acting jobs (my first role, we won an Emmy). I ended up leaving the airline because I made enough money acting and modeling.

Since then, I've basically created my own career. Everything was mostly in the creative field, but it also still ties back to my farm. I've been writing a weekly garden column for the newspaper for over 15 years. I have two books out on gardening, one of them is a *New York Times* bestseller, and it's all from the hands-on learning I did as a kid. My book deals came from meeting someone on a plane. I'm on my 10th book now. I started a charity and a radio show that's now in its 25th year. All my work with the charity is as a volunteer, it's my way of giving back. Oh, I still have the egg business, even now forty years later. The only time I wasn't raising chickens was the few years when I lived in Europe. Now I'm down to about 15 hens, but I still have five customers.

My advice to someone currently looking for their first job is … whatever you want to do in life, you can find a way to do it. You just have to get the tools and the skills that you need. Write down your plan, and then go into action and actually start doing it. Get a support person and believe in yourself and all the possibilities. Never say never. When people tell you something and compliment you on a skill that you have, pay attention to that. Maybe that's an avenue that you are going to excel in and you are going to love doing. I know people always say to me, I'm working so hard. Yes, but I enjoy it.

Another thing, get to be really good at in-person interviews. The key to that is neurolinguistic programming. It's modeling. It's looking and listening to the interviewer and their body language. See what their eyes are doing, and any twitches, and where they're putting their hands. Nowadays, all these interviews are on Zoom, and I find this completely challenging. I think that people today have a harder time, because yes, you can go on LinkedIn and see what's out there, but I don't know if people can really get to know who you are.

Also, don't compromise and think, "I'm going to just take the first job I can get." Before you go out for your job, think about what you are good at. Where do you have fun? What do you really love doing? What are your skills? Do a self-analysis of things that are enjoyable to you, and also give yourself a timeline or a time schedule of where you see yourself. It's a cliché, but when you love what you do, the money does follow. When you love what you do, you'll be really good at it, and other people will notice, and they'll come knocking on your door wanting you. Even in that first job, make sure it's something that you're going to look back on and be happy that you chose a job where you could learn, grow, and move on.

Lastly, work is work. We must show up and do the hard work. Some books say that everything is supposed to be easy, but it's not. It's still hard work. But once you figure out what your passion is, the work becomes fun.

2.59 On a Lifelong Career in Hospitality: Reagan's Story

When I'm hiring, I look for someone who has been committed to something. If there's someone that changes jobs every year, I'm thinking, "Okay, I'm going to hire them. I'm going to train them. They're going to be just at the point of producing what I hired them to do, and then they're going to leave to go look for something else." I look for a little bit of longevity.... So for me, if I see someone that did a job for three years, then the next move is a promotion, and they do that for three years, to me that's someone I would hire. They're committed. They get it. If I'm not promoting them, then shame on me. That's the boss's fault.

I had just graduated high school, and I needed to make some money to save up for college. I applied for a warehouse clerk position at a large downtown hotel. Actually, a relative of mine worked there and told me about the opening. The hotel was about 30 miles away from where we lived in the suburbs, but my relative was willing to drive me to work each day. Plus, it paid more than some of the suburban jobs that I knew of. Honestly, I was just looking for anything where I could make the most amount of money possible. So I got this job pretty quickly, it was all on the same day with an interview and the job offer, and I took the job and started the very next day.

My job was to unload trucks with food. I took them off the truck, dated the boxes, checked for expiration, put them onto carts, and pushed them around the building into different restaurants, bars, and kitchens. On my first day, I went through this long orientation learning about the hotel's culture, the benefits, touring the hotel, learning bits and pieces of all the jobs in the hotel, and so forth. That part excited me because I got to meet a lot of people and see all these different functions within the hotel. I got to be in awe of the hospitality industry. I remember checking through vegetables that I had never even heard of. I didn't know what bok choy was, for example. So there was a large learning curve for me, this young kid from the suburbs, but it was super exciting.

Sure, it got repetitive after a while, and it got really hot because they didn't have air conditioning even in the summer. But I started asking questions. I would ask the managers who were ordering food supplies, how did they know how much to order? They taught me their calculations on how to estimate what percentage of rooms that were booked would order breakfast, and that predicted how many croissants to get, for example. So that kept me motivated and interested in always learning more.

Anyway, I did the job for about four months, but once I started college, because I had a good relationship with the hotel, they transferred me to another location so I could work nights and weekends during college. I studied business economics, but then when I graduated, they had me come back to that first job as a supervisor of the warehouse, basically supervising my old role. It really went full circle in just a few years. Then every couple of years, because I was also so interested in learning, I would end up getting promoted or moving to another department, all within the same company. I worked in room service, in restaurants and bars, in stewarding, and eventually after about 20 years I was the food and beverage director for a massive hotel doing tens of millions in revenue. Then I took a leap of faith and changed careers into purchasing, overseeing all purchasing for eight states, and I worked my way up there. I went through multiple restructurings, layoffs, new openings, and more. Now, I'm a senior director in purchasing, and I've just celebrated my 40th anniversary working at this company.

My advice to someone currently looking for their first job is ... be open, and don't judge the book by its cover. You have no idea what's going to happen after you start this job. You may love it or you may hate it, but you can't go in with the pre-conceived notion of, "Oh, I know everything about this." Also, don't be afraid if you don't know everything. It's okay to not know. I tell my team this all the time. You should learn something every day, and you should teach something every day.

Also, I hate to say it now, but it's not all about money. I have three boys, and two of them are in college, so they're working in the summers. My recommendation to them is to like your job. You don't have to love your job, but you have to like it. Find something you like to do, not necessarily because it pays the most. When the alarm goes off in the morning, you don't want to wake up and say, "Ugh, I don't want to go to work today." Of course, we're all going to have those days. But if you're going to spend the majority of your time doing something, you should have some sort of enjoyment in it. Yes, there's going to be days that you don't like your job, but your output at work is going to be so much better if you don't hate it.

Lastly, when I'm hiring, I look for someone who has been committed to something. If there's someone who changes jobs every year, I'm thinking, "Okay, I'm going to hire them. I'm going to train them. They're going to be just at the point of producing what I hired them to do, and then they're going to leave to go look for something else." I look for a little bit of longevity. I tell my son, about his college experience, "Most people that are doing the hiring are looking at your college as a commitment. You committed to go to college for four years, and you got a degree." They're not as concerned about what your degree was, they want to know that you can commit to something for four years and get through it. So for me, if I see someone who did a job for three years, then the next move is a promotion, and they do that for three years, to me that's someone I would hire. They're committed. They get it. If I'm not promoting them, then shame on me. That's the boss's fault. If I can't train, develop, and move people up in my own organization, then I'm not a good leader.

2.60 On a Lifelong Career in Nursing: Barbara's Story

At one point midway through college, I did a missions trip to Mexico and loved it, and I wanted to stay there to be a missionary full-time. My parents told me that was a dumb idea, but we made a deal where I would come back to do one more semester. In my mind I was ready to drop out after that semester, but I ended up sticking it out. It was definitely wisdom coming from my parents, because I think I'm doing what I'm meant to do now, plus I've been much more effective at missions work now that I have a nursing degree and experience.

I had a lot of odd jobs growing up. I did some computer work making copies of CDs early on when they just started coming out, I worked in shipping and IT and learned some programming, and while I was in college for nursing, I worked as a summer camp nurse for a while. Some background here: no one in my family worked in any sort of medical profession. However, I found out in high school that I had an aptitude for biology, so that led me to take some human anatomy classes at the community college during high school. But then, at one point midway through college, I did a missions trip to Mexico and loved it, and I wanted to stay there to be a missionary full-time. My parents told me that was a dumb idea, but we made a deal where I would come back to do one more semester. In my mind, I was ready to drop out after that semester, but I ended up sticking it out. It was definitely wisdom coming from my parents, because I think I'm doing what I'm meant to do now, plus I've been much more effective at missions work now that I have a nursing degree and experience.

Anyways, in my last year of college in the early 2000s, I had a preceptorship, which is where I got paired with a nurse on a unit and worked their shift with them. After I did that at the local hospital, I knew I wanted to work in either labor and delivery or in the emergency room (ER). I applied to work at the same hospital as my preceptorship, and although I didn't get labor and delivery, I got the emergency room job.

Funny story, even when I was working there as a student, the director told me that I could stay after graduation, and I said yes. So they had me fill out the basic application, and I actually got a denial letter saying I wasn't qualified for the job. So I called the director, and he said he'd talk to HR and not to worry about it, then I got another letter the next week and eventually a third, all of them saying I wasn't qualified for the job. Back then, I was quite soft-spoken and timid, so I was definitely freaking out a little, very confused at what was happening. It turns out that part of the disconnect was that the director was on his way out, and the new one coming in didn't know my name. This actually became an issue later on when I worked there because we had seven different directors in the four years that I was there.

I'm a bit of an adrenaline junkie. The ER definitely fed that. You really need to grow up in the ER, otherwise you'll get eaten alive by everyone. It's a place where you can't follow all the rules neatly, you need to figure out whatever you need to do to save someone's life. So when do you play by the rules, and when do you not? You also need to really have the respect of the doctors, otherwise you could lose everything. So it's a ton of learning that comes with being at the ER. And I still love ER, but I didn't love the politics. I could go on and on about health care, but I'll say this: health care is so broken, ER doesn't help it and sometimes hurts it, but there's really no way to fix it. You can't turn anyone away in the ER, so when someone comes in on an ambulance for a hangnail, you have to take them. Things like that wear you out and make you jaded over time.

I should add, I think that nurses who are between two to five years out of school are the most dangerous, because they feel like they know what they're doing when they don't. They've been out of school for a year or so, so they feel like they have the experience and the latest education, so they know better. But you don't realize until year five that you've only just touched the surface of what you need to know in the medical field. Sometime around that year, you'll mess up and be humbled and knocked off your pedestal, and you'll realize you have a lot more learning to do.

Working in the ER was great for that, by the way. That's why most ERs won't hire a new grad, because it's too dangerous with all the autonomy that's in ER, you can mess up pretty badly. It's also a disservice to the new nurse's career. Especially if you're triage, which I loved doing, that's where you have to make order out of chaos. You have all this randomness in the waiting room, and you need to do some kind of prediagnosis to know who to prioritize, who's the most important, who's dying, and so forth.

Anyways, after that first job, I started working as an agency nurse, meaning I staffed hospitals when they had a shortage. You get paid a ton more, and you try out all sorts of different hospitals. I did that for a few years, then did some work as a nurse recruiter, some other stints at various hospitals, and then 10 years working for a large healthcare organization giving medical advice over the phone. That last job was while I was raising my kids, which was perfect for me. Then I quit that job and have been working with home birth midwives since then. This is now my dream job for me. There's some stress to it because I'm on call, but the hours work for my family, I have a lot of autonomy to schedule my own prenatal appointments, and I'm able to provide medical advice to friends and family.

My advice to someone currently looking for their first job is … this is not the advice anybody wants to hear, but listen to your parents. They're actually pretty smart. You don't have to do everything they say, but take it into consideration and really evaluate it instead of just being headstrong in your own decisions. You have your whole life in front of you. You don't have to make your life decision right now. My parents made me stay in school when I wanted to leave. But looking back, it was just two more years of school. What's two years? It's not that much, and if it honors your parents and keeps peace, why not?

I think personality tests actually are really helpful in giving you a list of ideas. I never would have thought of working in health care if it wasn't for that. I didn't know anybody who worked in health care, and I didn't do well in my first pharmacology class in college. However, the personality test gave me ideas to look through and consider trying. Also, find volunteer positions and use them to try them out to see what you think. Go volunteer in a hospital, and if that energizes you, maybe you should pursue something in health care.

If your career is in nursing, here's something to consider: once you're employed by a hospital, you can probably hop between floors pretty easily. People usually recommend that you start in medical surgery. If I had done that, I probably would have quit and never returned. You can start in whichever unit you want. Sure, some units give you a better foundation, but that doesn't mean you have to start there. And don't let yourself get pigeonholed in a single unit. Try to get some broad exposure when you first start out.

Lastly, be humble and learn. Don't come out of school thinking you're all that, that you have all the latest research and the people on the floor have antiquated information. No, actually, you don't know what you're doing, because you haven't seen the way things work on the floors. Now it is true that you can inform existing nurses of new information that's out there, but you also can't waltz in and change everything. These nurses who've been there for 20 years know a whole lot of behind-the-scenes information at a hospital that you can't study in school. Learn from the wisdom of these seasoned nurses.

2.61 On Just Starting a Career and Looking for Next Steps: Molly's Story

I enjoy this job, even though it really isn't in line with what I thought I wanted to do. I'm definitely fulfilled and I get to be outside a lot. I like the people I work with. We do some community outreach, and I end up talking to residents a good amount. But also, I'm applying. I applied to a coordinator job at a conservation organization that was awesome. But I'm not in a rush to move on. I guess we'll see where I go from here.

I went to college and studied biology with a minor in conservation studies. After my sophomore year, I did an internship with a tree service company. I wasn't really interested in it, but it was the only internship I could find. I really wanted to work with global communities to help them get more involved in conservation, especially people who are highly impacted by climate change and lower-income communities. I also did some nature camp counselor work over the summers, so I was looking for jobs like that. I remember applying for nature camp jobs, a preschool teacher job at a nature-focused preschool, and a grant coordinator job for a conservation organization. But I didn't hear back from much. It was a little stressful and overwhelming, with there being so many jobs I should apply to, and trying to do that on top of finishing school. I had a part-time job which took some of the stress off, thankfully.

Near the end of the semester, our housing coordinator sent around a flyer for a job with the county government's urban forest management division. It was pretty vague, it just said to email your resume to this address. I did that, and they scheduled an interview, and I got the job about a week later. So it was kind of just happenstance that I ended up in forestry after that internship with the tree company.

My job is Urban Forester I, which is a 1,560 position meaning you work 1,560 hours in a calendar year. I started in a co-op position working two days a week, then after a few months, I moved to full time. My job is pretty much exclusively watering trees around the county, mostly at schools and sometimes right off the roadway. I started part time because there were only so many trees to water. It was long, hot work, just me by myself driving this big truck with a water tank around, then standing there while the water drained on each tree. I liked being outside and being with trees and the routine, but it was also pretty boring. It got better when I went full time and started helping plant trees. I also started helping out with other branches in our division, such as forest pest management, which meant checking traps around the county for invasive species and doing pesticide applications. The place was very laid back. I basically just asked for more work and got it. But because it was laid back, sometimes the communication wasn't great. For example, even when I started, I could've worked more than two days a week, but they never told me until I asked.

I enjoy this job, even though it really isn't in line with what I thought I wanted to do. I'm definitely fulfilled and I get to be outside a lot. I like the people I work with. We do some community outreach, and I end up talking to residents a good amount. But also, I'm applying. I applied for a coordinator job at a conservation organization that was awesome. But I'm not in a rush to move on. I guess we'll see where I go from here.

My advice to someone currently looking for their first job is ... since I'm in a job that I didn't think was what I'd want to do but I actually love it, I'd say don't be too stressed about finding the perfect job right away. Apply to whatever sounds potentially interesting, and then just try it out. You never know if it'll end up being something you love. And if not, then that's just one more thing that you learn that you don't love. And often, a position could be like a stepping stone to something you love. Like for me, once you're in the county, it's a lot easier to move around within the county.

2.62 On Taking the First Step: Melinda's Story

I was just taking any job in my field [of health care] that would have me. Most places don't hire a new graduate for nursing, because there's a ton of training that needs to happen.... It didn't feel like a career when I started. Now, it looks a lot like a progression in a career, but not at the time. And that's ok, your first job doesn't have to be your career.

I come from an immigrant family, and where we came from, there were a lot of nursing schools. My mom started there. So the idea of nursing was passed down to me from my family. It was a bit of pressure, but it was about making sure that we had a secure job. In fact, I had a patient later on who recognized my mom's name from back in the country where she grew up.

I graduated college in May, I passed my board exams for my certification, and I got a job that August as a vaccinator for a city hospital clinic. I enjoyed my summer, working some part-time jobs and having fun with my college friends. But then when I passed my board exams, I ran out of money and came home, and I took the first available job. I applied to something like 20 different nursing jobs. This job was desperate for anyone with two fingers who could hold a syringe, so I got the job pretty quickly. It's not too hard to find a job in this area, especially when you're new and willing to do literally anything, including stabbing people with a needle 50 times a day. Again, I was just taking any job in my field that would have me. Most places don't hire a new graduate for nursing, because there's a ton of training that needs to happen. I remember interviewing at one hospital, which was actually my first choice, but it was like my first ever professional interview. I thought it went ok, but I didn't get the job, and I found out through one of those automated emails. So that sucked, and I was nervous about my other interviews after that, it was a blow to my confidence. But eventually, I got the vaccinator job at a different hospital.

I was pretty underqualified for the job at the end of the day. I was good at holding needles, but it got scary once it was with an actual person. I was lucky because they actually put me through this residency program where I was in the classroom for a month. We got a lot of practice with the things we needed to do. Also, customer service was important, so we learned how to handle patients.

I stayed in that job for 11 years and also completed my master's degree. I started with pediatrics, then crossed over to adults. I did some charge nurse work, which meant making sure patient flow worked smoothly when one patient left and another came in. I also was a resource nurse, helping others with higher acuity problems. Then eventually I left that hospital for a different hospital, where I'm a home care clinical analyst. I'm not a nurse right now, but I'm still using those skills as the only one on my team with clinical experience. Yeah, it feels like a career change, but it's never too late to change.

My advice to someone currently looking for their first job is ... send a lot of applications, even to places that aren't necessarily exactly what you're looking for. Like me, I was looking for nursing jobs, but I should've leaned into the fact that I did a lot of tutoring and babysitting, which is kind of like caregiving. Find something that's not exactly the same field, but similar, and that can make you stand out.

Going to your first job is like going to a new school. That's what it felt like for me. This was just going to be another thing that I had to do, and I'll see where I go from here. It didn't feel like a career when I started. Now, it looks a lot like a progression in a career, but not at the time. And that's ok, your first job doesn't have to be your career. Even though mine turned out to be, I distinctly remember not wanting it to be. So give the first job a chance, because I do know people who leave their first job very fast. They immediately think there's nothing to gain from it. But I didn't realize that I was getting a lot in those first couple of years. Even just the idea that I liked it. So give your first job a chance, as long as it's not mentally breaking you down.

CHAPTER III

Making Meaning of Career Narratives

> *Human life lives in story. Everyone has a story to tell and most of us want desperately to tell it. Story surrounds us as we tell our own stories, listen to those of other people, and construct them...*
> (Hartung, 2012, p. 1)

3.1 Introduction and Context

Hartung's (2012) thoughts on the power of life stories are one example of how career development scholars and practitioners rely on narratives to guide individuals' discernment of self and career goals. Hartung asserted that by "turning to narrative models and methods, career counselors aim to deliver career interventions that better account for the dynamic, diverse, and uniquely patterned nature of human life within a rearranged structure of work" (p. 1). Thus, we offer this book as a contribution to this conversation about narrative and the richness human stories of lived experience offer for meaningful career guidance. Part II of this volume shared the narratives of 62 unique participants' perspectives on their career paths from first jobs to their current professional and/or educational worlds. From these stories, myriad themes emerged that inform practical considerations for career development work. The most salient of these themes are noted in Table 3.1.

In this chapter, we will tease apart each of the seven themes highlighted in Table 3.1., discussing them briefly in the context of existing literature noted in Part I. In service to practicality, for each theme, we pose reflection questions for both career seekers and career development professionals to ask of themselves – and others – to ground the search and support in self-awareness. Additionally, we offer resources for further learning for each theme in the form of books, articles, web tools, and other media. Here, we note that these lists of resources are not exhaustive; they represent aspects of the authors' own toolkits in addition to recommendations offered by colleagues and subject matter experts.

Table 3.1 *Core career themes emerging from participant narratives*

Theme	Selected participant quotes
The first job does not have to be the forever job. It is not permanent.	"...the first job that you get doesn't have to be the end. Just because it's the job that you have, doesn't mean that you need to stay there for the rest of your life." – Sophie "I definitely didn't go into my first job thinking that it was what my first choice would have been. I was very happy about the job, but I was bummed that I wasn't starting grad school. But now, looking back on it, that experience that I had was really valuable to me." – Arlene
Engage personal connections and networks in career development.	"Somebody will call somebody. Every job I've gotten was because somebody made a phone call saying, 'Hey, you've got to hire this guy'." – Adnan "Also, connect with as many people as possible. Ask them where they work, so you can have a connection with them. In the future if you know somebody who knows somebody, it's easier to get into that company and to get a reference. As a hiring manager, getting an email that has someone's resume as an attachment, when you already have so many others in the system, makes a huge difference." – David
Identity (and intersections of identity) play a role in the career journey.	"I don't think the management at my first job recognized my full potential. I think I could've done well with more training and more responsibilities, but sadly I think there was some sexism where I was specifically not given opportunities because of my gender." – Macie "There's also all the complexities and concerns around race as well. I was just worried that anything that I didn't do well will be a negative, not just for me, but for everybody who looks like me. And so, it was just this pressure to really succeed." – Caleb
Take risks; value agility and the capacity to pivot as career situations and opportunities evolve.	"...but I realized that this was a rare opportunity that only comes across once or twice in a lifetime, such a special opportunity that could really lead to major success, even though it is a risky bet." – Taylor "We didn't build this thing called life, because if we did, we would make rounded corners on

Table 3.1 (*cont.*)

Theme	Selected participant quotes
	everything. But instead, life is full of sharp edges. You're going to get cut, hurt, bloodied, and bruised physically and emotionally. We didn't make life, but we adapt to it." – Tristan
Take time to explore the full landscape of what interests you and what speaks to your "why."	"Just try to get as many different experiences as possible. Don't pigeonhole yourself into one specific technique, computer science language, hardware platform, etc. Be willing to jump between different languages and different platforms. Just always be open to new opportunities." – Warren
	"This summer internship was probably the best experience I had in college. While I had the opportunity to see a couple of different companies and help the team with whatever they needed me to do, I wasn't working a busy season, so I had time to explore and learn different things. And they organized the internship well with our cohort, so we would do class activities together and have fun. It was amazing to get to see the inside workings of a business, to actually sit in their offices and see behind the scenes. It's like going behind the scenes of a movie." – Katie
Spend time with self-understanding and building self-efficacy. Believe that you have value.	"The only piece of advice I can give others is to not underestimate yourself. I did it back then. I remember my first team meeting with 10 to 12 others when I was introducing myself, and I said, 'I'm just a trainee.' My manager called me out on that and said, 'You are not just a trainee. You are a trainee who is going to bring a whole other mindset to our team, which we desperately need. You are going to be pipelined into being a future leader for us.'" – Kyla
	"I decided to go back to school to become a teacher, and I've been a high school teacher ever since. Even though that first job was difficult and so different than what I wanted to do or ended up doing, it at least taught me that I had to believe in my work and that I had to believe in the value I was adding to helping people." – Sara

Table 3.1 (cont.)

Theme	Selected participant quotes
Hone your capacity for resilience, perseverance, and persistence with respect to career undertakings.	"The bottom line is that you just got to be persistent. Failure is an ordinary and expected outcome in any endeavor. You can't sit there and be broken-hearted every time that somebody says, 'You suck, and you're never going to get to where you are.' You have to become resilient." – Nathan "[The job search] is super competitive. There're so many little things that matter. So, you have to persist, but you also have to overprepare. Make sure your resume is flawless, make sure your application is flawless." – Daniel

3.2 Core Themes and Resources for Practice

3.2.1 Theme 1: The First Job Does Not Have to Be the Forever Job

Many participants underscored that first jobs are just that – "firsts" – and that these beginnings do not represent the full potential or arc of a life but rather can open doors to other paths on the career journey. This observation echoes one of the main tenets of Super's (1990) Life-Span Life-Space Theory, which highlighted the point that career development is a process that evolves over a lifetime. This focus on learning was also embedded in Parsons' (1909) sentiments about the importance of building a strong understanding of self in career pursuits – and this understanding must start somewhere, even if that place is less than ideal. In fact, Dawis and Lofquist's (1984) Theory of Work Adjustment allows for this disruption to first job permanency by giving language to how individuals change work environments to align with who they are. Given the importance of normalizing the notion that career is a marathon and not a sprint, and that the first job may not be the "forever job," we encourage career counselors to shape conversations with clients with a life-span life space model in mind that accounts for an individual's life in an ecological context. As support, in Table 3.2, we offer resources for both career seekers and career guidance professionals with respect to contextualizing the first job. We pose self-audit prompts for both groups to spark reflective practice, and, in Table 3.3, we provide resources for navigating first job expectations and adjustments.

Core Themes and Resources for Practice   179

Table 3.2 *Self-audit prompts: the first job*

For career seekers	For career development professionals
• Though this job is not what I hoped for, what are three to five skills that I can develop here that will help me reach my career goals and/or prepare me for my eventual "dream" job? • What am I learning about myself in this job – my work values and/or my life values – that fit with who I want to be or that point me to areas in which I need to evolve? • What do I want my personal and professional brand to look like, and how can I leverage this first job to help me build my brand?	• How can I help my clients understand and value that career planning is a lifelong process, involves elements of compromise, and goes well beyond the first job? • How can I help my clients develop a plan for their first job that enables growth and development regardless of the circumstances? • How can I work with my clients to revisit the journey that led to this first job and reflect on lessons learned that might better support future career planning and decision-making?

Table 3.3 *Resources for navigating first job expectations and adjustments*

Resource type	Resource description
Books and articles	• *Designing Your Work Life: How to Thrive and Change and Find Happiness at Work* (Burnett & Evans, 2020) • *The Good Enough Job: Reclaiming Life from Work* (Stolzoff, 2023) • *First Jobs: True Tales of Bad Bosses, Quirky Coworkers, Big Breaks, and Small Paychecks* (Watts, 2015) • *What Color Is Your Parachute?* (Bolles, 2025) • "Education-Job Fit and Work-Related Learning of Recent Graduates: Head Start or Filling a Gap?" (Grosemans et al., 2021)
Websites and media	• CareerOneStop – GetMyFuture (sponsored by US Department of Labor). Employment and career resource site for young adults aged 14–24, www.careeronestop.org/GetMyFuture • O*NET OnLine (sponsored by US Department of Labor). Tool for career exploration and job analysis, www.onetonline.org/

3.2.2 Theme 2: Engage Personal Connections and Networks in Career Development

A considerable number of narratives in Part II of this volume speak to the importance of developing and maintaining personal connections and networks as part of the career planning and development process. For both new professionals and more seasoned folks, building and nurturing professional networks can be challenging. As we shared in Part I of this book, networks are part of social and cultural capital (Garriott, 2020) frameworks that vary significantly for individuals still developing "know how" about the web of work and how to build bridges between its various nodes. The capacity to build networks may also be reliant on where people are in their psychosocial development and their maturity in fostering relationships. This notion of relationship-building as a developmental task is central to Chickering (1969) and Chickering and Reisser's (1993) Seven Vectors Theory of college student development (see also Oxendine & Taub, 2023; Patton et al., 2016). Thus, we begin to wonder how career seekers and their helping professionals can engage in meaningful and strategic discussions about the importance of networks and the pathways for building them. Career development professionals could work to demystify the intimidating nature of "networking" and help clients focus on fostering meaningful relationships. In Table 3.4, we offer some ideas for engaging in helpful career discussions around networking and provide a broader set of resources in Table 3.5.

Table 3.4 *Self-audit prompts: networking*

For career seekers	For career development professionals
• What are some of the fears and worries that I have about "networks" and "connections" with respect to how I prefer to navigate the world and my existing relationships? • Who are three people in my current network (e.g., teachers, supervisors, friends, family, co-workers) who can help me think about my important career decisions? What stops me from reaching out to them right now? • Are there places that I need to grow with respect to how I build and maintain genuine relationships with people in my life? What do some of these places look like?	• How can I work with clients to help them understand the value of networking and how it applies to myriad life scenarios from professional to personal and educational? • In what ways can I support clients with varying social and cultural capital identify their strengths in relationship-building as the first step toward human-centered bonds that create a personal and professional network? • What are some ways in which I can support clients in creating a culture of network reciprocity in which they are clear on the value they bring to the table for others?

Table 3.5 *Resources for building meaningful professional networks and connections*

Resource type	Resource description
Books and articles	• *Never Eat Alone, Expanded and Updated: And Other Secrets to Success, One Relationship at a Time* (Ferrazzi & Raz, 2005) • *Friend of a Friend....:Understanding the Hidden Networks That Can Transform Your Life and Your Career* (Burkus, 2018) • *Find Your People: Building Deep Community in a Lonely World* (Allen, 2023)
Websites and media	• CareerOneStop – Networking (sponsored by US Department of Labor), www.careeronestop.org/JobSearch/Network • CareerOneStop – Professional Association Finder (sponsored by US Department of Labor). Professional association finder tool, www.careeronestop.org/Toolkit/Training/find-professional-associations.aspx • HBR IdeaCast Podcast: Stop Networking & Start Connecting, https://hbr.org/podcast/2021/07/stop-networking-start-connecting • WorkLife with Adam Grant Podcast: Brené Brown on What Vulnerability Isn't, https://shorturl.at/8cLdC

3.2.3 Theme 3: Identity and Intersections of Identity Play a Role in the Career Journey

A common thread that wove its way through many of the participants' narratives speaks to the role of identity and identity intersections in the world of work and in career decision-making. Participants pointed to marginalization due to gender identity, challenges given disabilities, pressure and fear associated with immigrant origins, difficulties holding dual roles as parents and employees, as well as finding agency in career planning when they shared in a collectivist culture with family urging a different career agenda. The participants' stories gave voice to some of the theoretical work shared in Part I – particularly identity-conscious frameworks such as the Psychology of Working Theory (Duffy et al., 2016). Duffy and colleagues embedded career development work in an understanding of systems and structures operating in individuals' ecology that influenced opportunity and decision-making. Research of scholars such as Souto and Sotkasiira (2022) aligned with this work, pushing career counselors toward a critical consciousness and a dismantling of identity and social "normatives" supporting dominant ideologies around career (see also Irving, 2020). We call on career development professionals to interrogate the social biases and assumptions that have silenced and othered, and to serve with a keen understanding of systemic influences on historically marginalized peoples. To support this charge, we share reflection question prompts in Table 3.6 and additional resources in Table 3.7.

Table 3.6 *Self-audit prompts: identity*

For career seekers	For career development professionals
• What do I know about my own identities (e.g., race, ethnicity, gender) and how have past experiences informed how I think about myself now in this current context? • What messages have I received and internalized about my identit(ies) from others and how might these messages contextualize how I think about my career decision-making and planning? • What does living an authentic life that speaks to the whole of me in personal and professional contexts look like? What are my fears and hopes as I envision this life?	• How do my own identities, biases, assumptions, and lived experiences affect the work that I do as a career development professional? How can I use this awareness to foster and model more inclusive practice? • In what ways can I grow my understanding of how individuals' identities and intersections of those identities within social systems affect my clients' career planning journey? • In what ways can I prepare to have identity-conscious conversations that do not further marginalize or other my clients but uplift and empower their capacities?

Table 3.7 *Resources for engaging in identity-conscious career conversation*

Resource type	Resource description
Books and articles	• *Playing Big: Practical Wisdom for Women Who Want to Speak Up, Create, and Lead* (Mohr, 2015) • *Lead from the Outside: How to Build Your Future and Make Real Change* (Abrams, 2019) • *Biased: Uncovering the Hidden Prejudice That Shapes What We See, Think, and Do* (Eberhardt, 2019) • *Closing the Opportunity Gap* (Pendakur, 2016)
Websites and media	• Human Rights Campaign Corporate Equality Index, www.hrc.org/resources/workplace • Higher Ed Immigration Portal: Career Counseling Support for Undocumented Students, https://shorturl.at/dmooR • Student Affairs Now Podcast: Identity-Conscious Supervision, https://studentaffairsnow.com/identity-conscious-supervision-2/ • Women Amplified Podcast with Celeste Headlee – Success, Leadership, & Authenticity: A Conversation with Stacey Abrams, https://shorturl.at/9bIrk

3.2.4 Theme 4: Do Not Be Afraid to Take Risks. Do Value Agility and the Capacity to Pivot

Advice on being bold and agile with respect to career risk-taking and pivoting was offered consistently by participants at the conclusion of their narratives. Risks included navigating and separating from familial expectations, leaping into the external job market after years of working inside the home as a parent and partner, and embracing work totally incongruent with training and experience in the hopes of making a life in a new country. Given that many of the narratives captured in Part II of this volume were shared during the COVID-19 pandemic, agility and comfort with pivoting was forced on myriad participants who had to unlearn and/or relearn elements of the world of work. These stories of change and chance help us recall Pryor and Bright's (2003, 2014) Chaos Theory of Careers from Part I, which was grounded in the understanding that career is enmeshed in micro and macro systems as well as the predictable and unpredictable events that influence career decision-making. Understanding the effects of this ever-changing career arena from a "chaos" perspective is critical to equipping career development professionals with skills to support clients as they navigate the unforeseen or decide to leap into the unknown. Yet, any counsel on risk-taking and agility should be informed by each client's unique story, comfort with risk-taking, and capacity to be free agents and architects of their own career trajectories. Irving (2020) underscored the importance of guarding against Westernized assumptions, noting that "the interests of family and community may supersede individual desires," (p. 186) and "expectations and obligations may conflict with dominant norms" (p. 186). In Table 3.8, we share reflection prompts for both career seekers and career development professionals aimed at unpacking risk. Additional resources to support the risk-taking conversation can be found in Table 3.9.

3.2.5 Theme 5: Explore Your Interests and Find Your "Why"

Participants' stories were rich with encouragement to readers of this volume to explore interests and passions as much as feasible. Some of the narratives extended this exploration into clarifying the very meaning of success and "career." These narratives echoed McMahon and Arthur's (2018) observation about the fraught nature of "career" with respect to how it is understood, valued, and enacted around the world. Thus, within and outside of US and Western-centric contexts, career counselors should

Table 3.8 *Self-audit prompts: risk-taking*

For career seekers	For career development professionals
• Where do I want this pivot or risk-taking to place me in the arc of my career? What goals and objectives do I have for myself? What are some of the nonnegotiables? • How can I create a network of trusted allies (e.g., career counselors, peers, family, teachers) to offer me feedback and advice? • In what ways can I pursue pivot-preparation activities in parallel with my current work or education so that I can be agile and prepared for a pivot (e.g., freelance projects, training, side jobs, volunteering)?	• In what ways can risk-taking look differently for clients in the context of lived experiences, identities, and privileging/oppressive systems? • In what ways can I reflect on the meaning of agency in each client's context? • How can I work with clients to nurture career agility and comfort with pivots? What are three to five key skills that each of my clients should grow regardless of goal or industry? • In what ways can I help clients think about careers as a tree with many branches rather than a straight line so that risk-taking, agile movements, and pivots are normalized?

Table 3.9 *Resources for navigating career risk-taking, career agility, and pivots*

Resource type	Resource description
Books and articles	• *The Pivot Year* (Wiest, 2023) • *Daring Greatly: How the Courage to Be Vulnerable Transforms the Way We Live, Love, Parent, and Lead* (Brown, 2015) • *Out of the Maze: An A-Mazing Way to Get Unstuck* (Johnson, 2018) • *Activate Your Agile Career: How Responding to Change Will Inspire Your Life's Work* (Konstant, 2018) • "Understanding Contemporary Career Success: A Critical Review" (Seibert et al., 2024)
Websites and media	• Stanford University School of Business: Think Fast, Talk Smart Podcast, www.gsb.stanford.edu/business-podcasts/think-fast-talk-smart-podcast • Lose Yourself: The Secret to Finding Flow and Being Fully Present, www.gsb.stanford.edu/insights/lose-yourself-secret-finding-flow-being-fully-present • Fast Company: The New Way We Work Podcast, https://podcasts.apple.com/us/podcast/the-new-way-we-work/id1393035987 • Fast Company: Adapting to Change, https://shorturl.at/186ig • A Bit of Optimism Podcast with Simon Sinek: Preparing for Change with Cassandra Worthy, https://shorturl.at/byWoe • A Bit of Optimism Podcast with Simon Sinek: Taking Comfortable Risks with Scott Galloway, https://shorturl.at/5sXiX

seek to understand what success and career looks like for each client by engaging with clients in meaningful exploration of interests and vocational purpose. Brown's (1995, 2002, 2016) Values-Based Career Theory offers scaffolding in this work as individual's values (e.g., cultural, work) are foregrounded in career choices and experiences *in tandem* with personal demographics and systemic norms. For example, while twenty-first-century notions of work highlight the protean career (Hall & Mirvis, 1995), the types of personal agency and self-directness underscored in protean pursuits may be incongruent with each client's journey. Further, how we typically think about "exploration" – particularly in higher education environments (e.g., internships, practica) – may not be possible for every student given time, resources, and personal obligations. Exploration is centered in the self-audit prompts we provide in Table 3.10 for career seekers and career development professionals. Table 3.11 highlights tangible resources around exploration for both groups.

3.2.6 Theme 6: Build Self-Efficacy and Believe in Your Value

While "self-efficacy" as an official term was not often articulated by participants in their narratives, its meaning and spirit flowed across many stories. Participants affirming the belief in themselves that they could "do" and achieve was a lesson learned through myriad avenues, to include

Table 3.10 *Self-audit prompts: exploration and finding your "why"*

For career seekers	For career development professionals
• What does "success" look like for me – how do I define it? What does it feel like and include? In what ways might my definition differ from what others want for me? • What do I care about and why? As I reflect on the arc of my career journey, how does my "why" connect to long-term purpose? • What are two or three areas of career interest for me? In what ways can my network of family, friends, teachers, and other allies help connect me to spaces to test these interests?	• What are some ways in which I can help clients reflect on their career "why" and then help them explore opportunities that connect that why to practice outcomes? • How can I serve clients who have limited time/resources for exploration given family and work contexts? In what ways can I help them to leverage current experiences to assess their career planning interests? • In what ways can I engage clients in discussions about their definitions of success that allow for breadth and honor differences?

Table 3.11 *Resources for navigating career exploration and finding your "why"*

Resource type	Resource description
Books and articles	• *You Owe You: Ignite Your Power, Your Purpose, and Your Why* (Thomas, 2024) • *Ten Feet Tall: Step into Your Truth and Change Your Freaking World* (Farbstein, 2018) • *Start with Why: The Inspiring Million-Copy Bestseller That Will Help You Find Your Purpose* (Sinek, 2011) • "Research on Work as a Calling ... and How to Make It Matter" (Thompson & Bunderson, 2019)
Websites and media	• O*NET Interest Profiler (sponsored by US Department of Labor). Suite of self-assessment career exploration tools, www.onetcenter.org/IP.html • CareerOneStop – Explore Careers (sponsored by US Department of Labor), www.careeronestop.org/ExploreCareers • Go Government Federal Internship Finder (Partnership for Public Service), https://gogovernment.org/federal-internship-finder/ • Dare to Lead Podcast with Brené Brown: Brené with Adam Grant & Simon Sinek on What's Happening at Work, Part 1 of 2, https://brenebrown.com/podcast/whats-happening-at-work-part-1-of-2

personal hardship, the guidance of good mentors, and experimentation. The through line in many narratives reflected elements of Lent and colleagues' (1994) Social Cognitive Career Theory, which – scaffolded by Bandura's (1977) conceptualization of self-efficacy – maintained that when individuals believe they possess (or can possess) a specific skill set (i.e., self-efficacy) and believe that fulfillment will come from using those skills (i.e., outcome expectations), they will foster a preference for certain activities and shift toward a career in an aligned field (i.e., personal goals) (Yates, 2020). While some participants were still searching for that alignment, many reflected on the roads taken and the connections of those paths to self-efficacy. In some of the narratives, we can feel the "lightbulb" moment happening right there in the interview. These narratives offer an example of the power of storytelling as a means through which career seekers can make meaning of their career paths and put language to their journey. Different from vocational assessments and choice-making, stories such as those shared in Part II enable folks to explore the full arc of what career construction might look *and feel* like – a concept supported by

Core Themes and Resources for Practice 187

Table 3.12 *Self-audit prompts: self-efficacy*

For career seekers	For career development professionals
• In what ways are negative thoughts about my own skills, abilities, and talents influencing my sense of self-efficacy and self-esteem (i.e., sense of worth)? • What tools can I use to combat the negative thoughts, especially in times when the career journey does not go my way, and I start to question my competence and capacity? • What kinds of support do I need from trusted others in my life to build more self-efficacy? How can I build these support networks with the folks who I value and who value me?	• In what ways can I help my clients identify their key strengths and how those strengths might be valuable to any future employer, supervisor, or stakeholder? • How can I support my client in minimizing the negative self-talk that keeps them from being the absolute best versions of themselves? What additional counseling resources might help? • In what ways can I provide clients with opportunities to see others who share their lived experiences model belief in self and mastery of career processes? How can I explore discussions about imposter syndrome?

Savickas' (2005) Career Construction Theory. Thus, with this learning in mind, career development professionals must consider ways (e.g., thinking through self-audit prompts in Table 3.12, engaging resources in Table 3.13) in which they can equip themselves and their clients to be mindful of the impact of story in teasing out the texture of self-efficacy for each client in service to current and future selves.

3.2.7 Theme 7: Hone Your Capacity for Resilience, Perseverance, and Persistence

Discussions of resilience, perseverance, or persistence would be incomplete without references to "grit" – a concept reintroduced into discussions of achievement by Duckworth's (2016) volume in which she describes grit as a driver of success comprised of a blend of passion and long-term persistence. While a deeper engagement with grit literature is outside the scope of this volume, we note it here both as an acknowledgement of its impact and appeal in larger circles *and* a caution that grit as a bootstrap concept and aspirational attribute can be problematic and contrary to much of the important discussions on the role of systems shaping, influencing, and – at times – suppressing individuals' educational and career paths (see Denby,

Table 3.13 *Resources for fostering self-efficacy*

Resource type	Resource description
Books and articles	• *Hidden Potential: The Science of Achieving Greater Things* (Grant, 2023) • *Social Cognitive Theory: An Agentic Perspective on Human Nature* (Bandura & Cervone, 2023) • *The Mountain Is You: Transforming Self-Sabotage into Self-Mastery* (Wiest, 2020) • "Effectiveness of Informational Interviewing for Facilitating Networking Self-Efficacy in University Students" (Kanar, 2023) • "Linking Protean Career Orientation with Career Optimism: Career Adaptability and Career Decision Self-Efficacy as Mediators" (Chui et al., 2022) • "Protean Careers at Work: Self-Direction and Values Orientation in Psychological Success" (Hall et al., 2018)
Websites and media	• TED Talk: How to Build Your Confidence – and Spark It in Others: Brittany Packnett Cunningham, https://ed.ted.com/lessons/H3Nrqfok • The Job Hunting Podcast with Renata Bernarde: Why You Should Stop Caring What Other People Think, https://shorturl.at/oFcvp

2016). While none of the participants referenced grit as a term, many spoke to resilience, perseverance, and persistence – in both proud recountings of their own actions or regrets not wished repeated. The advice to "never give up" is worthy and important, but it must be regarded in the context of everyone's sphere of influence and agency as well as individual definitions of success. Career counselors must embrace their roles as information-gatherers and story-keepers who support clients in unpacking the meaning of resilience, perseverance, and persistence in their own lives and ecologies – and this may be particularly true in how we think about work and its relationship to higher education. In Part I, we shared Eddy's (2023) assertion that a singular focus on a particular type of education or a particular type of career privileges paths (and persistence) in certain directions. Thus, we encourage career development professionals to instead foster the "capacity to aspire" (Mann et al., 2020), which meets clients where they are and honors the types of achievements that matter the most. In Table 3.14, we offer prompts to shape some of this work and, in Table 3.15, share potentially helpful texts and web material.

Table 3.14 *Self-audit prompts: resilience, perseverance, and persistence*

For career seekers	For career development professionals
• What do I perceive as "failure" in my career planning and decision-making journey? How can I reframe failure to be about learning? • What does perseverance mean to me and why does it matter? How has perseverance looked like for me in the past? What lessons can I take from those moments? • What does resilience look like in my life? How do I become resilient in a manner that is consistent with who I am and how I want to live life as my authentic self?	• In what ways can I help my clients identify their motivations to persist and persevere? How can I keep identity and lived experiences as the center of this discussion for clients? • How can I support my clients in teasing apart notions of perseverance to distinguish between healthy resilience and self-directedness and persistence which may jeopardize well-being? • In what ways can I help my clients value lifelong learning as a principal component of the career development journey? How do I incorporate lifelong learning into my work?

Table 3.15 *Resources for fostering resilience, perseverance, and persistence*

Resource type	Resource description
Books and articles	• *Atomic Habits: An Easy & Proven Way to Build Good Habits & Break Bad One* (Clear, 2018) • *The Gifts of Imperfection: Let Go of Who You Think You're Supposed to Be and Embrace Who You Are* (Brown, 2010) • "Toward Trauma-Informed Career Counseling" (Powers & Duys, 2020) • "University Students' Future Time Perspective and Career Adaptability: The Mediating Role of Grit" (Diaconu-Gherasim et al., 2024)
Websites and media	• TED Talk: Success, Failure and the Drive to Keep Creating – Elizabeth Gilbert, https://shorturl.at/jBbAb • The Resilience Institute Podcast, https://resiliencei.com/podcast • The Job Hunting Podcast with Renata Bernarde: Starting a New Career Over 40 – Dr. Marianne Roux, https://shorturl.at/JvFnA

3.3 Summary and Conclusion

As we close this Part III – and the text writ-large – we recall Hartung's (2012) reflections on the importance of stories and narrative to career development work that is holistic and acutely conscious of the varied lived experiences of job and career seekers. In this book, we attempted to create a bridge from the theoretical underpinnings of career development to the narratives of 62 unique individuals, and, finally, to the realistic application and/or translation of theory in the context of those narratives. As we noted in the Introduction to this text, our hope is that this work and the invaluable stories shared here serve as a reminder that there is no singular route to the "right job" or to the "right kind of success" or to the "perfect career," and that, at times, there is no clear route at all. And, in the not knowing, we experiment together and forge the way.

APPENDIX A

Methodology

The interviews collected in Part II of this book followed a set of research protocols outlined in detail in this appendix. First, we obtained institutional review board approval under category #7 for research employing interview and oral history methodologies. Participants signed an informed consent document at the start of every interview detailing the process and consenting to have their interview audio recorded.

Participants

Participants were recruited using snowball sampling from the lead authors' personal and professional networks. The inclusion criteria were as follows: (a) 18 years of age or order, and (b) hired for their first full-time job, defined as regular (not contract) employment, hourly or salaried, for 32 or more hours per week for a nonfamily employer. Efforts were made to recruit a range of participants based on their employment industries (both in their first job and their current job) and their self-reported demographic details. Participants were aware that their participation was completely voluntary and could exit the interview at any time. No reward or compensation was provided for participation. Due to our snowball sampling method, we do not make a claim that our sample is representative of the population; rather, we hope that our sample provides examples of people's career journeys with which a wide range of readers can relate.

Study Procedures

After signing the informed consent form, participants were asked a series of questions in a 30- to 60-minute audio-recorded interview (almost all interviews were conducted on Zoom). The primary authors of this book conducted most of the interviews. We thank Lauren Campbell, John Aitken, Renee McCauley, and Stephanie Atkins for assisting and conducting interviews as well. Interviewers were guided by a standard set of questions, which are listed here. However, interviewers were encouraged to engage in natural conversation with the participants, depending on the stories that the participants wished to share.

1. How old were you when you got your first job?
2. How long had you been searching before you got your first job?
   a. What did your search look like? Tools? Resources? Feelings?
3. What were your qualifications (education and experience) prior to receiving your first job? Did you feel like you were over- or underqualified for the roles you were pursuing?
4. What were some of the methods you used in applying for your first job? Describe in detail the various methods you used and the amount of effort you put into each one. Describe which ones worked and which ones didn't.
   a. Did specific folks help? School counselor? Family? Friends?
   b. What were some jobs you applied for that you didn't get, if any?
   c. How did that make you feel?
   d. How did you make sense of your feelings?
5. Ultimately, how did you get your first job? What application method did you use? Describe in detail your process of getting your first job, including what interviews you had to go through, any assessments used, etc.
6. What was the job title of your first job? Who was the employer?
7. Tell me about how you felt walking into your job on the first day.
8. Describe your first job in detail. What was it like? Was it good or bad, and why? What were some of the strengths and weaknesses?
   a. What kind of people did you meet?
   b. Did you have any regrets?
9. What advice would you give to individuals currently seeking their first job?
   a. What do you wish you would have known?

If the individual had moved on from their first job to another role, we explored the following:

10. What is your current job title and employer?
11. How long has it been since you got your first job?
12. How many promotions have you received since you got your first job? How many job changes?

13. Please describe, in general, your path from your first job to your current job. Please focus especially on what skills or experiences, if any, from your first job that were particularly helpful in your future success.
14. Looking back, what advice would you give to individuals currently starting their first job?

After the interview was completed, the author team used either the Otter.ai or Transcription Panda service to transcribe the audio interview into a raw text transcript. The author team then read the transcript carefully to remove all personal identifiers (e.g., names, specific locations, specific years) and, where necessary, replace them with proxies and/or pseudonyms. Each deidentified transcript was then sent back to the participant for a final review and member-check. Each transcript was carefully reviewed and revised into paragraph form. The final interviews that appear in this book have been modified and edited for clarity and conciseness. Where possible, we retained the participant's original voice, language, and tone while facilitating a smoother delivery of the primary storyline. Participants were also invited to complete a brief, anonymous postinterview survey that asked basic demographic questions (see Appendix B).

APPENDIX B

Participant Demographics

Of the 62 interviewees, 52 participants completed the optional follow-up survey to provide their demographic information. For transparency, we offer the details in Table B1.

Table B1 *Participants' self-reported identity and demographic details*

Self-reported item	No.
Gender	
Man	30
Woman	22
Nonbinary	0
No response	10
Race/ethnicity	
African American or Black	6
American Indian, Alaskan Native, Indigenous, or First Nations	0
Asian or Asian American	8
Arab or Middle Eastern	3
Hispanic or Latino/a	2
Multi- or biracial	0
Native Hawaiian or Pacific Islander	0
White, Caucasian, or European American	32
No response	10
Highest education level (at the time of the first job)	
High school/general educational development (GED)	11
Bachelor's	25
Master's	10
Doctorate	6
No response	10
Income (at the time of the first job)	
Lower income	18
Middle income	15
Upper income	3
No response	26

Note: Mean age for participants = 40 years with standard deviation = 13.78 years, minimum = 21 years, and maximum = 78 years.

References

Abes, E. S., Jones, S. R., & Stewart, D.-L. (Eds.). (2019). *Rethinking college student development theory using critical frameworks*. Taylor & Francis. https://doi.org/10.4324/9781003446835
Abrams, S. (2019). *Lead from the outside: How to build your future and make real change*. Picador.
Allen, J. (2023). *Find your people: Building deep community in a lonely world*. Waterbrook.
American Council on Education (ACE). (1937). *The student personnel point of view (1937)*. www.naspa.org/articles/student-personnel-point-of-view-1937
American Psychological Association (APA). (n.d.). *APA dictionary of psychology*. https://dictionary.apa.org/identity
Arnett, J. J. (2000). Emerging adulthood: A theory of development from the late teens through the twenties. *American Psychologist, 55*(5), 469–480. https://doi.org/10.1037/0003-066X.55.5.469
  (2015). *Emerging adulthood: The winding road from the late teens through the twenties*. Oxford University Press.
Athanasou, J. A., & Perera, H. N. (Eds.). (2019). *International handbook of career guidance* (2nd ed.). Springer. https://doi.org/10.1007/978-3-030-25153-6
Bandura, A. (1977). Self-efficacy: Toward a unifying theory of behavioral change. *Psychological Review, 84*(2), 191–215. https://doi.org/10.1037/0033-295X.84.2.191
Bandura, A., & Cervone, D. (2023). *Social cognitive theory: An agentic perspective on human nature*. Wiley.
Bauman, Z. (2017). *A chronicle of crisis: 2011–2016*. Social Europe Edition.
Bengtsson, A. (2022). On epistemic justice in career guidance. *British Journal of Guidance & Counselling, 50*(4), 606–616. https://10.1080/03069885.2021.2016614
Bolles, R. N. (2025). *What color is your parachute?* Ten Speed Press.
Brown, B. (2010). *The gifts of imperfection: Let go of who you think you're supposed to be and embrace who you are*. Hazelden.
  (2015). *Daring greatly: How the courage to be vulnerable transforms the way we live, love, parent, and lead*. Avery.

Brown, D. (1995). A values-based approach to facilitating career transitions. *The Career Development Quarterly, 44,* 4–11. https://doi.org/10.1002/j.2161-0045.1995.tb00524.x

(2002). *Career choice and development* (4th ed.). Jossey-Bass.

(2016). *Career information, career counseling, and career development* (11th ed.). Pearson.

Brown, S. D., & Lent, R. W. (Eds.) (2020). *Career development and counseling: Putting theory and research to work* (3rd ed.). Wiley.

Buford, M. V., Sharp, M. J., & Stebleton, M. J. (2023). *Mapping the future of undergraduate career education: Equitable career learning, development, and preparation in the new world of work.* Routledge. https://doi.org/10.4324/9781003213000

Burkus, D. (2018). *Friend of a friend . . .: Understanding the hidden networks that can transform your life and your career.* Harper Business.

Burnett, B., & Evans, D. (2020). *Designing your work life: How to thrive and change and find happiness at work.* Knopf.

Carnevale, A. P., Smith, N., Van Der Werf, M., & Quinn, M. C. (2023). *After everything: Projections of jobs, education, and training requirements through 2031.* Georgetown University Center on Education and the Workforce. https://cew.georgetown.edu/wp-content/uploads/Projections2031-National-Report.pdf

CEDEFOP & Organisation for Economic Co-operation and Development. (2021). *Career guidance policy and practice in the pandemic. Results of a joint international survey: June to August 2020.* Publications Office. http://data.europa.eu/doi/10.2801/318103

Chickering, A. W. (1969). *Education and identity.* Jossey-Bass.

Chickering A. W., & Reisser, L. (1993). *Education and identity* (2nd ed.). Jossey-Bass.

Cho, S., Crenshaw, K. W., & McCall, L. (2013). Toward a field of intersectionality studies: Theory, applications, and praxis. *Signs, 38*(4), 785–810. https://doi.org/10.1086/669608

Chui, H., Li, H., & Ngo, H.-Y. (2022). Linking protean career orientation with career optimism: Career adaptability and career decision self-efficacy as mediators. *Journal of Career Development, 49*(1), 161–173.

Clear, J. (2018). *Atomic habits: An easy & proven way to build good habits & break bad ones.* Penguin.

Collins, P. H. (2009). *Black feminist thought: Knowledge, consciousness and the politics of empowerment.* Routledge (Original work published 2000).

Collins, P. H., & Bilge, S. (2020). *Intersectionality* (2nd ed.). Polity Press.

Cooper, A. J. (1892). *Voice from the South: By a Black woman of the South.* The Aldine Printing House.

Covacevich, C., Mann, A., Santos, C., & Champaud, J. (2021). *Indicators of teenage career readiness: An analysis of longitudinal data from eight countries* (OECD Education Working Papers, No. 258). OECD Publishing. https://doi.org/10.1787/cec854f8-en

Crenshaw, K. (1989). Demarginalizing the intersection of race and sex: A Black feminist critique of antidiscrimination doctrine, feminist theory and antiracist politics. *University of Chicago Legal Forum*, *1*(8), 139–167. http://chicagounbound.uchicago.edu/uclf/vol1989/iss1/8

Dawis, R. V., & Lofquist, L. H. (1984). *A psychological theory of work adjustment*. University of Minnesota Press.

Denby, D. (2016, June 21). The limits of "grit." *The New Yorker*. www.newyorker.com/culture/culture-desk/the-limits-of-grit

Dey, F., & Cruzvergara, C. Y. (2014). Evolution of career services in higher education. *New Directions for Student Services*, *2014*(148), 5–18. https://doi.org/10.1002/ss.20105

Diaconu-Gherasim, L. R., Țepordei, A.-M., Labăr, A. V., Vîrgă, D., & Măirean, C. (2024). University students' future time perspective and career adaptability: The mediating role of grit. *The Career Development Quarterly*, *72*(2), 121–134.

Duckworth, A. (2016). *Grit: The power of passion and perseverance*. Scribner.

Duffy, R. D., Allan, B. A., England, J. W., Blustein, D. L., Autin, K. L., Douglass, R. P., Ferreira, J., & Santos, E. J. R. (2017). The development and initial validation of the decent work scale. *Journal of Counseling Psychology*, *64*(2), 206–221. https://doi.org/10.1037/cou0000191

Duffy, R. D., Blustein, D. L., Diemer, M. A., & Autin, K. L. (2016). The psychology of working theory. *Journal of Counseling Psychology*, *63*(2), 127–148. https://doi.org/10.1037/cou0000140

Duran, A., Abes, E. S., Stewart, D.-L., & Jones, S. R. (2024). Looking back, moving forward, and everything in between: Revisiting student development's relevance and enduring concepts. *Journal of College Student Development*, *65*(2), 121–136. https://doi.org/10.1353/csd.2024.a923524

Duran, A., & Jones, S. R. (2019). Using intersectionality in qualitative research on college student identity development: Considerations, tensions, and possibilities. *Journal of College Student Development*, *60*(4), 455–471. https://doi.org/10.1353/csd.2019.0040

Eberhardt, J. L. (2019). *Biased: Uncovering the hidden prejudice that shapes what we see, think, and do*. Penguin.

Eddy, J. (2023). *Crisis-proofing today's learners: Reimagining career education to prepare kids for tomorrow's world*. Rowman & Littlefield.

Farbstein, B. (2018). *Ten feet tall: Step into your truth and change your freaking world*. Ten Feet Tall.

Ferrazzi, K., & Raz, T. (2005). *Never eat alone, expanded and updated: And other secrets to success, one relationship at a time*. Crown Business.

Flores, L. Y., Martinez, L. D., McGillen, G. G., & Milord, J. (2019). Something old and something new: Future directions in vocational research with people of color in the United States. *Journal of Career Assessment*, *27*(2), 187–208. http://doi.org/10.1177/1069072718822461

Fu, M., Zhang, L.-F., & Li, B. (2019). Revisiting the congruence–satisfaction relationship: The role of external forces. *Journal of Career Development*, *46*(3), 203–218. https://doi.org/10.1177/0894845317737379

Garriott, O. (2020). A critical cultural wealth model of first-generation and economically marginalized college students' academic and career development. *Journal of Career Development, 47*(1), 80–95. https://doi.org/10.1177/0894845319826266

Garvey, J. C., Harris, J. C., Means, D. R., Oerez, R. J., & Porter, C. J. (Eds.). (2020). *Case studies for student development theory: Advancing social justice and inclusion in higher education*. Routledge.

Grant, A. (2023). *Hidden potential: The science of achieving greater things*. Viking.

Grimmett, B., & Severy, L. (2024). Career services. In N. Zhang (Ed.), *Rentz's student affairs practice in higher education* (6th ed., pp. 129–163). Charles C. Thomas.

Grosemans, I., Vangrieken, K., Coertjens, L., & Kyndt, E. (2021). Education-job fit and work-related learning of recent graduates: Head start or filling a gap? *Journal of Career Development, 48*(5), 638–665.

Guan, Y., Deng, H., Fan, L., & Zhou, X. (2021). Theorizing person-environment fit in a changing career world: Interdisciplinary integration and future directions. *Journal of Vocational Behavior, 126*, online first. https://doi.org/10.1016/j.jvb.2021.103557

Guichard, J. (2022). From career guidance to designing lives acting for fair and sustainable development. *International Journal for Educational and Vocational Guidance, 22*(3), 581–601. https://doi.org/10.1007/s10775-022-09530-6

Gutowski, E. R., Blustein, D. L., Kenny, M. E., & Erby, W. (2020). The decline of decent work in the twenty-first century: Implications for career development. In P. J. Robertson, T. Hooley, & P. McCash (Eds.), *The Oxford handbook of career development* (pp. 23–35). Oxford University Press. https://doi.org/10.1093/oxfordhb/9780190069704.013.3

Hall, D. T. (1996). Protean careers of the 21st century. *The Academy of Management Executive, 10*(4), 8–16.

Hall, D. T., & Mirvis, P. H. (1995). Careers as lifelong learning. In A. Howard (Ed.), *The changing nature of work* (pp. 323–361). Jossey-Bass/Wiley.

Hall, D. T., Yip, J., & Doiron, K. (2018). Protean careers at work. *Annual Review of Organizational Psychology and Organizational Behavior, 5*(1), 129–156. https://doi.org/10.1146/annurev-orgpsych-032117-104631

Hartung, P. J. (2012, June 21–23). *My Career Story: An autobiographical workbook for life-career success* [Paper presentation]. National Career Development Association, Atlanta, GA. www.careerconstructionnetwork.org/uploads/1/1/2/3/112370035/mcs-article.pdf

(2019). Life design: A paradigm for innovating career counselling in global context. In J. G. Maree (Ed.), *Handbook of innovative career counselling* (pp. 3–18). Springer. https://doi.org/10.1007/978-3-030-22799-9_1

Hofstede, G. (1991). *Cultures and organizations: Software of the mind*. McGraw-Hill.

Holland, J. L. (1959). A theory of vocational choice. *Journal of Counseling Psychology, 6*(1), 35–45. https://doi.org/10.1037/h0040767

(1973). *Making vocational choices: A theory of vocational personalities and work environments*. Prentice-Hall.

(1985). *Making vocational choices: A theory of vocational personalities and work environments* (2nd ed.). Prentice-Hall.

(1997). *Making vocational choices: A theory of vocational personalities and work environments* (3rd ed.). Psychological Assessment Resources.

Hooley, T. (2023). The future isn't what it used to be! Revisiting the changing world of work after Covid-19. In M. V. Buford, M. J. Sharp, & M. J. Stebleton (Eds.), *Mapping the future of undergraduate career education: Equitable career learning, development, and preparation in the new world of work* (pp. 38–51). Routledge. https://doi.org/10.4324/9781003213000-5

Irving, B. A. (2020). The positioning of social justice: critical challenges for career development. In P. J. Robertson, T. Hooley, & P. McCash (Eds.), *The Oxford handbook of career development* (pp. 181–192). https://doi.org/10.1093/oxfordhb/9780190069704.013.14

Jehangir, R. R., Moock, K., & Williams, T. B. (2022). In support of first-generation and working-class students' career development: Navigating the hidden curriculum of the workplace. In M. V. Buford, M. J. Sharp, & M. J. Stebleton (Eds.), *Mapping the future of undergraduate career education: Equitable career learning, development, and preparation in the new world of work* (pp. 104–121). Routledge. http://doi.org/10.4324/9781003213000-10

Johnson, S. (2018). *Out of the maze: An a-mazing way to get unstuck*. Portfolio.

Juntunen, C. L., Motl, T. C., & Rozzi, M. (2019). Major career theories: International and developmental perspectives. In J. A. Athanasou & H. N. Perera (Eds.), *International handbook of career guidance* (pp. 45–72). Springer. https://doi.org/10.1007/978-3-030-25153-6_3

Kanar, A. M. (2023). Effectiveness of informational interviewing for facilitating networking self-efficacy in university students. *The Career Development Quarterly*, *71*(2), 147–159.

Kantamneni, N., & Fouad, N. A. (2023). Multicultural vocational research: critique and call to action. *Journal of Career Assessment*, *31*(1), 3–26. https://doi.org/10.1177/10690727221084002

Keshf, Z., & Khanum, S. (2021). Career guidance and counseling needs in a developing country's context: A qualitative study. *SAGE Open*, *11*(3). Online first. https://doi.org/10.1177/21582440211040119

Knefelkamp, L. L. (1982). Faculty and student development in the 1980s: Renewing the community of scholars. In H. F. Owens, C. H. Witten, & W. R. Bailey (Eds.), *College student personnel administration: An anthology* (pp. 373–391). Charles C. Thomas.

Konstant, M. (2018). *Activate your agile career: How responding to change will inspire your life's work*. Konstant Change.

Lee, D., Lee, H.-S., Na, W., & Hwang, M. H. (2022). Gender differences in the structure of Holland's personality model in South Korea. *Journal of Career Development*, *49*(4), 875–889. https://doi.org/10.1177/08948453211004780

Lent, R. W., Brown, S. D., & Hackett, G. (1994). Toward a unifying social cognitive theory of career and academic interest, choice, and performance. *Journal of Vocational Behavior*, *45*(1), 79–122.

Lent, R. W., Morrison, M. A., & E. Ijeoma. (2014). The career development of people with disabilities: A social cognitive perspective. In D. R. Strauser (Ed.), *Career development, employment, and disability in rehabilitation* (pp. 113–124). Springer.

Lund, S., Madgavkar, A., Manyika, J., Smit, S., Ellingrud, K., & Robinson, O. (2021). *The future of work after COVID*. McKinsey Global Institute. www.mckinsey.com/featured-insights/future-of-work/the-future-of-work-after-covid-19

Malach-Pines, A., & Kaspi-Baruch, O. (2008). The role of culture and gender in the choice of a career in management. *Career Development International*, *13*(4), 306–319. https://doi.org/10.1108/13620430810880808

Mann, A., Denis, V., & Percy, C. (2020). *Career ready? How schools can better prepare young people for working life in the era of COVID-19* (OECD Education Working Papers No. 241). OECD Publishing. https://doi.org/10.1787/e1503534-en

Maree, J. G. (2020). *Innovating counseling for self- and career construction: Connecting conscious knowledge with subconscious insight*. Springer. https://doi.org/10.1007/978-3-030-48648-8_4

McClellan, G. S., & Kiyama, J. M. (Eds.). (2023). *The handbook of student affairs administration* (5th ed). Wiley.

McEwen, M. (1996). The nature and uses of theory. In S. R. Komives & D. B. Woodard (Eds.), *Student affairs: A handbook for the profession* (3rd ed., pp. 147–163). Jossey-Bass.

McMahon, M., & Arthur, N. (2018). Career development theory origins and history. In N. Arthur & M. McMahon (Eds.), *Contemporary theories of career development: International perspectives* (pp. 3–19). Routledge.

McWhirter, E. H., & McWha-Hermann, I. (2021). Social justice and career development: Progress, problems, and possibilities. *Journal of Vocational Behavior*, *126*, 103492. https://doi.org/10.1016/j.jvb.2020.103492

Mohr, T. (2015). *Playing big: Practical wisdom for women who want to speak up, create, and lead*. Avery.

Nuss, E. M. (1996). The development of student affairs. In S. R. Komives & D. B. Woodard (Eds.), *Student affairs: A handbook for the profession* (3rd ed., pp. 22–42). Jossey-Bass.

Oxendine, S., & Taub, D. (2023). An overview of student development theories. In G. S. McClellan & J. M. Kiyama (Eds.), *The handbook of student affairs administration* (5th ed., pp. 115–135). John Wiley & Sons.

Parsons, F. (1909). *Choosing a vocation*. Houghton Mifflin Company.

Patton, W. (2019). *Career development as a partner in nation building Australia: Origins, history and foundations for the future*. Brill.

Patton, W., & McMahon, M. (2021). *Career development and systems theory: Connecting theory and practice* (4th ed.). Brill.

Patton, L. D., Renn, K. A., Guido, F. M., & Quaye, S. J. (Eds.). (2016). *Student development in college* (3rd ed.). Jossey-Bass.

Pendakur, V. (2016). *Closing the opportunity gap*. Routledge.

Perera, H. N., & Athanasou, J. A. (2019). Introduction: An international handbook of career guidance. In H. N. Perera & J. A. Athanasou (Eds.), *Interntional handbook of career guidance* (pp. 1–15). Springer. https://doi.org/10.1007/978-3-030-25153-6

Pope, M. (1997). History and development of career counseling in the USA. In W. Evraiff (Ed.), *Caring in an age of technology: Proceedings of the 6th International Conference on Counseling in the 21st Century, Beijing, China*. Beijing Normal University Press. https://files.eric.ed.gov/fulltext/ED439332.pdf

(2000). A brief history of career counseling in the United States. *The Career Development Quarterly, 48*, 194–211. https://doi.org/10.1002/j.2161-0045.2000.tb00286.x

Powers, J. J., & Duys, D. (2020). Toward trauma-informed career counseling. *The Career Development Quarterly, 68*(2), 173–185.

Pryor, R. G. L., & Bright, J. E. H. (2003). The chaos theory of careers. *Australian Journal of Career Development, 12*(3), 12–20. https://doi.org/10.1177/103841620301200304

Pryor, R. G. L., & Bright, J. E. H. (2014). The chaos theory of careers (CTC): Ten years on and only just begun. *Australian Journal of Career Development, 23*(1), 4–12. https://doi.org/10.1177/1038416213518506

Ribeiro, M. A. (2020). Career development theories from the global south. In P. J. Robertson, T. Hooley, & P. McCash (Eds.), *The Oxford handbook of career development* (pp. 225–238). Oxford University Press. https://doi.org/10.1093/oxfordhb/9780190069704.013.17

Robertson, P. J., Hooley, T., & McCash, P. (Eds.). (2020). *The Oxford handbook of career development*. Oxford University Press. https://doi.org/10.1093/oxfordhb/9780190069704.001.0001

Saunders, T. (2024, January 5). How many countries are there in 2024? *BBC Science Focus Magazine*. www.sciencefocus.com/planet-earth/how-many-countries-are-there

Savickas, M. L. (2005). The theory and practice of career construction. In R. W. Lent & S. D. Brown (Eds.), *Career development and counseling: Putting theory and research to work* (pp. 42–70). John Wiley & Sons.

(2013). Career construction theory and practice. In S. D. Brown & R. W. Lent (Eds.). *Career development and counseling: Putting theory and research to work* (pp. 147–183). John Wiley & Sons.

Savickas, M. L., & Savickas, S. (2019). A history of career counselling. In H. N. Perera & J. A. Athanasou (Eds.), *International handbook of career guidance* (pp. 25–43). Springer. https://link.springer.com/chapter/10.1007/978-3-030-25153-6_2

Schuh, J. H., Jones, S. R., & Torres, V. T. (2016). *Student services: A handbook for the profession*. Jossey-Bass.

Seibert, S., Akkermans, J., & Liu, C. H. (2024). Understanding contemporary career success: A critical review. *Annual Review of Organizational Psychology and Organizational Behavior*, *11*(1), 509–534.
Severy, L. (2018). Career development in emerging adulthood. In J. L. Murray & J. J. Arnett (Eds.), *Emerging adulthood and higher education: A new student development paradigm* (pp. 75–88). Routledge. https://doi.org/10.4324/9781315623405
Sheu, H.-B., & Bordon, J. J. (2017). SCCT research in the international context: Empirical evidence, future directions, and practical implications. *Journal of Career Assessment*, *25*(1), 58–74. https://doi.org/10.1177/1069072716657826
Sinek, S. (2011). *Start with why: The inspiring million-copy bestseller that will help you find your purpose*. Penguin.
Solberg, V. S. H., Donnelly, H. K., Park, C., Esquivel, L. E., Blake, M., & Temurnikar, M. (2023). *2023 report on the condition of career readiness in the United States*. Coalition for Career Development Center. www.ccd-center.org/2023-career-readiness-report
Souto, A. M., & Sotkasiira, T. (2022). Towards intersectional and anti-racist career guidance. *British Journal of Guidance & Counselling*, *50*(4), 577–589. https://doi.org/10.1080/03069885.2022.2073583
Stolzoff, S. (2023). *The good enough job: Reclaiming life from work*. Portfolio.
Sultana, R. G. (2011). On being a "boundary person": Mediating between the local and the global in career guidance policy learning. *Globalisation, Societies and Education*, *9*(2), 265–283. https://doi.org/10.1080/14767724.2011.577326
(2023). For a postcolonial turn in career guidance: The dialectic between universalisms and localisms. *British Journal of Guidance & Counselling*, *51*(2), 262–273. https://doi.org/10.1080/03069885.2020.1837727
Super, D. E. (1990). A life-span, life-space approach to career development. In D. Brown, L. Brooks, & Associates (Eds.), *Career choice and development: Applying contemporary theories to practice* (2nd ed., pp. 197–261). Jossey-Bass.
(1994). A life span, life space perspective on convergence. In M. L. Savickas & R. W. Lent (Eds.), *Convergence in career theory: Implications for science and practice* (pp. 6–74). Consulting Psychologists Press.
Terkel, S. (1974). *Working*. Pantheon Books.
Thomas, E. (2024). *You owe you: Ignite your power, your purpose, and your why*. Rodale Books.
Thompson, J. A., & Bunderson, J. S. (2019). Research on work as a calling . . . and how to make it matter. *Annual Review of Organizational Psychology and Organizational Behavior*, *6*, 421–443.
Thomsen, R., Hooley, T., & Mariager-Anderson, K. (2022). Critical perspectives on agency and social justice in transitions and career development. *British Journal of Guidance & Counselling*, *50*(4), 481–490. https://doi.org/10.1080/03069885.2022.2106551

US Central Intelligence Agency (CIA). (n.d.). *The world factbook: Explore all countries*. www.cia.gov/the-world-factbook/countries/

Watts, M. (2015). *First jobs: True tales of bad bosses, quirky coworkers, big breaks, and small paychecks*. Picador.

Wiest, B. (2020). *The mountain is you: Transforming self-sabotage into self-mastery*. Thought Catalog Books.

(2023). *The pivot year*. Thought Catalog Books.

Yates, J. (2020). Career development theory: An integrated analysis. In P. J. Robertson, T. Hooley, & P. McCash (Eds.), *The Oxford handbook of career development* (pp. 131–142). Oxford University Press. https://doi.org/10.1093/oxfordhb/9780190069704.013.10

Index

accounting jobs, 35, 37
alumni connections, 35
American Council on Education, 22
Americans with Disabilities Act, 8

bad managers, 43, 110–111, 126, 155
Bandura, Albert, 13, 186
Bilge, Sirma, 25
boundaryless careers, 6
branding, personal and professional, 123–124, 179
Bright, Jim, 13, 183
broadening horizons, 30, 34, 50, 103, 140, 158
Brown, Duane, 11, 185

Career Construction Theory, 13, 187
Career Development Quarterly journal, 7
career development theories, 9
career readiness, 20
career trajectories, 1–2, 22, 183
CareerOneStop, 179, 181, 186
changing world of work, 6, 8, 21, 26
Chaos Theory of Careers, 13, 183
Civil Rights Movement, 7
Collins, Patricia Hill, 25
community-building at work, 33, 55
computer science jobs, 102, 109
construction jobs, 157, 163
constructionist paradigm, 15
consulting jobs, 102, 117, 124, 127, 129
content theories of career development, 9
Cooper, Anna Julia, 25
COVID-19, 6, 183
Crenshaw, Kimberlé, 25
critical consciousness in career counseling, 181
cultural relevance, 11, 18
culture and career choice, 17
customer service jobs, 27–29, 100, 153

data jobs, 46–47, 59, 111
Dawis, René, 11

depression and anxiety, 42, 138, 144
disability and work, 118, 146
disappointment, 60, 73, 76–77, 91, 118, 120, 122
Duffy, Ryan, 9, 12, 181

education jobs, 49, 55, 68, 84, 96, 100, 103, 106, 110, 123, 129, 160
engineering jobs, 67–68, 108
entertainment jobs, 44, 80, 164
entrepreneurship, 128, 136, 141, 163
equity, 15, *See* power
exploration and the career process, 76, 177, 183

family connections, 28, 59, 130
family pressure in the job search process, 83, 86, 128, 137, 140, 170
farming jobs, 149, 164
finance jobs, 46, 50, 64, 90, 121
first impressions, 68
first job, 176
first-generation college student, 97
flexibility in the job search, 37, 82, 92, 176
food service jobs, 42, 125, 134, 145, 167
frustrating job search, 48, 56, 69, 78, 125

gardening jobs, 139
gender and work, 59, 110, 129–130
GI Bill of Rights, 7
gig economy, 6
Global North career perspectives, 19
Global South career perspectives, 19
government jobs, 66, 68, 119, 128, 132, 134, 172
graduate school, 27, 29, 31, 45, 50–51, 55, 57–59, 67, 82, 105, 108–109, 114, 123, 129, 142, 146–147, 159

Hall, Douglas, 11, 185
higher education, career guidance in, 22, 188
history of careers research, 5, 26
Hofstede, Geert, 17

Index

holistic career development, 23
Holland, John, 9–10, 17
hospitality jobs, 167
human resources jobs, 38, 40, 48, 57, 69, 87, 145
humility, 41, 81–82, 112–113, 126, 135, 171

identity and work, 9, 11, 13, 15, 176, 181–182, 189
immigrant origins and the career process, 15, 82, 86, 92, 127, 138, 162–163, 173
imposter syndrome, 63, 187
international jobs, 65, 86
internationalism, 16–19
internships, 35, 38, 46, 64, 74, 86, 90, 116, 119, 127, 147, 185
intersectionality, 12, 16, 25

job fair, 50, 116
journalism jobs, 131, 150

K-12 education, 20, 72
Knefelkamp, Lee, 23

lack of qualifications, 61
later in life experiences, 95, 109, 137, 139, 149
law jobs, 84, 149
Lent, Robert, 13, 18, 186
life-design model of career counseling, 15
Life-Span Life-Space Theory, 12, 178
lifelong learning, 46, 52, 102, 116, 167, 189
limitations of career theory. See underrepresented, marginalized communities
Lofquist, Lloyd, 11, 178
lucky break, 32, 59, 82, 84

maintenance jobs, 113
marriage and family therapy (MFT), 27, 30
medical jobs, 146, 154, 159, 168, 170, 173
mental health. See depression and anxiety
mentors, 73, 80, 125
military jobs, 52, 55, 64, 92, 103, 133
Mirvis, Philip, 11, 185

narratives of career, storytelling, 1–2, 23, 175
National Career Development Association, 7–8
negotiating salary, 153
networking, 38, 40, 48, 58, 66, 81, 85, 89, 99, 103, 107, 112, 120, 158, 160–161, 176, 179–180
nonprofit jobs, 62, 74, 114, 160

O*NET, 11, 186
Omnibus Trade and Competitiveness Act of 1988, 8

Parsons, Frank, 7, 10, 178
Perkins Vocational Education Act of 1984, 8
perseverance. See resilience
persistence, 72, See resilience
person-environment fit, 10, 178
philanthropy jobs, 51
policy jobs, 31, 60, 74, 83, 148
Pope, Mark, 6
power, 12
proactivity in the job, 34, 40, 68, 80, 85, 125, 134, 147
process theories of career development, 9, 12
protean careers, 6, 11, 185
Pryor, Robert, 13, 183
Psychology of Working Theory, 12, 16, 181

racial identity and work, 32, 34, 89, 91, 102
real estate jobs, 43
reflection questions for career seekers and career counselors, 3, 175, 179–180, 182, 184–185, 187, 189
relationship-building. See networking
religion, faith, 79, 81, 119, 169
religious jobs, 77, 163
remote jobs, 115
resilience, 56, 97, 133, 143, 145, 156, 178, 187
resume and cover letter, 124, 161
RIASEC vocational interests, 10–11
risk-taking, 27, 63, 66, 74, 85, 140, 151, 158, 176, 183

sales jobs, 113, 128, 144
Savickas, Mark, 6, 13, 15, 187
Savickas, Suzanne, 6, 15
scholarly research, 3, 5, 9
self-efficacy, 13, 89, 107, 177, 185
self-employed, 134
self-worth, 60, 63, 101, 132, 154, 156, 177, 187
sense of failure, 41, 44, 59, 123, 143, 189
small companies, 114–115, 117, 157
social and cultural capital, 23, 180
Social Cognitive Career Theory, 13, 18, 186
social services jobs, 49
soft skills, 37, 61
sports jobs, 113, 121
stages of career counseling, 7
stay at home parent, 109, 138
staying at the same job long-term, 37, 67, 131, 166
stepping stone, first job as a, 48, 105, 129, 154, 171
student affairs, 22
student development theory, 23–25, 180
student loans, 39
success, meaning of, 2, 183, 185, 188
Super, Donald, 9, 12, 178

technology for career advising, 21
temporary jobs, 31, 45, 58, 80, 128, 133, 148
temporary work, 49
Terkel, Studs, 2
Theory of Vocational Choice, 10, 18
Theory of Work Adjustment, 11, 178
transferrable skills, 79, 140, 145, 154

underrepresented, marginalized communities, 5, 14–16, 19–20, 25, 181

unemployment, 98, 142
unexpected career paths, 31, 44, 72, 75, 100, 105, 137, 144

values, work and life, 116, 179, 185
Values-Based Career Theory, 11, 185
Vietnam War, 7
Vocation Bureau in the Civic Service House, 7, 10
Vocational Education Act of 1963, 7

For EU product safety concerns, contact us at Calle de José Abascal, 56–1°, 28003 Madrid, Spain or eugpsr@cambridge.org.